Freeing
Sexuality

"Thank you, Dr. Miller, for calling out the cultural hypocrisy that creates mass psychological abuse. You help us see through the shaming and religious fear mongering that distorts and perverts our sexual and erotic birthrights. Those who delve into the pages of *Freeing Sexuality* will be blessed with their revolutionary insights into sexual terrain unfettered by shame. And they will benefit from your reasoned perspectives as an esteemed psychologist. Your readers now possess access to a paradigm shift that can liberate and heal their connection to self, to those they love, and to their broader community."

VERONICA MONET, AUTHOR OF *SEX SECRETS OF ESCORTS*
AND FOUNDER OF THE SHAME FREE ZONE

Freeing Sexuality

PSYCHOLOGISTS,
CONSENT TEACHERS,
POLYAMORY EXPERTS,
AND SEX WORKERS
SPEAK OUT

Dr. Richard Louis Miller

Park Street Press
Rochester, Vermont

Park Street Press
One Park Street
Rochester, Vermont 05767
www.ParkStPress.com

Park Street Press is a division of Inner Traditions International

Cataloging-in-Publication Data for this title is available from the Library of Congress

ISBN 978-1-64411-541-1 (print)
ISBN 978-1-64411-542-8 (ebook)

Printed and bound in the United States by Lake Book Manufacturing, LLC

10 9 8 7 6 5 4 3 2 1

Text design and layout by Debbie Glogover
This book was typeset in Garamond Premier Pro with FreightBig Pro, Gill Sans MT Pro, and Rival Sans used as display typefaces

To send correspondence to the author of this book, mail a first-class letter to the author c/o Inner Traditions • Bear & Company, One Park Street, Rochester, VT 05767, and we will forward the communication.

This book, Freeing Sexuality, *is dedicated to my dear friends Margo St. James, sex workers' rights activist/founder of COYOTE (Call Off Your Old Tired Ethics), and sex activist/former porn star Annie Sprinkle, Ph.D., as well as all the sex workers of the world who have suffered ignominiously from misguided public policies and belief systems based on hypocrisy, distorted morality, and superstitious religions.*

Though vital to sustaining life on Earth, humankind has so distorted our views of sex that it became a commodity. Water is also now being sold, and it is quite possible that someday—if we pollute the environment enough—we will have to pay for the air we breathe. As soon as sex became a commodity, not an expression of life, men and women went into the business of selling.

Unfortunately, purveyors of sexual delights are denigrated and castigated—sometimes celebrated on a superficial level, but most often ostracized. Like professional athletes, they have relatively short careers, after which they spend the rest of their lives living down their reputations while their children suffer humiliation and shame.

Let us celebrate the sex workers of the world and help them elevate to a profession of distinction, for not only do they offer up their bodies, their toil, and their sacrifice, but, when we look at their work with the courage to suspend judgment and accept the naked truth about ourselves, we must recognize that they grace us with their very souls.

Editor's Note

The interviews in this book were all conducted by Dr. Richard Louis Miller on his podcast *Mind Body Health & Politics*. While some took place earlier, many of the interviews transpired during the peak of the COVID pandemic. As such, the conversations contained herein reflect a specific moment in time. Due to the sensitive and evolving nature of the issues that recur throughout this book as well as the casual nature of these interviews, we've added editor's notes as footnotes where updates and further clarifications were needed, where sources are difficult to substantiate, or where statistics may be out of date.

These interviews represent important conversations with experts in sensitive subject areas. The views expressed are the speakers' own and do not represent those of the publisher.

Contents

GENDER IDENTITY & NON-MONOGAMY

THE SEX INDUSTRY

CONSENT

Foreword

Dr. Lea Lis

Freeing Sexuality is composed of exploratory interviews with an expertly curated group of researchers, teachers, authors, and sex workers. Dr. Miller starts his book by honoring his first wife and great love, Stella Resnick. This book embodies a beautiful collaboration between these two one-time spouses whose mutual respect as friends, peers, and researchers still abounds. The spirit of their rapport helped illuminate the path of inquiry engaged by the author. Resnick provided her invaluable expertise on a range of topics—from why women sublimate their desires to be more "ladylike," to the importance of masturbation in sexual satisfaction. Along with Stella Resnick and other contributors to *Freeing Sexuality,* Dr. Miller isn't afraid to address topics within the realm of human sexuality that often prove difficult and awkward for subjects to discuss.

As Dr. Miller says on his *Mind Body Health & Politics* podcast, "human beings are friendly tribal animals and basically nice to one another. We tend to be collaborative, but we must also acknowledge that a small percentage of people are greedy and avaricious. Those who fall into the latter category would have us live as subjects rather than citizens. How can a few subjugate many? There are undoubtedly many dimensions to that question, but as we look back throughout human history, an oft-employed—and highly effective—tactic used to control people's behavior is shame.

Shame and sex are so intertwined that it is almost impossible to separate them. Many scholars and theologians interpret the story of Adam and Eve not as "original sin," but as the birth of shame—an emotion that is effectively unique to our species. While shame does seem to have utility, functioning as a kind of social glue that upholds the mores and standards of our culture, unfortunately, it goes without saying that shame is used to suppress and control women and sexual minorities the world over.

Why is this? One answer is that a sexually evolved woman is a powerful being endowed with not only the ability to create and sustain life, but embrace *her own* pleasure. This can be intimidating to those who seek to wield power over women. It's telling that, in spite of our prodigious appetite for technical advancement, relatively little is known, for example, about the human female's capacity for multiple orgasms. Dr. Miller hardly needs to explain the hostility toward female sexual freedom that continues to seethe like a hot ember within our collective consciousness.

How can women be suppressed? Controlling women's bodies through outdated laws regarding abortion and denying access to health care and birth control are but two clear examples. Some societies even go so far as to cover women's entire bodies or mutilate their pleasure centers. In her book *Creating Cutltures of Consent,* Dr. Laura McGuire describes attempts made by others to exert dominion over the sexual essence of her being, recalling, for example, how she was made to wear a bathing suit that covered her from neck to knees to spare her male teenage counterparts from temptation.

This type of social coding—rampant across cultures and time periods—revolves around the presumption that men are bestial creatures with an inherent inability to control their sexual desires. As one would expect, the onus then falls on women to forestall male transgressions by denying their own innate sexuality and beauty. Today, we see this take many forms, from the *Burqa* in Taliban-controlled regions of Afghanistan to school dress codes in the West.

As far as it concerns men, their particular burdens with shame are clearly articulated by Veronica Monet, in the chapter where she discusses her book, *Sex Secrets of Escorts.* She considers the shame men feel when they do not think they perform well enough. It is a fallacy that male performance is dependent upon maintaining long-lasting erections. Consider that most women achieve orgasm through clitoral stimulation that is not reliant on intercourse. Most men still have their fingers and tongues.

Veronica illustrates the notion that the antidote of shame is vulnerability. She states that, "Sometimes they (men) would cry in my arms after they had an orgasm. I was touched and moved by this, and I was thinking, *Wow, men are far more vulnerable and sensitive than I ever thought.*"

WHY DOES SEX CONTINUE TO DRIVE SHAME?

In his groundbreaking work as the originator of the concept of the collective unconscious, Carl Jung pointed to a reserve of impulses and information that reside outside of our awareness. These impulses are common to all people and distinct from the personal unconscious, which arises from an individual's experiences. The collective unconscious applies to sex in that we all have deep desires that are common throughout our species and manifest in the form of universal themes or archetypes.

One way or another, the overwhelming majority of religions and societies have been structured in opposition to desire, which finds its root in this collective unconscious. These desires are easily subdued and manipulated by societal forces and frameworks, especially when people do not understand those desires or where they come from. Denying our sexuality, however, is akin to denying our right to be human. In these pages, Dr. Miller embraces the collective unconscious, unpacks its components, and theorizes about its origins.

The chapter on sexual data science with Ogi Ogas is especially fascinating in this regard. Ogas analyzed a large amount of internet data in order to determine some common themes in what the average person searches for. For example, men were more interested in healthy or overweight women (perhaps because they looked more fertile) than skinny women. Regardless of sexual orientation, almost all men like to watch pornography that includes another man's penis. These are interesting examples of collective unconscious sexuality stemming from our vestigial primate behavior related to social hierarchy.

I wholeheartedly loved part II, Gender Identity & Non-Monogamy, which details how some forward-thinking people are implementing new sexual models and managing to make them work in relationships. Many couples I work with suffer from either monogamy-induced boredom or *cheating*, which significantly impacts the integrity of their marriages, as well as the lives of their children.

As a result, the only culturally accepted exit ramp from non-monogamy typically comes in the form of serial monogamy, divorces, and remarriage. Divorce often yields horrific circumstances that wreak havoc on the family structure, causing children to suffer trauma and parental alienation when vindictive ex-partners deploy a draconian legal system to come down with all its wrath for the crime of venturing outside the traditional relationship structure. Parental alienation* frequently occurs against the parent who "cheats," the reaction simplifies blame, which is often more nuanced, as anyone who is in a long-term relationship can attest.

Living according to the principles of polyamory, ethical non-monogamy, or any of the other labels described in that section of the book presents a new set of challenges for the pioneers who embark on them. Non-monogamy allows for what's known in polyamory circles as "new-relationship energy," which—as proponents of this lifestyle argue—invigorates longer-term partnerships whether or not one ever takes the plunge into polyamory. Managing jealousy, meanwhile, can heal many traumas and allow for greater communication in partnerships and marriages.

---

*Editor's note: A controversial subject, parental alienation is called child psychological abuse by Craig Childers, Ph.D. It is when a vindictive parent creates a cross-generational alliance with a child against the former partner. The alienating parent manipulates the child into rejecting and fearing the target parent. The subject is controversial because it is sometimes also used by abusive parents to steal custody of their children from protective parents utilizing the aforementioned legal system.

Nevertheless, the stigma of venturing outside society's prescribed parameters has its consequences. According to Janet Hardy, "There have been numerous stories about people who have lost jobs, friends, connections to families of origin, and even the custody of children—because of their lifestyle. It's not a safe world yet for people whose sexual path is not heterosexual monogamy."*

Dr. Miller and his guests examine how sex and therefore sex work has been exiled, vilified, and made illegal. Sex work has been consigned to the margins, rarely taught or discussed in mainstream culture. Recently, for example, sex outside of marriage was made illegal in Indonesia, which could greatly curtail the modern millennial's vacation to Bali. Will it now be illegal for a worn-out American escaping the cold to have a fling with a local guru without risking being jailed for six months? If this seems absurd, it's because it is.

In contrast, in the Netherlands, sex is openly talked about and sex work has been legal since the year 2000. Sex education there starts in kindergarten, with discussions about bodies, boundaries, love, and even "crushes"—which happen during adolescence, well before sexual desire kicks in. These open discussions have led the Netherlands to having the best statistics for teen pregnancy rates, lower rates of STIs, and better overall health measures.†

In *Freeing Sexuality*, Dr. Miller unabashedly attempts to take the subject of sex out of the proverbial closet. Through his series of expert interviews, he pierces through the veil of "red light" and allows the very idea of sexuality to be tested and viewed as safe in the light of day. Dr. Miller has tapped into the collective unconscious by presenting the many varieties of sexual expression without shame or judgment, while celebrating the diversity of sex for pleasure and sexual expression.

Speaking on what I learned about the Dutch approach to teaching children about sex and consent I must admit that I have a "crush" on Dr. Miller. He is an expert on human sexuality and a master interviewer.

---

*Editor's note: Additionally, we have no reason to assume that a non-monogamous family unit is safer or healthier for children, specifically.
†See the book *Beyond Birds & Bees* by Bonnie J. Rough for some great resources regarding sex education in the Netherlands.

He transcends most psychologists in his field with his unique insights and ability to ask the right questions of his experts. In the spirit of *Freeing Sexuality,* and the part on consent, I hope you approach this book with an emphatic *Yes!*

DR. LEA LIS is the author of *No Shame: Real Talk with Your Kids about Sex, Self-Confidence, and Healthy Relationships* and is known as the Shameless Psychiatrist. She is a double board certified adult and child psychiatrist who has been working with nontraditional family arrangements since the beginning of her psychiatric career. She has appeared as an expert on parenting in programming by ABC, CBS, NBC, and other news outlets as well as newspapers such as *The Chicago Tribune* and *The Washington Post.*

What has the sexual act, so natural, so necessary, and so just, done to mankind, for us not to dare talk about it without shame and for us to exclude it from serious and decent conversation? We boldly pronounce the words kill, rob, betray; and this one we do not dare pronounce, except between our teeth. Does this mean that the less we breathe of it in words, the more we have the right to swell our thoughts with it?

For it is a good one that the words least in use, least written and most hushed up, are the best known and most generally familiar. No age, no type of character, is ignorant of them, any more than of the word bread. They impress themselves on everyone without being expressed, without voice and without form. It is also a good one that this is an action that we have placed in the sanctuary of silence, from which it is a crime to drag it out even to accuse and judge it. Nor do we dare to chastise it except roundaboutly and figuratively. A great favor for a criminal, to be so execrable that justice deems it unjust to touch and see him: free and saved by virtue of the severity of his condemnation.

—MICHEL DE MONTAIGNE,
ON SOME VERSES OF VIRGIL,
TRANSLATED BY DONALD M. FRAME

INTRODUCTION

How We All Got Here

How comfortable are you with sex? Can you speak openly about it? Are you turned off or on when sex comes up in conversation?

What about your actual sexual behavior? Are you open to doing anything sexual so long as there is respect, dignity, and sober mutual consent? Are certain sexual behaviors taboo for you? What are they? Are you willing to look at—and perhaps reevaluate—your personal sexual taboos?

Where do you think your beliefs about sex came from? Do you think you were born with your sexual beliefs or did you learn them? If you learned your sexual beliefs, who were your instructors? Was it your parents? The kids at school? Your religious leaders? Your teachers? Books? Movies? The internet? Pornography? All of the above?

When and how did it come to pass that sex lost its place as simply a natural act engaged in for procreation and pleasure?

Witness the place of drugs and sex in the biblical Garden of Eden. The apple contained the drug and, before long, the garden's human inhabitants—Adam and Eve—were hiding their genitals. And, with that, the concept of sin was attached to sex, with shame as a foundational element in the origin story of the entire Judeo-Christian world.

With the help of religion, we have moved sex from the garden of delights to one of—if not *the*—most conflictual topics and behaviors on the planet. We all know that sexual behavior is critical for the preservation of the species. Without it, we wouldn't be here and our species would die off.

Since sexual activity is a given, therefore, the hiding of it and the sanctioning of those who make no apologies for it make for a perverse kind of mass psychological abuse.

Cultural hypocrisy is detrimental to mental health because it twists and conflicts the mind and creates what psychologists call neurosis. All too often, cultural hypocrisy turns something pleasurable and positive into something conflictual and *bad*.

Our American culture is so hypocritical about our sexuality that I believe our entire nation, if not the world, is suffering from post-traumatic sexual stress disorder (PTSSD).

Those of us who have engaged in some form of sexual behavior—with ourselves, or others—know that the feelings generated by sexual contact are often quite pleasurable.

A person can sit just about anywhere, and by touching or rubbing their genitals, they can pleasure themselves. Two or more people can touch one another's genitals and create pleasure. Being able to derive pleasure from contact with the genitals is, when all is said and done, part of the human experience.

Looking at genitals is pleasurable and sexually stimulating. Looking at pictures and movies of people engaging in sexual acts can also be sexually stimulating. Watching people fornicate can be sexually stimulating.

In our culture, if a woman shows a great deal of cleavage in public, she is considered sexy; however, if she also bares her nipple, she may be arrested. During the 2004 Super Bowl halftime show, in an incident that was broadcast live to a massive international audience, singer Janet Jackson infamously revealed a nipple. Major controversy ensued, mostly focusing on Jackson, and the event was still being discussed in the halls of the American Congress a year later. Although it was ultimately thrown out, the FCC issued a whopping fine of $550,000 to CBS for the incident.

The obsession and condemnation of a single "nip slip" on live television in the U.S. stands in ironic contrast to our culture's utter obsession and utter fascination with women's breasts.* It is estimated that about 5 percent of all women, or over 5,000,000 women, have had their breasts made larger with implants. Looking at, touching, and pos-

---

*Editor's note: More recently, sexual trends have swung around to embracing bigger butts on women.

sessing a large penis is likewise sought after. Men use various methods of enlarging their penis, including implants, pumping with a vacuum pump, pulling on it, placing weights on it, shocking it, and injecting it.

Male anxiety about sexual *performance* is epidemic. Men live in fear of not "achieving" an erection, not "maintaining" an erection, or having a "premature" ejaculation.* Note the language commonly used: achievement, maintenance and premature. Can we achieve breathing, maintain urination, be prematurely thirsty? Hungry? Pregnant? Does one achieve thirst? Do we maintain our urges to defecate? Have you ever witnessed a person prematurely breathing?

While there's no question that trouble awaits anyone brave enough to have sex in public, we rarely discuss sex in public either. Although we are obsessed with sex, as a culture, we don't speak honestly about our sexual lives. The closest we have come to open discussion of a sexual body part is the breakthrough play, *The Vagina Monologues* by Eve Ensler (who now goes by the one-letter moniker *V*).

Even the scientific study of human sexuality is frowned upon. Alfred Kinsey, Ph.D., Indiana University professor and the world's foremost sex researcher of the past 100 years, was ridiculed and disgraced for his monumental works *Sexual Behavior in the Human Male* and *Sexual Behavior in the Human Female*. Kinsey, founder of the world-renowned Kinsey Institute at the University of Indiana, was punished severely for having the audacity to study sex. His research defunded, and his academic career halted, Kinsey died a broken man.

We talk as though we are meant to mate for life, but most of us have more than one mate during our lifetime. We talk as though we are meant to be monogamous, but many of us are not, and have never been monogamous. We talk as though sexual behavior is sacrosanct and yet watching pornography is a national pastime. Indeed, pornography is the most viewed material on the internet.

And then there is what we call prostitution or selling sex. Men have made the selling of sex illegal. Why? What is the basis of this legislation?

---

*A study published in the *Journal of Sex Research* in 2020 found that 38.2 percent of men reported experiencing sexual performance anxiety.

Ideology? Morality? Control? It certainly can't be reason. What is the fundamental basis for men not allowing women to sell sexual activities, especially considering that it's mostly men who patronize women for sex in the first place? Can we attribute this phenomenon to dominance? Control? Money?

Our hypocritical and distorted attitudes regarding sex have also created the horrendous business of sex trafficking whereby adults and children are transported and sold as sex slaves for profit. When the slaves lose their youthful attractiveness, they are often sold, put out on the streets, or murdered.

It is quite possible that, left to their own devices, most people would prefer to have consensual sex with anyone, anytime, anywhere. And many do. But they are far from honest about it. We don't even really know if we are meant to mate in twos, threes, fours, or in groups.

For over 200 years, Americans have suffered the inheritance of a group of people—Puritans—who thought *dancing* was sinful, to say nothing of sex.

Lest we dismiss this as a laughing matter, George Washington—a superb dancer—did not dance at public events for fear of group criticism and harm to his reputation. Today, in many parts of the world, one can lose one's life for dancing in a way that might be considered too *suggestive*.

For thousands of years, we have suffered the impact of religion's attitudes toward sex. This has caused human suffering on a scale so large that measurement is impossible. I say again that we all suffer from post-traumatic sexual stress disorder. Because of our national cultural hypocrisy and outright suppression of sex research, we know very little about human sexuality and the interactions surrounding that sexuality. We do not teach young people in school how to engage in sexual activities.

Sex education in schools is mostly focused on preventing pregnancy and sexually transmitted diseases and explaining bodily changes during puberty.* This leaves our young to learn about sex from parents, peers,

---

*That is, when it's not teaching an abstinence only model.

books, photographs, and movies, of course: Hollywood, yes, but mostly pornography.

From pornography, we learn that after rapid, pounding sex, the man strokes his penis frantically and then ejaculates semen onto the woman's face. Pornography teaches its viewers that women enjoy it when men make them gag with forceful oral sex. Porn teaches that women like to be slapped, choked, and spanked hard enough to leave red markings on their buttocks while engaging in intercourse.*

Hollywood movies show us a version of sex that is a frenzied activity in which people tear off one another's clothing, madly and passionately. They "go at it" for less than two minutes, before a jump cut has them landing back on the bed, sweaty, to light up a cigarette.

This book is not about that. In these pages, we will investigate sexual customs and beliefs from a wide variety of perspectives, ranging from sexpert clinical psychologists to sex workers.

It is my wish that this book will contribute toward an evolutionary cultural change. We need to free our species from the shame, control, and hypocrisy spiral, and restore sex to what it truly is: procreation or how we all got here, a way of enhancing interpersonal intimacy, a biochemical/electrical healing modality, and a source of the most incredibly pleasurable sensations available to humankind.

---

*Which is not to say that with mutual, sober consent, any of these behaviors are sick, bad, or crazy. But without clarification, a male entering a sexual encounter with a female, assuming that she wants to be treated in that rough manner will usually result in a terrible time at best (abuse at worst).

Sexperts

Through our language use, we frame human sexual activity as performance that we must optimize. We *achieve* and *maintain* an erection. We *reach* orgasm. In this way, we mutate what should be enjoyable, satisfying behavior into anxiety-producing effort. Picture a man doing all he can to *achieve* an erection in order to *perform*. Can you imagine a woman then *reaching* for her orgasm? How high must she reach? Does she need a special sex ladder? Do some women stand on their tippy-toes in order to climax, and is that what high heels are for?

Human sexuality is like breathing air, eating food, drinking water, defecating, and urinating—only better, because besides serving procreation, sex provides unique pleasure. Sexuality, a human process necessary for the survival of our species, bonds us with our mates, and provides us with a modicum of pleasure in what can be an otherwise harsh, uncaring world, has a bad rep! We have distorted sexuality so markedly, for so long, that we have turned our most beautiful gift into tragedy.

Hypocrisy, the practice of claiming to have moral standards or beliefs to which one's own behavior does not conform, is a national security issue and we should treat it as such. When leadership is hypocritical, it undermines the moral fabric of society.

How many politicians have we watched rail against homosexuality, only to be caught in public toilets soliciting sexual favors from young men? How many evangelists have we heard screaming hellfire and brimstone only to be caught with prostitutes and drugs? (Or, for that matter, watching their wives having sex with other men?) It's clear to us from the outside of these scandals that the problem is not the behavior itself, but the oppression of others caused by this suppression of the self.

This hypocrisy seems to be caused by a tragic and unnecessary cognitive dissonance, one that we'll revisit throughout the book. *How can we indulge lustful desires, and still be good people?*

Scientists who study human sexuality are most often clinical psychologists and are referred to colloquially as sexperts. These sexpert psychologists are few and far between because our morally misguided and hypocritical culture is so powerful that even the sacred halls of academia look down upon those who study sex. The courageous scientists who do study sexuality do so at risk of jeopardizing their professional careers. In this chapter, I bring you sexpert scientists who have contributed hugely to our understanding of sexuality.

When I met Lonnie Barbach sometime in the 1970s, at the Health Sanctuary I created at Wilbur Hot Springs in Northern California, I was smitten by her intellectual vitality and physical beauty. Alas, the event I met her at was a women's group, so all the men living and working at Wilbur Hot Springs were asked to leave. This may seem puzzling, but that's how it was in the 1970s . . . we men got off campus.

The next time I saw Lonnie was in the early 1990s, when her daughter, Tess, and my daughter, Evacheska, were classmates in grammar school. By then she had become world famous for her pioneering book, *For Yourself: The Fulfillment of Female Sexuality,* which helped open the tightly-closed door to female masturbation. Lonnie's lifelong life partner, David Geisinger, was the prominent psychologist, artist, and author who was to become my closest male confidant until his untimely death in 2021. Their book, *Going the Distance*—which, indeed they did—is a must-read for anyone who cohabitates.

I met Stella Resnick at a restaurant in San Francisco's North Beach neighborhood. She looked like a Jewish beauty, pronounced words like an Italian mobster, and spoke like an intellectual. I fell in love and quickly fell into calling her Stella, which brought to mind images of Marlon Brando's iconic *A Streetcar Named Desire* performance, every time I called out to her. In our twenties at the time, we were both clinical psychologists filled with idealism, and there was a profound resonance in our shared views about people and politics. We were soon married. We had found our ideal. I introduced Stella to Dr. Fritz Perls, the founder of Gestalt therapy, and they took a liking to one another. I immediately sensed his attraction to her. Aside from her being married, Perls was more than twice her age. Being territorial, I openly showed my irreverence by teasing this much older man in spite of his professional seniority. In retaliation, Fritz put a curse on us. It worked. We were divorced before a year of marriage. But no, they didn't run off together. Fritz died soon thereafter, and Stella and I remained friends for life.

In her book *The Heart of Desire: Keys to the Pleasure of Love,* Stella teaches us that it is necessary for us to learn—by ourselves—exactly what turns us on sexually, so that we may inform our partners of how best to pleasure us.* Now in our 80s, we email and sometimes see one another at Esalen, where she continues to lead seminars. We have recently acknowledged how much we loved one another. This acknowledgment gives me a very sweet feeling and reminds me that Stella will always be my *shayna punim.**

Katherine Rowland spent five years talking with 120 women about sexuality and desire. In her book, *The Pleasure Gap,* she argues that women should take inequality in the bedroom as seriously as they would take it in the boardroom, and that they need to understand its causes and effects. Katherine reports that, just as there is an enormous gap between how much money males and females earn, there is also a large gap between how much sexual pleasure and actual orgasms males and females experience—hence, the pleasure gap.

Diana Richardson is known as the pioneer of the slow sex movement. In her book *Slow Sex: The Path to Fulfilling and Sustainable Sexuality,* Diana teaches us that while fast, hot, orgasm-driven sex can

---

*"Pretty face" in Yiddish.

bring momentary satisfaction, it can in the long run become boring and mechanical, causing many couples to lose interest and stop making time for physical intimacy. She advocates for making sex a conscious decision, which awakens the body's innate mechanism for ecstasy, unlocking the door to extraordinary realms of sensitivity, sensuality, and higher consciousness.

It has been my privilege to know these courageous women who have successfully risked their professional lives to advance the study of human sexuality, thereby bringing it to its rightful, dignified, and important place in the world of science.

You will also read an interview with Ogi Ogas, Ph.D., author of *A Billion Wicked Thoughts* (with Sai Gaddam, 2011), a fascinating book, about their findings gleaned from combing through a treasure trove of user data analyzing trends in sexual interest and online behavior.

Read on and you will find the very latest information about what the sexperts are saying about sex, what sex is, and how to best *enjoy* it.

1

Stella Resnick

Keeping the Sensuality

Stella Resnick, Ph.D., is a clinical psychologist, Gestalt therapist, certified sex therapist, and developer of the Embodied Relational Sex Therapy (ERST) process and therapist training. Stella's holistic approach recognizes sexual health—capacity for pleasure and play—as intertwined with self-development throughout life, and as basic elements in emotional, physical, and relational health and happiness.

She developed this "full-spectrum" approach over many years of experience. It is a body-based, present-centered, experiential method for individuals and couples, centered on personal and relational healing and growth and focused on enhancing the capacity to enjoy greater physical, emotional, and sexual pleasure. The process involves looking into early programming, not as an intellectual process of mere understanding, but as felt-sense memories that are locked in the body through chronic physical tension, withheld breathing, and unresolved old emotions that trigger programmed reactions to stress.

Through breath and body awareness in the present moment, we learn to become more mindful and self-aware in the moment. By breathing *into* painful emotions and experimenting with new ways to respond in emotionally fraught situations, we can access inner resources that we may not even know we have and call forth more loving and pleasurable responses from others.

Stella believes this is especially true in romantic and sexual relationships, viewing relational and sexual problems as opportunities to heal from early emotional pain and shame, to broaden the ability to love and be loved, and to share emotional and sexual pleasure with a lover or mate.

Dr. Richard L. Miller (RLM): Today, we're going to have an exciting interview with Dr. Stella Resnick, one of our country's foremost certified sex therapists. Stella is a clinical psychologist who has a private practice in Beverly Hills, California. She is a certified sex therapist, she teaches and trains therapists, and has appeared on many television programs, including *Oprah*, CNN, and *The O'Reilly Factor*, and she's also the author of several books. One of her previous books is: *The Pleasure Zone: Why We Resist Good Feelings and How to Let Go and Be Happy*. Her most recent book is *Body-to-Body Intimacy: Transformation through Love, Sex, and Neurobiology*.

THE DILEMMA OF LOVE AND LUST

Richard Louis Miller (RLM): Stella, you've been working with couples for decades. You talk about something fascinating at the beginning of your second book, *The Heart of Desire: Keys to the Pleasures of Love*. You call it the "love-lust dilemma." You say that due to our sexual programming the commitment of love itself can undermine sexual desire. Tell us more about that.

Stella Resnick (SR): It's true that sex is important for our physical health and for the health of a relationship. I love what you've been talking about in promoting health. When we look at promoting health, an important but overlooked factor is promoting *pleasure*. Pleasure has a bad reputation. People think of pleasure as selfishness and associate it with guilt. They don't look at how health is about vitality and that vitality itself is a result of pleasure. It feels good to be healthy. And pleasurable feelings contribute to our physical, mental, and relational health.

Sex is an important part of an intimate relationship. Of course, we have relationships with people that are pleasurable without sexual contact. With friends and family, we might have hugs or a squeeze. Intimacy is about closeness, and intimate closeness is skin to skin, face to face, looking into each other's eyes, touching each other, and experiencing pleasure and desire for one another.

Most intimate relationships that end in living together or marriage involve sexual contact. A lot of people have discovered that the sex is great before they make a commitment to one another. Frequently, that's what brings two people together. The sex is so good, they say, "What else do we have going for us?" But when two people make a commitment to one another, not uncommonly they discover that their sexual relationship changes.

In some cases, the sexual experience and the desire for one another can die shortly after moving in together. One couple I saw had been together for ten years and had great sex together. They finally decided to live together. She told me, "The day after we moved in together, the sex and the magnetism between us were gone." When we love someone, we may want to touch them, be with them, and hug them—but not necessarily have sex with them. When we fall in love, that new person arouses us sexually. What makes us fall in love with them is that we're playful together; we're in sync. This is somebody who understands you. So you decide to live together or get married. At that point, we sometimes get into the difficulty of sharing a space with someone or of getting into an attachment. Two people's attachment styles may be very different. One person may be secure in their attachment; another may be insecure. If they're insecure, they may be anxious, avoidant, or ambivalent. So it may be difficult to maintain an attachment solely based on our love because we may start to trigger each other. We trigger in each other some of the old wounds that haven't been resolved. That tends to interfere with our sexuality. Sex is either for procreation or recreation. In the first case, we bring new life into the world. In the second case, we bring new life into ourselves—re-creation. The latter requires the ability to play together, and that can get lost, based on what people witnessed in their own home, whether or not their parents showed any signs of playfulness, affection, or sexiness.

RLM: After ten years of good sex, they moved in together and, all of a sudden, it was gone?

SR: Before they moved in together, they were sexually playful, but once they were committed, their expectations of each other changed, and sex became more of an obligation. The excitement—the enthusiasm—was gone.

THE IMPACT OF CHILDHOOD ON MARRIAGE

RLM: I see. You talk about the effects of early childhood history on sexual pleasure. Tell us about that.

SR: We know that babies are born sexual. We know little boy babies have erections in the womb, we know little girl babies lubricate by three days of age. We know that babies delight in touching their genitals. We know that toddlers may touch their genitals in front of other people and it can be embarrassing for parents. Many teenagers discover the pleasure of masturbation.

It's typically programmed into our brain at an early age that if we're caught in sexual activity at home, it can meet with punishment. Of course, the incest taboo is important in the sense that we do want to discourage family members from having sexual contact. But that can lead to overgeneralizing the incest taboo, turning off our sexual feelings at home, and directing sexual desire to outsiders. This is good to propagate a healthy species, but when people declare their commitment to one another, the beloved becomes family, particularly if they move in together.

They begin to treat each other like a parent/child, or a brother/sister. Even among gay and lesbian couples, the same factors take root. They treat each other as sisters or mother/daughter, father/son, or brothers. The familiarity of living together begins to breed a non-sexual relationship.

RLM: So the object of our romantic attachment becomes like a family member and sexual desire can drop off because it's become incestuous?

SR: It drops off because of the dynamic between the two people. The wife asks the husband for permission to spend money and then he asks her permission to go out with the boys. You ask permission of a parent, not an equal. They have quarrels about money; they get into the mundane things about fixing the leak in the sink. Their day-to-day life becomes more family driven.

This is particularly pronounced when they have babies and see one another as parents rather than lovers. You see your beloved man, that sexy stud you were having great sex with, as a father. Or you see the beautiful woman that you were so turned on by as a mother. Many people don't recognize the programming, but this change in dynamic brings up past learned responses. I call it *family transference*.

RLM: Yes. We were taught at Best Parents not to show signs of sexual interest in each other in front of our children. Is that still going on?

SR: It's still going on and it's a terrible idea. Now, I don't recommend that parents get overtly sexual in front of children because that will offend the children. But even when children protest, it's important for parents to talk about sex and to acknowledge children's sexual interests. They should not say, "Don't touch yourself," or, "What are you doing?" or, "That's disgusting." They should ask, "How does that feel? Does it feel good?" They should tell children not to stop masturbating, but to do it in private and certainly not do it at school. There are ways of channeling behavior without suppressing it, yet much of the training around sexuality is suppressive rather than channeling.

RLM: Correct me if you think differently, but don't religions basically denigrate pleasure?

SR: Yes. A lot of adolescents are discouraged from being in touch with their sexual pleasure. There's a limited realm of pleasure available for adolescents unless they're willing to go against their parents or religious teachings. We think that young children and teens should be nonsexual. As children explore their bodies and sexuality, they're typically discouraged from touching themselves, from being curious about sex. They may ask questions about sex and get limited answers. So there isn't a steady developmental growth with regard to sexuality in the same way that there is with other aspects of our physical and emotional growth. Sex is one kind of pleasure. There are other kinds of pleasure as well. But religion bans pleasure itself, and pleasure in our culture still doesn't have a place.

RLM: How would you teach us to educate our children about sexuality differently, Stella? How might parents best approach their children when they walk in and find the children playing with their genitals?

SR: You might simply smile and leave the room. I had a woman in therapy with me who described an event between her and her son. She had knocked on her eleven-year-old son's door and said, "Honey, dinner is ready—will you come downstairs?" He said, "Not right now, Mom." She asked, "Why not? What are you doing?" His answer: "I'm masturbating."

RLM: Well, good for him.

SR: She said to him, "Okay, honey, come downstairs when you're finished."

RLM: How do you think parents should show affection for each other in front of children? How much affection is okay for a husband and wife to show—kissing? Hugging?

SR: It's not only okay, it's *important* to allow children to recognize that physical affection and attraction is okay to see among parents and people committed to one another. This will shape their own programming. They will think that people who love each other, who live together, who are married to each other and have children are still sexually interested in one another.

RLM: So often in life, we see couples who are dating, holding hands, putting their arms around each other, and kissing. Yet it's also the experience of many patients I've talked to that when people get married they stop showing affection.

SR: They stop acting like lovers. Lovers not only kiss and show affection, they are also playful with each other, which brings them into emotional and physical synchrony with one another. When they stop being playful, they stop feeling romantic toward one another, and when they stop kissing as lovers their sexual feelings begin to wane.

RLM: What happens then?

SR: It may be that they don't think they need to do that anymore; but it is unfortunate because the quality of their relationship will suffer. It's not just about having intercourse. You're treating one another as a lover—as somebody attractive, desirable, and as somebody you want to touch. It's important to get close to one another. A lot of times, when people are raising kids, much of their contact is shoulder-to-shoulder rather than face-to-face, eyeball-to-eyeball, chest-to-chest, belly-to-belly.

KISS, NOT KISS-OFF

RLM: I just started something different with my wife that has been helpful and I think it's appropriate to mention: Typically, when we leave the house or arrive at the house we give each other a kiss. We hold the kiss for six seconds and we are noticing that it makes a difference. In your book, you talk about the value of holding on to a hug for a certain period. Tell us about that.

SR: That's true. But I hope when you're holding that kiss that you're not counting up to six, because that takes you away from the present moment.

RLM: No, we're not counting the numbers while kissing. I'm trying to figure out whether it's okay to touch her with my tongue while I'm kissing.

SR: In my book, I talk about "little wet kisses." I talk about the fact that those little pecks "hello" and "goodbye," are part of the problem. That's the way you would kiss a relative. When my husband and I first moved in together he gave me one of those little pecks. I grabbed him and I said, "Stop! That's not a kiss—that's a kiss-off."

I want a *real* kiss, at least a little wet kiss. I want one in the morning, one in the evening, and one if we're around during the day. I want a hug to linger. I want us to press our bodies against one another. I want us to breathe together. When we break our embrace, I want us to look into each other's eyes. I want to smile at you; I want your smile. Those are the kinds of body-based experiences of intimacy that make a big difference in a relationship.

Keep in mind that sex is not just intercourse, it's sensuality and playfulness. That means looking into each other's eyes, getting close enough to draw in the pheromones in their scent that affect the behavior and the desire of one for the other. Touching each other and feeling skin-to-skin is so important. A lot of people don't get naked with each other, except when they're having sex, but it's important to feel skin on skin at other times so that sex cannot be compartmentalized. It's certainly not something that should begin in a bed, because a bed is a place where we go to sleep. This is especially true when much of your lovemaking is at night before your usual bedtime. Once in bed, your body will naturally fall into the need for sleep, not for sex.

Playfulness begins the experience of sexual arousal. Good sex needs to include flirting and playfulness. It is like going for a meal. You have talked about obesity. Many times obese people are eating too much. They're eating it too fast and not even enjoying it. If we sit down to a meal, we want to look at the presentation and smell that food. The digestive process begins before we even put the first forkfull of the food into the mouth. We begin to salivate. Playfulness is a major factor in good sex. We want to be flirtatious, dance together, hold each other, say loving things to one another, put on some music, and light some candles. The worst time and place is right before you go to sleep. You can *finish* sex in a bed—when you want to get prone and comfortable, by all means, get into bed. But before that, so much can be done more energetically in any other room. It makes it more fun and interesting. This way, you're treating each other as lovers, as opposed to merely performing a marital duty.

TOOLS TO IMPROVE YOUR RELATIONSHIP

RLM: In your book, you talk about various exercises a person can do with their partner. "Step one: body-mind basics—name three qualities you would like more of in your emotional life." You go on to say, name three qualities you would like more of in your sexual and emotional life with your partner. Give some examples of how that might look.

SR: You might want to share these things with your partner. For example, some key aspects of your personal health have to do with breathing. Breathing is an involuntary activity. You don't have to remind yourself, "I better take a breath or I'll pass out." It's automatic.

However, most people have learned to hold their breath and breathe in a shallow way—especially when were stressed or in our heads. Breath is an important part of down-regulating stress. When we're stressed, the body's tension and contraction narrows your experience, raises your heartbeat, and gives you tunnel vision.

If we want to be in a loving, sexual, *sensual* experience with our partner, we have to breathe together. We need to learn how to take nice, deep sighs to tune in to our body rather than our head. In order to be sexual with our partner, it helps to get in touch with our breath, to feel our chest rising and lowering; we need to feel our ribcage expanding and relax our bellies. People who are self-conscious about their bodies may hold their bellies in. But doing so can block sexual arousal because it limits blood flow into the pelvic region, which depends on blood flow to get turned on. So, breathing is important. I suggest exercises to my clients that involve taking deep breaths and relaxing the belly.

When two people hold each other, it's important to learn to breathe together. In one of my exercises, two people hold each other as close to one another as possible, lie down, and breathe together in nice, deep sighs. It's a tantric exercise called "breathing the one breath." It has also been called "matching breaths." In essence, you're bringing your bodies into sync.

On a side note, saliva is an important way of syncing your bodies. When two people kiss they're sharing saliva, which contains dopamine, which is involved in the biochemistry of reward. They're sharing testosterone—the hormone of sexual desire for both men and women. They're sharing serotonin. All of this shared biochemistry is bringing them together.

DAILY PROXIMITY

RLM: Some people might read this and think, *Gee, I breathe all the time. What is there to learn about breathing?* But there's a lot to be learned, as you discuss at length in your book. I'm moving on now to something you call *the daily proximity.* You talk about how too much proximity can dampen sexual interest. Tell us a little about that.

SR: There's proximity and there's *proximity.* It's not great if you feel like you're tied at the hip and that you have to ask permission to be apart. We do need to be individuals, but sometimes people deny their individuality in order to be able to get along with one another.

We need to be able to not only tolerate each other's differences, but *respect* our differences because that's a big part of what brings us together. Our individual differences are what attract us to one another. It's also essential for intimate couples to spend time together daily, face-to-face. When you talk to each other, don't just shout at each other across the room—or, even worse, from another room than where your partner is. Talk while looking into each other's eyes. Only then can you be sure your partner fully hears you. And you can read his or her face and know if they empathize or understand what you are saying, or if they agree with what you're asking for.

I get my clients to do most of their sessions with me facing each other and talking to each other rather than to me. I may interject a comment to describe what I'm seeing, or I may suggest a little experiment on how they might say or do something differently and then ask, "How did that feel?"

Some therapists have the couple sitting side by side on a couch facing the therapist. Then the entire session consists of each person talking separately to the therapist and the therapist responding with "How do you feel about that?" And, "How do you feel about what he or she just said?"

When I start to work with a couple, they typically begin by telling me the issues that have brought them into couples therapy. But, as we proceed, I ask them to face each other, and to share with one another how they feel about the other right this moment. I bring them into the present, into face-to-face, eye-to-eye communication. I encourage them to focus in on their felt-sense—what they are experiencing right now in their bodies. You can't be in your body if you're in your head thinking. Our bodies are where we feel our feelings, our desires, our truth, and our vitality.

AVOIDING EMOTIONAL CONTAGION

SR: You talked about obesity before on the show. Obesity anesthetizes the body from pain. We need to be able to feel the pleasure of being alive and in a connection with somebody else. Being in a relationship is not just about a division of labor—having a partner to do chores. It's also the ability to achieve a quality of life that involves pleasure, excitement, interest, curiosity, and joy—and to share those, not only on special occasions, but every day.

Many of us think laughter is even better than sex in a relationship. I like both myself, but laughter is important—and, of course, laughter is all about *breathing*. When you're conscious of your breathing you're making involuntary behavior voluntary. So instead of being triggered with anger when your partner says something that hurts your feelings, you can take a breath, feel the trigger, and respond in a more effective way. You may choose to say, "That hurt my feelings." That way, you can talk about what just happened in a way that injects love or even humor, rather than react in a negative way and perpetuate anger.

When partners trigger each other, it's called emotional contagion. They're awakening in their partner old wounds from earlier times. One person gets angry and shouts, "Screw you!" Then the other shouts, "Oh, go to hell!" And they're off and running. There's no learning there, no growth. A loving relationship is a *growing* relationship. You're each *learning* how to perpetuate love in close proximity. It's very important when you raise a family for everyone to know how to keep the love between all family members—between parents, between parents and children, and between siblings.

If you breathe and take time to downregulate your anxiety or anger—you may be able to then talk to one another. Instead of having contagion of a negative feeling, you'll have contagion of a positive feeling—empathy. When we begin to empathize with another's feelings, we can work things out. It starts with taking a few deep breaths before reacting out of our old fears and wounds. It's about taking the opportunity to do things differently from what never works. I like to say, "You can't use negative means to gain positive ends." You can quote me on that!

SOLO SEX REVISITED

RLM: A lot of what you've been talking about so far has been pleasure, sex, fun, flirting, and sexual life in the context of having a partner. I'd like you to spend some time on solo sex, or masturbation. How can one have fun with oneself? Why is it important to learn how to pleasure oneself?

SR: The key to being sexually active is having a sexual relation with oneself. The big study, *Sex in America,* shows that the people with the best sex life are also the people who tend to masturbate the most. Now, we don't know whether the libido caused masturbation or vice versa; but we *do* know that to be good lovers and enjoy sex with a partner, we need to understand our own bodies. The best way to understand our own bodies is to touch our bodies in ways that give us pleasure.

It's important for children not to be shamed about touching their genitals or masturbating—I can't stress that enough. I know it is going to seem crazy to a lot of people, but children have a right to sexual pleasure. In fact, Sigmund Freud talked about how little was known about the erotic life of children. When I read that phrase, "the erotic life of children," I was astounded. I had never read that anywhere else. You still don't read that in contemporary books.

Boys are more likely to masturbate than young girls, which may be a factor in women having more difficulty with reaching orgasm. Unfortunately, boys often learn to masturbate as quickly as possible because they're afraid of getting caught. That reduces their ability to have lingering, lovely sex with a woman. They finish before she's even getting started. So it's important for both men and women to have an active sex life with themselves in order to have one with a part-ner. "Active" does not mean every day, but that, when you get turned on, sometimes you may want to be with your partner, sometimes you may want to get off by yourself. It's especially important for women to learn how to touch themselves. Women can have orgasms from three different parts of their genitalia, including the uterus, so they need to learn how to find and stimulate the clitoris. The clitoris is not just the little pea-shaped organ at the top of the vaginal opening, but a rather long wishbone-like organ. That "pea" is sometimes vis-ible but not always.

RLM: That's right, not always. I've read that the clitoris averages about seven inches in length.

SR: Seven to eight inches in length.

RLM: Isn't that remarkable?

SR: Yes, it's a large organ. It can be stimulated by touching the glans, which are like the glans of the penis. But because the clitoris has a shaft, like a small penis, it can be stimulated in more ways. The clito-ris and the penis are analogous in the fetus. What's visible above the vaginal opening is the clitoral glans, which is analogous to the head of the penis. But besides the glans, there's a shaft that's analogous to the shaft of the penis, as well as a wishbone area that we might describe as being like two legs, called *crura*—one on each side of the vaginal opening. The whole area can be stimulated not just by touching the head of the clitoris, but by squeezing the entire female organ, the vulva, which squeezes the crura and stimulates every part of the vulva.

Male genitals are external, female genitals are mostly internal. Studies show that many girls think that their vulva and vagina are ugly. Can you imagine the mindset of thinking your genitalia are ugly? What can that be? How do you get an orgasm out of a rejected part of your body?

RLM: Where is this negative indoctrination coming from, Stella?

SR: No idea. I never thought that when I was growing up. But I didn't have a close relationship with my mother. I think that was good when it came to my sexuality.

RLM: You were spared that particular grief. One of our other guests, sexologist Lonnie Barbach, told us that before she wrote her book, *For Yourself*, 75 percent of the women in the United States had never looked inside of their vaginas. They had never explored or taken a look with a mirror. Women had no idea what their vaginas looked like inside. They were scared about what they saw of their vagina on the outside and it turned them off or scared them. But they weren't born afraid of their vaginas. Somebody taught them to be put off by what they saw.

SR: Exactly. So masturbation is important to discover what turns you on, or how to touch yourself, what kind of touch you like. Exploring different ways of touching yourself brings out different feelings. Also, masturbation is healthy. It's good creative energy because it's arousing, and it keeps us in a state of overall vitality, in terms of our emotional and physical energy as well as being able to access our sexuality.

RLM: If you had a magic wand and could direct the curriculum of schools, at what age would you have proper teachers teaching students about masturbation—how to masturbate, enjoy it, and allow it to be pleasurable?

SR: No one has to teach a child how to masturbate, or even should. As the child's body matures, it goes through a developmental stage when genital feelings become more intense and the infant or young child naturally begins to touch him or herself. It's essential for sex education to begin with parents and not teachers. Parents can begin to talk about sex as soon as a child starts to show interest in their genitals. Talk in simple terms, guide and channel that child's sexual energy, rather than discourage it. That means if you catch your child masturbating, instead of freaking out, you can take a couple of breaths, and say something like, "Excuse me, dear, I don't want to intrude on your privacy." Wouldn't that be nice! As soon as they show curious sex, parents need to be able to talk to them. Don't just show them pictures in a book.

Don't just talk about the plumbing and what goes where. Talk to them about the pleasurable aspects of sex and desire. Allow them to feel the urge to desire but learn to channel it and not do that in front of others. You don't want a child to begin touching his or her body in school or in front of the family. So you need to be able to say, "It's nice that you enjoy touching your body. But it's better to do that when you're by yourself than in front of anyone." Also, you want to set other boundaries like not touching other children's bodies unless the other child wants to play, not allowing oneself to be bullied into any sexual activity, or not allowing any adult to be sexual with them.

RLM: Listening to you talk about the large gaps in sex education, it occurs to me that we need internet programs for teaching parents how to talk to their children about masturbation. You're right in saying it should start with the parents—not with the schools—but parents won't know how to educate their children about sexuality.

SR: Parents usually don't know how to do it because they themselves may not be in touch with their sexuality due to their own upbringing. We know from the literature on neurobiology that there can be an intergenerational transmission of trauma. We experience sexual trauma from not having sufficient information about sex when we really do want to reach out. From birth until about age three, sexuality is autoerotic—although a fetus begins to explore its body in the womb. When they get to the genital area, they tend to linger there, and they tend to go back there more frequently than other areas of the body. So, even then, they're curious and receive some pleasure in touch.

RLM: What you said is right out of our psychology laboratories: do something rewarding and you want to do it again. People stumble upon some place in their body that feels good when touched and they want to touch it again. Makes perfect sense.

SR: Exactly. It begins in the womb. It's natural, a part of fetal and neonatal development. Obviously, it's natural! One woman told me that her mother was looking over her shoulder watching one day as she was diapering her son. He developed an erection, and her mother automatically raised her hand to hit the little boy's hand away. My client grabbed her mother's hand and said, "Don't you ever do that to my son." She told me she felt like she had prevented a form of sex abuse.

RLM: Very moving. We're so very messed up as a culture with regard to sex.

SR: It's not just the culture; it's the entire world, I must say. I think it started with the ancient Greeks actually. I thought the Romans and Greeks were a bit ahead of us in their sexual practices, and that the real problems began with Christianity. But maybe you're correct. Even the ancient Greeks were screwed up sexually.

RLM: Men are also cheered on by the culture for having sex. Sexually active men are called studs. However there's still a lot of slut-shaming going on.

SR: Yes, a lot of slut-shaming.

RLM: But again, our story always comes back to a denial of pleasure. Pleasure has gotten a bad reputation, and pleasure keeps getting pushed down further and further.

SR: There's a series of books by the French philosopher Michel Foucault, who wrote about the history of pleasure. He talks about how pleasure has been denied all the way back to the Greeks—and, I would assume, by the Romans as well, because the Romans were a warlike people. That's very left-brain, which is not sexual. It's the right brain where sexual desire, discovery, and creativity blossom.

THE FEMALE ORGASM

RLM: In preparing for today's interview and doing some research, I read that the average size of a man's penis is somewhere between five and six and a half inches. As you just pointed out, the average size of the clitoris is somewhere between seven and eight inches. So the clitoris, rather than being tiny, is actually longer than a man's penis. Yet, we only found this out in 1998. We put a man on the moon before we had an anatomical description of the clitoris. The clitoris—a great source of female pleasure—has been ignored by science for millennia. This has contributed to the orgasm gap.* Males orgasm significantly more often than females.

SR: There are a couple of reasons. First, when boys learn to masturbate, they learn to masturbate as quickly as they can—and they *aim* for ejaculation. That's good for perpetuating the species, but not for being a great lover. It's not even good for enjoying the nuances of sex, because there's more to sex than just coming. When a man orgasms so quickly, he's not getting as much out of this experience as he could. He's getting an experiential sleeping pill, not the full experience of being aroused to the point where an orgasm fills his body. Men can learn to have multiple orgasms. One of the best ways to learn how to do that is by masturbating and stopping just prior to the point of an inevitability. That enables him to learn to relax back into the pleasure of the experience, to allow the experience to spread through the body, so that the final result isn't just a local sensation in the genitals. What makes it so difficult for females to have an orgasm is that a lot of females don't masturbate as girls. That is a great limitation.

---

*See Katherine Rowland's book *The Pleasure Gap*.

RLM: You're saying that masturbation is a kind of training for later lovemaking with another person?

SR: That's right. Women learn to turn off their sexual desire because it's not "ladylike." Having an orgasm for a man, we might say, is ego-syntonic, in harmony with their sense of self. A man feels like a stud. But for some females, it's ego-*dystonic,* because they don't feel lady-like, pure, or chaste.

RLM: You're saying that we're still dealing with suppressive morality?

SR: It's in our bodies, and it's been passed down from body to body. It's an intergenerational transmission of sexual shame. Men have it as well. The second reason women seemingly take longer to orgasm is that the female anatomy takes much more blood engorgement to fully engorge the whole area for an orgasm. But for the same reasons, when fully turned on, the female is capable of a far more intense orgasm—and even of multiple orgasms—until they are physically exhausted and call it quits. Men have an orgasm and they're kaput.

RLM: Human sexuality suddenly sounds like a cruel joke, where the rapid male orgasm is like a sleeping pill, and women are capable of going on to having multiple orgasms for a long time, but who do they go on with when their guy falls asleep after a minute and a half of sex?

SR: I would like to add one other important note: men are often focused on performance, on getting it on, getting it off, and getting to sleep. Getting it on means having an erection and an orgasm. That's a performance. When men get more into the experience of what's taking place—into the sensuality of it—everything gets better, both for them and their partner.

MAINTAINING SEXUAL INTEREST
IN LONG-TERM RELATIONSHIPS

RLM: Let's talk about how sexual dynamics change in long-term relationships, because that's something that has held your interest.

SR: Yes. When people come in and tell me they don't have sex, I ask them first, "Do you kiss?" Very simple, because kissing is essential to maintaining a physical connection in a long-term partnership. It's not just dry kissing, which I call kiss-offs. A real kiss is with tongues and swapping saliva, because there are testosterone, estrogen, dopamine, and all sorts of biochemistry in the saliva. That starts a form of arousal.

Also, people don't kiss if they're angry with each other. So when people are not kissing, what grudges are they holding on to? That has to be resolved. When you talk about parents being able to teach kids about sexuality, they have to get in touch with their *own* sexuality. That means they need to get in touch with their love and desire for their partner, as well as their playfulness.

RLM: We know from sexpert research that sexual frequency in a relationship decreases over time. When analyzing the data, we find that sexual activity does decrease as a function of the longevity of a relationship. But isn't that contrary to our self-interests? Those of us who are partnered have a willing partner whom we live with, who cares about us, and—hopefully—loves us, offering us an opportunity to experience pleasure. Instead of engaging in more sex as we get older, though, we engage in less.

SR: Yes, because one of the difficulties in long-term relationships is when people stop being playful with each other. If there's no sex play, sex becomes a ritual or an obligation.

RLM: Back to your point on the difference between real kissing and a "kiss-off." Some couples just give each other a quick peck. We need to take time to kiss each other.

SR: Kiss each other and breathe together. When you're kissing somebody what happens to the breath? You're breathing together, and you're breathing each other's air in and tasting each other's saliva. Of course, you want to brush your teeth so that everything is nice and clean.

RLM: I use Listerine myself. But what you said about what's transmitted in the saliva is important, Stella, and I want to come back and underline it.

SR: Okay. But before we do I want to say more about what happens in the long-term relationship. I think it's important that people do get into a routine. A lot of people get into the routine where they meet together, touch, and kiss a few times, and then they go right into intercourse or oral sex. It's the same thing all the time. It's a ritual; one thing follows the other all the time, and it gets boring.

RLM: Even when it feels so good.

SR: Even when it feels good, it's still boring. People even say, "The sex is good, but I'm not interested anymore. It's the same-old, same-old." I have a joke about that. A son says to his father, "Dad, how do you feel about same-sex marriage?" The father says, "I know all about it. Your mother and I have been having the same sex since we were married."

RLM: Very cute. So good sex is like tending a garden, Stella—you can weed one year and put all kinds of beautiful things in the garden, but the next year, you have to weed again. And you have to also plant more beautiful flowers. You can't just create good sex once and have it sustain you forever.

SR: Exactly. What turns us on sexually is the play. We have that when we first get together, and we first get turned on. It's the newness—the discovery—of the other person's body. But even if you've been with somebody for ten or twenty years, you can still discover places in that body that feel wonderful to the touch, the nibble, or the lick. Where else can you discover each other's bodies? I also tell people never to make love without music.

RLM: Tell us more about that.

SR: Music is how we dance together. Music enables us to get into a rhythm together, into interpersonal synchrony. Making love relies on synchrony on being able to get into resonance with one another. When we're in resonance, our hearts entrain to synchronize our heartbeats, our breathing comes together, and we can feel each other. We get into synchrony. We can feel what's turning our partner on and what's not working. We want to be attuned to each other's bodies in that way—not just go through the motions that we've gone through in the past, but to delay orgasm as long as possible, for females as well as males, so that we can build the arousal. That's what counts.

RLM: When you're building a sex life that way and you're in synchrony and you're in a long-term relationship, is there value to doing different activities in order to maintain the spirit—maybe making love in the kitchen or living room?

SR: There's value in just saying that you're getting out of that routine of, "We're going to make love now; we gotta get into bed." I tell people all the time: the bed is a place where sex ends, not where it begins. Start anywhere *but* the bedroom. People even say to me, "I want to work on what happens for my husband and me in the bedroom." The first thing to do is get out of the bedroom. The bedroom is the place where we go unconscious, where we go to sleep. Get out of the bedroom. Start by putting music on, dancing together, kissing, and playing with each other and put some candlelight on. Create an environment that's sexy for you. Don't just do it as a routine. Do it as a way of creating *art*.

RLM: So you're saying eroticize the whole house—not just one room in the house—and create an erotic atmosphere? An erotic environment.

SR: Right. If one of you is washing the dishes, the other person can come in and stand behind him or her and massage their body or kiss the back of his or her neck. Anything but saying, "Wanna get into bed and have sex?"

RLM: Now what about those people who have two kids in the house? What do you say to them about how to eroticize the environment in a way that makes them still feel like they're not perverts for doing weird things in front of their kids?

SR: You don't do weird things in front of the kids, and you don't have to eroticize the environment, just *be with your partner* in your environment. Being sweet, huggy, and playful is enough. It doesn't have to involve red lights, gauzy fabric, and all that nonsense. That's not necessary unless you like it. You don't have to do anything special in your environment, and you certainly don't want to be overtly sexual in front of your children, because that also has unpleasant ramifications. I once had a client who had a lot of difficulty with sexuality, and he attributed it to the fact that his mother was flirtatious, even with him. He witnessed a lot of sexual play between his parents, and he felt threatened by it. He attributed some of his sexual issues to that very openness, an open sexuality between his parents in front of him. So you have to be careful, obviously.

RLM: So much of what you're saying, Stella, sounds so reasonable and natural. But, sadly, it sounds like it's going to take fifty to a hundred years to get our culture to the place you're describing. It stretches my imagination to think of the American public allowing their children to masturbate, or allowing themselves to learn—from a *class*—how to teach their children to masturbate.

SR: You don't have to teach your children that it's okay to masturbate. All you have to do is not shame them. Masturbating is very natural, and we're born with that ability. We know about childhood development that there are critical periods for everything, and that there's one for sexuality. The critical period for sex play starts at around age three or four. Many cultures share the term: *playing doctor*. I asked all my clients from Iran, Brazil, Germany, and England. It's amazing. I asked my Iranian client, "How do you refer to 'playing doctor' in Iran?" She thought about it and said, "Playing doctor."

MALE VERSUS FEMALE ORGASMS

RLM: Because the doctors are the only ones that are allowed to look at your genitals. Let's talk about male and female orgasms.

SR: Yes. One of the ways in which I describe the difference between male orgasm and female orgasm is that a male orgasm is more like a sneeze whereas a female orgasm is more like a yawn. Does that make sense to you?

RLM: The sneeze I get because it's explosive. But why the yawn?

SR: Because when a woman orgasms, her vagina opens and her uterus drops down like a *V.*

RLM: In order to receive the sperm.

SR: But this is called a valley orgasm and it's the most intense kind of vaginal orgasm for a female. A clitoral orgasm feels more like a male orgasm because it's localized. But with a vaginal orgasm, it's like the entire vulva opens. It's a more intense orgasm. When you have the clitoral orgasm followed by a vaginal orgasm, that's the most intense of all. A lot of women don't want to have intercourse until they've had their first clitoral orgasm, and then they're ready for a vaginal orgasm. Don't believe any writing that says women do not have vaginal orgasms. That is absolutely false.

RLM: You' mentioned earlier that the clitoris is not a button, but that it's actually a wishbone. I discussed this with Katherine Rowland, but an Australian urologist named Dr. Helen McConnell did anatomical dissections in 1998 and informed the world that part of the clitoris goes down in circles into the vagina.* She says anatomically, the entire vaginal wall is made up of clitoral material. So that little button has an eight-inch root, which then becomes barrel shaped.

I'm asking myself, "How the heck is it that we figured out how to go to the moon, we invented electric cars, we discovered penicillin, and it took until 1998 for a female Australian urologist to describe what the clitoris actually *is?*" I want to talk to you about the *orgasm gap*. Have you heard that term? Sex researcher, Katherine Rowland is saying there's a direct relationship between the relative amounts of money that males and females make and the discrepancy between

---

*Reported in an article "Get Cliterate: How a Melbourne Doctor is Redefining Female Sexuality" in *The Sydney Morning Herald* on December 8, 2018.

the percentage of males and females who have orgasms. The number of men who have orgasms is about 80–90 percent, whereas the percentage of women who have orgasms is about 20 percent. They believe the suppression of female orgasms is politically motivated. In other words, over hundreds—maybe thousands—of years, women's orgasms have been suppressed.

SR: It's suppressed through childhood development in that girl children are much more protected from their sexuality, the idea being that their sexuality can be abused, or that they have to be careful because males want virgins. You know the philosophy of, "If you can get the milk for free, why buy the cow?" So there are many reasons why female sexuality is suppressed, but I don't know whether it's related to their income.

RLM: Katherine Rowland is saying, "You see how women make less money than men? Women also have fewer orgasms than men. Both of those events are a symbol of male dominance." It's not that the money is related directly to the orgasm, but they're correlated in the sense that they're symbolic of male domination and male control of women—controlling the money, controlling the orgasms, controlling power—not a far cry from when we owned you.

SR: Right. Males tend to be controlling. There's no doubt about that.

RLM: We're raised to be controlling.

SR: But some women like that. Some women like a strong male. Certainly, women tend to prefer strong men. I talked earlier today about a client, a couple. The male was a big, strong-looking guy, very handsome, and the woman was very attractive. But she lost interest in him. As I was working with them, I saw how careful he was with her and how he treated her like a porcelain doll. The way he touched her was so careful. As I saw that, I thought, *Gee, how come he's coming on like such a wimp?* I could understand why she wasn't attracted to him. So I gave them a little exercise. Each could say one word to the other partner. They were going to take turns saying that word to each other, and they needed to lean into it and give it an emotional expression. I gave her the word "Yes" and him the word "No." I asked, "Who wants to start?" He said, "I will," and yelled, "No!" I thought to myself, *Finally!* It's so important to be able to say no to her, to show her his strength because women do like men with muscles and power. We do enjoy that aspect. We also like them to be tender with us, but not only tender and careful. Have a little *oomph*.

RLM: Part of females liking male muscularity is deeply built in, in terms of being protected. At the animal level, coming out of the caves, men had to be large enough to protect a woman. I wonder if we're still dealing with that inheritance.

SR: Essential.

DON'T HOLD YOUR BREATH, DON'T SUCK YOUR BELLY IN

RLM: I want you to talk to us about the place of breathing in enjoying sexuality.

SR: There's nothing that kills sex more than holding your breath. If you get together with your partner, your partner is touching you and you're holding your breath, you're aiming for a particular place, and they're not getting there, that's going to kill any sexuality. If you're holding your breath, you're typically not only holding your chest but your belly. We carry a lot of tension in our bellies, we somatize our emotions in our belly. If you hold the belly during sex, you're preventing the blood from flowing deeply into your genital area. This is particularly important for people with body image issues. Blood flow in the genital area is responsible for both male erection and female lubrication. So it's important to breathe into your belly, have your belly open and feel it moving when you're making love. When you're kissing, get into a rhythm together. That's the value of having music. You're both listening to the same music, almost choreographing your lovemaking.

RLM: That's beautifully said. I'd like to ask you to take a pause and think of anything relevant that you might want to discuss that we missed.

SR: Oh, great. One of the issues that happens between partners—it could be two males or two females—is winning versus loving. I remember one time I was with my husband, Alan, and we were having a spat. He was really fighting me on it, and I didn't want to fight with him anymore. So I said to him, "Honey, would you rather be right, or would you rather get laid?"

RLM: I think that's a perfect place to end our interview, and let every male read it. *Would you rather be right or get laid?*

SR: I also want to point out the importance of humor. People who laugh together stay together.

2

Katherine Rowland

Bridging the Gender Gap in the Bedroom and the Boardroom

Public health researcher and journalist Katherine Rowland spent five years talking with 120 women about sexuality and desire. The result, her book *The Pleasure Gap: American Women and the Unfinished Sexual Revolution,* is out now.

Rowland believes it's time to take inequality in the bedroom as seriously as we take it in the boardroom. This is the premise of her book, based on extensive interviews with women.

Why are we so afraid, as a culture, of talking about women's sexuality? In her book, Rowland considers how factors like education, bias in scientific research, social messaging, long-term monogamy, and sexual and gendered violence contribute to women's sexual malaise. She finds no silver bullet to close the pleasure gap, but her wide-ranging foray into women's sexuality clarifies that the epidemic of sexual dissatisfaction is about more than a few missing orgasms. It's about the complex interaction between culture, biology, capitalism, history, and our shifting ideas about what is right and natural. It's symptomatic of an unfinished revolution—and nobody should settle for it.

Rowland is based in Brooklyn, New York, and her work has appeared in *Aeon,* the *Financial Times, The Guardian, Psychology Today,* and *Nature,* among others. She is currently a contributing editor at *The Guardian,* the host of *Seeking,* a podcast from Sony Music

Entertainment, and is writing a biography of Anaïs Nin, forthcoming from Crown. She is also formerly the publisher of *Guernica Magazine*. You can find her other work at *katherinerowland.com*.

THE ORGASM GAP

Dr. Richard L. Miller (RLM): I'm excited to be talking to you about your book, *The Pleasure Gap*. It's a great book with an amazing amount of material. Let's begin with your talking to us about the orgasm gap.

Katherine H. Rowland (KHR): The orgasm gap describes the differential rate at which men and women achieve sexual satisfaction during their interactions. A lot of research suggests that, in your run-of-the-mill heterosexual encounter, a man will reach orgasm about three times as frequently as his female partner. Crucially, these numbers begin to shift and appear less unsettling when the sexual dynamic includes more than penetrative sex. In instances where couples engage in fondling, deep kissing, manual or oral stimulation, you start seeing women begin to attain pleasure at a much higher rate. We also know that when it's a couple's first time or a one-off hook-up, women tend not to fare so well.

That said, experience goes a long way and women experience orgasm more regularly when they've been with someone for six months or more. These numbers also change significantly when you look outside of heterosexual couples: queer women report consistently higher rates of pleasure, which means that what we're seeing isn't some cruel expression of biology that renders women less capable of enjoying themselves—as many have suggested—but, rather, that social and relational factors play a huge role in how and what we feel.

RLM: Give us some numbers in terms of the percentage of heterosexual males and females who achieve orgasm compared to lesbian women.

KHR: For heterosexual men, orgasm is near universal; it happens around 90 to 96 percent of the time. But for heterosexual women, orgasm occurs around 65 percent of the time—bearing in mind, this improves when couples are more familiar or include oral sex or a vibrator. Women who have sex with women experience orgasm at a much higher rate, around 85 percent of the time.

RLM: So what do gay women know that heterosexual couples don't know?

KHR: Many things, but the overwhelming issue on the table is that sex looks different. You're dealing with a different set of assumptions about what pleasure should look and feel like and about parity and who is supposed to attain pleasure in an encounter. Sex between two women often lasts much longer. It's not focused on penetration as the ultimate expression of an erotic encounter. It's much more wide-ranging. It can be more curious, which is not to say that lesbian sex can't also fall into the same ruts that beset heterosexual couples. But you're proceeding from the outset that sex is something different than, "Man mounts woman, penetrates her a few times, groans, and then the act is done," which leaves both partners unhappy.

RLM: What you just described about the man mounting the woman, jumping around, having an orgasm, ejaculating, and leaving the woman, sounds exactly like the animals on my little farm. You're describing what my dogs, cats, and chickens do. The chickens are the fastest, by the way. So you're describing animal behavior without a sense of empathy or care for the other person. It's almost like sex has been relegated to being some form of relief mechanism.

KHR: I think you could certainly say that—though, interestingly, among some other primates, females are highly sexually expressive and will go around trying to satisfy that itch by moving through a suite of male partners. What you're seeing between humans is a diminishment of the real possibility that we have this rich, erotic potential. That potential, perhaps a gift to ourselves as humans, is being squashed down and reduced to transactional encounters that don't yield any lasting satisfaction for anyone.

ORGASM GAP AND INCOME GAP
INTERLINKED

RLM: Let's take a look at this from a political perspective. We have the income gap, whereby when two people, male and female, have the exact same merits and skills, the female makes significantly less money.

In human sexuality, when we have two people, male and female, with similar sexual plumbing, the males have much more satisfaction. The two graphs—income and sexual satisfaction disparity—look quite similar. Does the research appear to indicate that men have suppressed women's orgasms and subjugated them to a position where the men "get off," have their pleasure, and the women are having significantly less pleasure just as they are making less income?

KHR: I love that we're framing this as a political issue because that's important. I think that the idea of women's perceived and experienced social value in a sexual situation tracks closely with what we're seeing in terms of women's economic standing. But we need to complicate this question of suppression, because I would argue that it's historical. In Western Europe, just a few hundred years ago, women's orgasm was often seen as a necessary component of reproduction. If men had to achieve a certain level of heat to release their seed, women, too, were believed to need to experience orgasm in order to be receptive to that seed and to become pregnant. This was so strong in the medical understanding that it shows up in early court documents. If a woman's rape resulted in pregnancy, that was seen as the outcome of a pleasurable encounter, and therefore it could not be persecuted as rape. So while there is a long-standing subjugation of women through the ages, the way that has played out in terms of sexual understanding has shifted considerably. This shows up, too, in twentieth-century American politics. There was a moment in the sixties and seventies—before the rise of the religious right in the eighties and nineties—when women's orgasms and the orgasm gap looked different than it does today.

RLM: Orgasm is an act and an expression of intense human pleasure. Talk to us about how pleasure itself got such a bad rap in our culture.

KHR: Yes, why did pleasure become something that we became wary of as opposed to celebrating? I have a couple of ideas. One returns to social control. When people own their pleasure, they're able to exert more authority and decision-making power in a way that doesn't necessarily hew with current social conventions. If a woman felt fully empowered and said, "I relish my body and the pleasure it's able to give me," would she be content in a loveless marriage filled with drudgery? I would argue, no. But the larger reasons why pleasure has gotten such a bad rap have to do with politics and the rise of extremist religious values in our culture today, which has filtered into the ways in which we educate young people about what is good, normal, and healthy. We've removed pleasure from a public-health dialogue and turned it into a vice—to the detriment of everyone.

RLM: Yes, pleasure is considered a vice. I can't help but think that religion is creating these terrible misconstructions. The endemic hypocrisy is regrettable. I'm not comfortable appearing to attack religion, but it seems to be the boldface truth that the Judeo-Christian and Islamic traditions have undermined human pleasure, while at the same time there are all the atrocities that are going on in the world. In addition, fear is being spread—and now, even the possibility of nuclear war. It seems so sad that we're putting one of our biggest positives, namely pleasure, into a garbage heap and shaming ourselves and calling ourselves bad.

KHR: Yes, that we condemn rather than educate around our body's essential functions and undermine what pleasure can give us is remarkable. I hate to speak in blanket terms around Judeo-Christian or Islamic faiths. But I do feel comfortable speaking about political developments in the U.S. starting in the late seventies and early eighties. They continue at pace today, and they have stripped women and women's bodies of their autonomy, increased women's social and political vulnerability, and presented sex as something that we should flinch in the face of and greet with shame—something that should only take place in a highly restricted container. It's hard to tease that stringency and surveillance apart from the other larger, incredibly disturbing developments in the world today, wherein our very humanity appears so disposable and indispensable.

DENIGRATION OF FEMALE SEXUALITY IN RESEARCH AND CULTURE

RLM: I want to read something from your book:

"Among first-time hookups, the orgasm gap reflected the national average. The men had three orgasms on average for every one of the women. However, the likelihood of orgasm among the women did increase over repeat encounters. Moreover, when sexual interactions entailed more than penetration, the women's orgasms increased dramatically."

Now, this is interesting to me, because you and I both know the work of Helen McConnell, the Australian urologist. Part of what's so important about Helen's work is that she brought it to us in 1998. At that time, we had already been on the moon for thirty years. We already had cars, we had penicillin, and, then, for the first time in history—*in 1998*—an Australian urologist diagramed the full female clitoris. Then I read that, in 1985, *Grey's Anatomy*—the number one anatomy book on the planet—completely ignored the clitoris. This is not science fiction. These are political acts, not accidents. McConnell taught us that the clitoris isn't just a little button sticking out from a hood at the top of a woman's vulva. Furthermore, it isn't a wishbone, with two little roots going down the side from that button. The clitoris goes all the way down into the vagina and creates the vaginal wall. McConnell then documents how in development, the same material makes the clitoris and the penis. One of the wonderful funny things about all this, especially considering all the cultural emphasis on the big penis and the tiny clitoris, is that as it turns out, the clitoris is much longer than the penis. The clitoris is a big organ in itself. What do you make of all this?

KHR: It's mind-blowing that this information arrived so late. By the time the world finally realized the clitoris was a complex organ, the federal government was in the process of mandating that Medicaid cover Viagra—this just months after the wonder drug hit the market. The history is so fascinating because you see the clitoris flicker in and out of focus for hundreds of years preceding Helen's research. It was documented by early anatomists who varied in their interpretation of what it was. To some, it was this miraculous flower, this seed of pleasure, this perfume of women's feminine expression. Others reviled it as the devil incarnate and this horrible seed that led men astray like sailors to sirens. What's so remarkable in more recent history is that despite this discovery, the clitoris remains largely absent from education. It remains neglected in medical textbooks. You have volume upon volume, elaborating the anatomy of the penis—how to preserve it, fortify it, and create compounds to strengthen its sexual power. Yet, there's such scant literature on the clitoris. Where are the equivalent tomes that tell us what this organ is? Even terming it an organ and not shrugging it off as an accident of evolution—let alone the accidental discovery of naughty fingers traversing one's own body, which is how it continues to be perceived popularly—speaks so loudly toward our continued denigration of women's physicality and sexuality.

RLM: Yes, I agree, we see the denigration of women's sexuality and pleasure. I'm going to read something else from your book:

> Anthropologists have observed that in cultures that expect women to enjoy sex as much as men do, women have regular orgasms, whereas cultures that question the propriety of female pleasure are home to greater orgasmic difficulties.

Talk to us about that sentence.

KHR: I'll add the caveat that a lot of the research around this area can be less firm than one would like because it's so hard to get at. What do we mean by pleasure across cultures? Who are you talking to? But in broad strokes, you see that in cultures that don't view women's pleasure as an aberrant phenomenon, something attained with one's mistress or outside of sanctioned loving, male partners engage in a way that is supportive of sexual expression. You're able to be more curious about one's body, and curiosity isn't accompanied with damnation or criticism; it's nurtured. Where the expectation of sexual enjoyment exists, it changes the entire terrain of intimate interactions. But on the flip side, if the cultural script reads that women's pleasure is dirty or secondary to male pleasure, or that women's bodies are hard to operate and their desire occupies tenuous ground, and we assume that women are naturally less sexual creatures than men, then their pleasure isn't going to feature prominently during sexual interactions, and as a consequence women will experience orgasm less regularly.

RLM: You quote a researcher named Roy F. Baumeister, who talks about *erotic plasticity*. When we talk about *cognitive plasticity,* we talk about the brain being able to bring in new material, change itself, and grow intellectually. Baumeister reports that women are even more susceptible than men to the peer pressure that comes from the culture.* When females live in a tribe, in which it's expected that they'll have more pleasure, they do. When women are in a suppressive culture, their pleasure is suppressed. In other words, women are more sensitive to what the culture is pressing on them. Is that correct?

KHR: That's correct. Women's desire and pleasure appear far more vulnerable to shifting social context and social mores. A number of questions surround why that might be the case and whether that's built into women's physiology or whether it's a learned state. That's because of the inequitable way in which women are punished for deviating from social expectations, or the inequitable way in which women have to perform certain duties for the home and community, leaving little room for their pursuit of sexual pleasure. More research to that end is warranted.

---

*See "Gender differences in erotic plasticity: The female sex drive as socially flexible and responsive" by R. F. Baumeister, published in *Psychological Bulletin* 126(3) in 2000.

POLICING YOUR OWN PLEASURE

RLM: I want you to talk to us about researcher Carole Vance, who says that women's impulses are being poisoned. Their desire is poisoned, which creates self-doubt and anxiety. She even says that pleasure for men is giving men their due—whereas, for women, it's an accidental aside.

KHR: Carole's work does a great job at pointing out that, for women, pleasure and danger are often hideously commingled so that women can often come to associate their desires as incurring bodily or social harm. So you start policing yourself from the get-go because you anticipate that, should you express who you fully are sexually, you're going to be castigated.

RLM: You quote another scientist, Nicole Prause, who says that the National Institute of Health accused her of being an immoral person because she wanted to study sexuality.

KHR: Nicole's research is amazing. She was running a prestigious lab at UCLA. She wanted to ask sensible questions about how orgasm and pleasure contribute to health. In one study, she wanted to look at orgasm as having a mediating effect on depression, and her university review board said, "Hey, the depression study is great, as long as you remove the orgasm component." When her federal grant proposals were under review, reviewers termed them immoral and not worthy of public funding. It returns to the question of what this says about women's worth, and why we're so willing to segregate women's health from their sexuality. Why is women's sexuality not seen as an essential component of their overall health and well-being? Instead, it becomes this dirty, untouchable domain. That should give all of us pause. There's no reason why research into orgasm, a natural bodily function—which is the outcome of healthy sexuality in healthy sexual interactions—should be considered immoral. We should know as much as we possibly can about it.

RLM: Richard von Krafft-Ebing was the leading sex researcher in the nineteenth century. Some consider him the first sex researcher. He was ostracized and took a tremendous amount of abuse. Alfred Kinsey, arguably the greatest sex researcher of the twentieth century and the founder of the Kinsey Institute at the University of Indiana, had his career ruined for studying sexuality. The Rockefeller Foundation took away his research money and he died a broken man. Now, you're bringing information about this particular researcher, Nicole Prause, taking heat for doing sexual research. A Massachusetts Institute of Technology researcher that I've also interviewed for this book, Ogi Ogas—who wrote an important book called *A Billion Wicked Thoughts*—has also taken heat for engaging in sex research. Are you familiar with the book?

KHR: Yes. He used AI to identify people's search patterns.

RLM: Exactly. He literally identified a billion different pieces of data on what pornography viewers are looking at. But the heat he took for doing the research is just as important. This is a prominent researcher at a prominent university in the year 2022, and he's taking heat for doing sex research. I don't even know how to put words to what a serious, painful, sad position we've gotten ourselves into. Which brings us to the absence of real sex education in this country.

KHR: It's glaring, and this issue has worsened over the past decades, with politics playing an increasingly large role in determining who learns what and where. Some sex ed has taken a hearteningly progressive turn in certain schools and pockets of the country, but this is far from representative. Elsewhere, we are stripping information of its scientific integrity, depriving children of knowledge that they should have every right to and giving them horror stories, or simply presenting sex as something that either results in reproduction, disease, or pathology. In the meantime, issues of the orgasm gap are reified in early education. Because we see that men's pleasure is discussed—men have erections and ejaculate and have orgasms, but women's sexuality is considered only in terms of its reproductive potential—there is no mention of women's entitlement to pleasure or how that might remotely be achieved during the course of sex.

THE POLITICS OF FAKING IT
AND CARETAKING

RLM: I'm going to wrap up this section with another quote from your book. This is a quote from the American Psychological Association, the largest association of psychologists on the planet. You are talking about the consequences of the cultural attitudes towards women, and the APA psychologists say the consequences are ghastly. They include body dissatisfaction, eating disorders, low self-esteem, depression, anxiety, a range of physical health problems, and even impaired and fragmented consciousness. The APA authors state that, taken together, these detriments suggest that the sexualization practices in the United States may function to keep girls "in their place" as objects of sexual attraction and beauty, significantly limiting their free-thinking and movement in the world. That is a powerful statement. Let's talk about what you call the politics of faking it, and what women are telling you.

KHR: We all know what faking it is—when a woman is in bed with a man and instead of actually experiencing any kind of pleasure, she feigns arias of delight to bring the experience to a close. I have to admit that when I began this research, my exposure to faking it had always been in the context of humor, be it appropriate or not. It's so often made fun of, and often the man is presented as the humiliated party hoodwinked by a performance. So he is the poor guy because he is subject to this misleading transaction. As I started talking to women, faking it became an almost ubiquitous feature of their sexual experiences, and the research certainly pointed this out, as well. The surveys aren't great; a lot have been conducted by mass media outlets. But these suggest a significant number of women are faking half the time, if not all the time. As I had these conversations, I realized that this wasn't a jokey matter. Women are the injured party here, and they feel that expectation to perform for their male partner so strongly, that even when they're in pain or discomfort—or not sexually engaged at all—they feel like they have to *perform* pleasure for their partners. This played out to such an extreme that women could be in acute physical pain. Rather than feeling like they could say, "I need you to stop, I'm uncomfortable," they follow through with this pressure to act out delight. That to me was horrifying and suggested that we need to reframe our conversation around what faking it is. We need to equip women with the ability to dictate the course of their sexual interactions more clearly, and also diminish the expectation that women have orgasms that follow the track of their male partners.

RLM: Talk to us about how faking it relates to what you call caretaking.

KHR: What I mean by that is that women are oftentimes *groomed*. I don't think that term is too strong. They're brought up with the idea that they need to minister to the sexual and emotional needs of their male partners. This might show up in a variety of domestic ways, but also in tending to their male partners' sexual satisfaction. It falls under the larger canopy of emotional labor that women are taking on. Not only do they need to assure their partners experience orgasm and pleasure, but they also need to sustain the illusion that their partners have performed in such a way that they too have experienced pleasure. What an enormous caretaking burden that is to take on.

RLM: An enormous burden. You say that 70 to 80 percent of middle-class women are deprived of orgasm, because of the excessive speed of the husband's orgasm and concomitant ejaculation. Now, everything I've read over the last half-century seems to agree that the average male in the United States has an orgasm, during sexual activity, in under five minutes. Does that meet with the research that you've done?

KHR: It's not an encouraging number. I think the quote you shared aligns with the findings of early researchers like Kinsey. You have these floundering marriages and unhappy couples because the men aren't lasting long enough to bring women into a state of excitement, and for them to get going enough to enjoy what their bodies have to offer them. As expectations continue along these inequitable lines of who deserves pleasure, who should expect pleasure, then that jackrabbit-y response is allowed to persist.

RLM: Yes, it's connected to what we said about the lack of education and the perspective on sexuality, of whose pleasure this is for. Obviously, we need to teach men, "Hey guys, here's the situation: you come in four to six minutes, and the women are left hanging because they are genetically built to require ten or twenty minutes. So we've got a little problem with nature here. We've got to do something about it. What you guys need to do is, after you come in like a jackrabbit, you need to hang in there a little while longer, do oral and other things with your fingers, make love with your whole body, not just with your penis." A lot of male sexuality is about putting their penis in, finishing, and being done. It's not about "making love."

KHR: Right. It's important in this conversation to emphasize that men, too, are missing out. They're missing out on not only the full range of sexual possibilities of their female partners but on their own range. If they think all they're capable of is four minutes of penetration resulting in a humdrum orgasm, that's limiting their experience to a devastating degree.

AMERICA'S UNRECOGNIZED RAPE EPIDEMIC

RLM: Let's move on to something even more difficult: rape statistics in the United States. It's breathtaking, as you point out in your book, that roughly 36 times in every hour of the day, a woman is raped in the United States. I guess I'm a softy. I read that, and I start to cry. I can feel tears welling up thinking that I live in a world like that. We're not calling this an epidemic, yet it *is* an epidemic. If 315,000 people, each year, contracted any kind of illness by comparison, you'd call it an epidemic.

KHR: Exactly. And why is this metabolized as the status quo, as an acceptable state of affairs? Why are we not out in the streets, demanding to see this as the crisis that it is? I think I'm a bit of a softy, too. I felt, in the course of my interviews, almost ill-equipped to meet with this devastating reality being articulated over and over again—almost as ubiquitously as faking it. Women are either having direct experiences with some form of sexual or physical trauma or near exposure to it.

RLM: I'm scratching my head and I'm thinking, how does this happen politically? How are we not calling 315,000 rapes per year an epidemic? How are we not calling attention to it? Then I read, in your book, that marital rape wasn't considered illegal in all states until 1993. So what you're telling us is that, prior to that, a man could rape his wife.

KHR: Rape laws through the 1970s excluded spouses—if coercive sex took place between a husband and wife, it wasn't considered actual rape.

RLM: Lingering on the books, as legal laws, is a way of saying that certain kinds of rape are okay. There's no red line. Rape is not okay. Yet the law, in these states, was such that if you marry a woman, you can rape her. We've gotten through that painful chapter in history, which was less than just thirty years ago. Maybe we'd better go on to something easier to deal with—talk to us about boring sex.

KHR: Boring sex, I think, is crushingly common. Again, what people expect to see in sex doesn't look particularly interesting, experimental, or attuned to what people want. The corollary to boring sex is when you talk to people about their sexual imaginations, they're far more wide-ranging. They often flirt with taboo elements that run up against the power dynamics that contour the relationships they're in. Somehow, that is all abandoned when you come together with someone else. So boring sex is such a crushing phenomenon. It plods alongside this rich realm of imagination that many quietly harbor and yet don't feel empowered to express.

RLM: How is boring sex related to your concept of *dead bedrooms?*

KHR: *Dead bedroom* is a rather odious term that has been applied to a lot of long-term relationships where all sex, all activity, all interest, and all heat have steadily been extinguished until the relationship is almost sexless and the partners have drifted apart. Sexless marriage is now understood as couples who come together less than ten times per year. But I would argue that part of why that happens is sex becoming unsatisfying. When this is commonly explained, women are frequently positioned as being at fault. Indeed, I started this research to investigate female sexual dysfunction, the idea that women's desire had grown pathologically low and should be treated. What I came to believe was that low libido and a resulting disinterest in sex was oftentimes a healthy response to sex that was boring, unfulfilling, unchanging, and not oriented towards women's pleasure.

THE PATHOLOGY OF INHIBITED SEXUAL DESIRE

RLM: The DSM stands for *Diagnostic Statistical Manual.* This is the book that psychologists and psychiatrists all over the United States, if not the world, use for diagnoses. It names the diagnostic label along with the behavioral description. You bring to our attention that the DSM has a category called "inhibited sexual desire."

In itself, if you make it into the DSM, you're in a pathological condition because the DSM is a categorization of pathology. The DSM isn't meant to be a health book—this is a pathology book. Inhibited sexual desire is now officially considered pathological. Please talk to us about inhibited sexual desire or what is now officially categorized in the DSM as the highly sanitized new category, *hypoactive sexual desire disorder.* This new nomenclature is important because the older label, *inhibited sexual desire,* implies there is sexual desire, which is being held back by inhibitions. This further implies that the person is inhibited, which implies that if the person were less inhibited their sexual desire would improve. The implied inhibition is then pathologized by inclusion in the DSM, opening the door for psychotherapy. That the culture itself caused the lowered female sexual desire is not considered.

The new diagnostic label switches the focus from the psychological "*inhibited* sexual desire"—requiring verbal therapy—to the physiological "*hypoactive* sexual desire," which requires medicine. In changing the diagnosis, the medical profession moved in on patient turf held by the psychotherapy profession and brought with them the pharmaceutical industry, who have searched—so far in vain—for a female Viagra.

KHR: This is a relatively recent addition to the DSM. You didn't see these labels crop up until the early 1980s—a time when there were a host of new ideas circulating around women's sexuality, as well as their civic and economic participation more broadly. If we can agree on some level that diseases—what we understand as normal and healthy versus sickly and suboptimal—are cultural, we need to look at shifting ideas about sexuality and womanhood to get at this question. The assumption is there's something wrong with a woman when sexual desire doesn't look the way it should. At that point, we need to stop and ask ourselves, "What do we mean by *should*? What is the entity that we're pathologizing? What are we expecting of a normal and healthy sexual response?" From that point, we've had almost three decades of trying to determine what healthy desire is. How do we qualify—let alone quantify—something as elusive, subjective, and vulnerable to the changing tides and seasons as desire? How do we treat that? Can it be approached in a standardized manner, in a way that does not pathologize a woman's healthy response to her circumstances? The other piece that we see at work is that so many of those labels around sexual response or female sexual interest and arousal disorder, which I believe is the current diagnostic term, are divorced from the social context in which a woman is expressing low desire. So even though this pathetic parade of treatments that are steadily pushed into the consumer market addresses female desire as an empowering act of reclaiming your health, it's still not addressing the underlying concern that women feel *vulnerable*. Society remains not sexually educated. Lives are endangered, and you come home and women are still tasked with having a professional career but also doing all that caretaking in their relationships or their families. Ultimately, that's what's sapping their desire.

RLM: There's also the fact that New York psychiatrist Dr. Julie Holland reports in her book, *Moody Bitches,* that 26 million women in the United States are on antidepressant drugs. Tell us about anti-depressant drugs and sexual desire.

KHR: It feels like a chicken-egg situation. Part of why we started investigating low sexual desire was in response to the uptick in women taking anti-depressant drugs. But we're also living in an overmedicated moment when not just the 26 million women are on antidepressant drugs. A battery of other pharma is piled on top of that. With antidepressants, too, we're treating one symptom with a pill and not looking at the larger universe of concerns. Since we render women's sexuality secondary socially, it's seen as an acceptable sacrifice in the name of ministering to mental health needs.

RLM: Yes, and anti-depressants numb sensation. I remember one of the first published articles about Prozac, which appeared in *The New York Times* many years ago, in which the author says, "Oh, what a wonderful feeling. I'm feeling better. I don't seem to care about things anymore. But I did note that at my mother's funeral, I wasn't able to cry." How is such a drug going to affect one's *sexuality?* Our culture ignores the woman's seat of pleasure, the clitoris. We slut-shame a woman when she has a sexual appetite. We're calling men studs when they have the exact same appetite. We're telling scientists that if they research women's sexuality, they're immoral. It's amazing women have any sexual appetite whatsoever. One could easily get to a place of "Why bother with all this sex? It's too much trouble."

KHR: That calls our attention to how powerful the female sexual drive is that it's still able to overcome this tremendous baggage—the shaming and the pathologizing, the danger and the threat—and still, women are expressing their appetite to an incredible degree.

QUANTITY OVER QUALITY

RLM: Extremely astute point. People of all ages ask themselves, "What's a normal amount of sex? What's okay?" You talk about it in terms of how the frequency of sex develops through different stages of life. Tell us about the relationship between age and sexual desire.

KHR: So much of this conversation still tends to overemphasize sexual frequency in place of sexual quality. We're so hung up on how much sex we "should" be having, how much sex is "normal," or whether we're "healthy." We're constantly playing this weird numbers game to figure out where we're positioned on what is already a fictive bell curve. I pause in trotting out numbers because I don't know how healthy they are. Conditions change so much. What we tend to see is gathering sexual energy in your youth that continues to play out with greater sexual frequency in your twenties and early thirties. But in your thirties and fourties, especially if you drift into the latter years of a longer-term, monogamous partnership, those numbers fall off. By your fifties and sixties, you might see sex happening once a week, once every other week, petering out a bit more. Should we be concerned about that? Say you only have sex twelve times a year. But when you have sex it's spectacular, transcendent sex that puts you into communion with the mysteries of your soul and the universe not to mention with the other person. We should celebrate that, not term that as *too little* sex. If you're having constant sex, but it's those sledgehammer three minutes that result in relational despair, we shouldn't be applauding that.

RLM: Call me greedy in saying that the kind of spectacular sex you're talking about experiencing once a month would make one want to switch to once a week or once a day. I mean why get out of bed? However, I will read something else from your book. It says, "If bedroom life revolves around a modest preamble, leading up to penile penetration, women may become increasingly uninterested in intimacy because, so far, it has routinely left them underwhelmed—if not sad, angry, or frustrated."

Another powerful statement. How can we expect anybody to want to do something and reignite themselves when they're being left underwhelmed, sad, angry, or frustrated? You're saying that's happening quite a bit.

KHR: It's not a tiny number; I think that is the norm rather than the deviation. Yet, that does not have to be the case. We can have resplendent sex that we'd want to have every day or at least every week.

RLM: We've created a negative situation in our sexual activity. It's clear from you and other authors and researchers that we have created non-beneficial attitudes about sex. Morality interferes with our pleasure. Men are wired to finish with sex quickly. We have women being put down, by name-calling, societal rejection, or boring sex. As we're doing with our planet, we've taken something beautiful, and we've undermined it. What do we do with the bedroom now? What should women and men do? How do we turn this around?

KHR: That's the question. I'm so glad you mentioned this allegory to the discard with which we treat the earth. The way we storm the planet and trash this miraculous vehicle that we're all on shows up in our lack of empathy and compassion and disdain for fellow humans. This is obviously going to require a much larger cultural shift. But it fundamentally begins with women learning about their own bodies, listening to their bodies, figuring out what their pleasure feels like to become deeply familiar with it. We need to become truly fluent in ourselves because we so often mistake pleasure for something that we derive from our partners. But ultimately it emanates from ourselves. So women becoming versed in how to achieve that on their own— feeling strong and empowered—is going to be the first step. How we give women a sense that they have the entitlement to know their own bodies goes back to our conversation about education. It needs to be a big component of early learning and then revisited over the course of the life span. I don't think you simply learn about anatomy in a scientific, nonshaming way and move on. We need to continually revisit that conversation, just as we should be continually revisiting consent throughout the life span. But we start with women's bodies, and we ensure that all members of society are exposed to that in a way that's grounded in science and human rights.

OVERCOMING SEXUAL INERTIA
BY "JUST DOING IT"

RLM: Women are going to read this interview, and some of them are going to say, "Okay, that's great—but what should I do *tonight?*"

KHR: They should touch themselves.

RLM: That's right in line with other researchers I've interviewed, who emphasize the importance of masturbation and of learning to pleasure oneself. If you don't know how to make yourself feel good, how can you possibly indicate to the other person how to make you feel good? What else might women do with regard to having sex with a guy, if they're heterosexual? One of the things you say in your book is, *just do it*. What does that mean? I don't know how to relate to "just do it."

KHR: I didn't relate to it either. Many women received that advice from therapists, and they balked in the face of "just do it." But once you get in the boat and start paddling, you might actually get somewhere in overcoming that initial inertia around sex. If you're open to the possibility that sex might look and feel differently from the "same-old, same-old" sex that hasn't given you much, you might be able to experience *something*. I initially took issue with the just-do-it philosophy. It's a tall order, but we need to trash that old narrative about the sex that we've been having. If you've been having that boring, old penetrative sex, "just do it" is going to lead you into an encounter where you're going to expect boring, old, penetrative sex, and you're not going to derive any pleasure from it. But you can try to thoroughly destroy old assumptions about sex. Say, for example, that you share a fantasy: some women I spoke to took bold steps outside of their marriages, either having affairs or opening up their partnerships and being with new partners. Some even suspended normative sex and said, "You know what? For tonight or for this week or month, you're not going to orgasm. This is going to be just about me, and maybe I'll orgasm or not, but I need to know that all the focus is on me and we're both going to relearn what's possible in this dynamic and what can transpire in this place."

RLM: Twenty-five hundred years ago—before Christianity—some excellent Chinese books instructed men on how to withhold orgasm and explained to them how it built up their charge and excitement, eroticized their daily life, and gave their women more pleasure. We need to learn about those old Chinese customs. And asking women to "just do it" is a tall order, given their many subjugations we've been talking about. If you don't want to answer the following personal question you're welcome not to: How did writing, five years of research, interviewing, all the work you did, and all you learned affect your personal sex life?

KHR: It's not a straightforward answer. I thought it was going to throw open the doors of my own sexual potential. On a personal level, one of the questions I was investigating is how good it can get. Is there a ceiling? Is transcendent sex available to everyone? I wanted to push the boundaries of what was possible. I'm married, and I've been in a long-term, monogamous partnership for some time. I wanted to look within that container. In the course of researching this book, becoming a mother twice over altered my sexuality. I also lost my brother and my father. So while I was researching pleasure, there was also this deep dive into grief. What came out of it was a more nuanced and productive understanding of pleasure, that pleasure isn't just the pursuit of a good, wonderful feeling. It's the richness of feeling *in general* and being open to feeling the full spectrum of human emotion. Pleasure in all of its tones originally emanates from that receptiveness to the fullness of our *lives*.

RLM: Coming back to your book, is there anything more you'd like to share with us before we conclude?

KHR: Going back to the point that beautiful sex is available and that we don't have to content ourselves with this sad status quo—it's not a matter of altering one's biology or working your way through perceived pathology or deep-seated inhibition. It's learning to tap into gifts that you already possess. I approached this book as a journalist. My background is in public health, so I tended to embrace a scientific mindset for much of this text. Yet, as I heard more stories of beautiful transcendent sex, it was hard to resist the pull of what felt mysterious and sacred. I arrived at a place where I thought, *We need to include a discussion about sacredness in a way that doesn't make people flinch.* We live in a time where we don't want to hear words like *soul* and *sacred* because it sounds too woo-woo, or it's undergirded with religious ideas that make people uncomfortable. But finding a way to incorporate that beauty feels truly fundamental towards restoring our sex to the marvelousness that it can really be.

3

Lonnie Barbach

How Communication Keeps Sex Alive

Lonnie Barbach, Ph.D., is one of the country's foremost experts of human sexuality. Barbach's books have sold over 4 million copies worldwide. Her breakthrough book, *For Yourself: The Fulfillment of Female Sexuality,* opened the closed door to female masturbation and was voted the most important self-help book by 5,000 psychologists.

The 1993 publication of *Going the Distance: Finding and Keeping Lifelong Love,* written with David Geisenger, Ph.D., her partner of thirty-two years, secured Barbach's place as an authority on intimate relationships.

THERE IS NO NORMAL

Dr. Richard Louis Miller (RLM): How much is a normal amount of sex for a particular age? Is there a normal amount?

Lonnie Barbach (LB): There is no "normal" when it comes to sexuality. A normal amount is what feels good for you. The thing about sexuality is that there is an incredible range. What people like to do, how often they like to do it, where they like to do it, and so on varies from person to person. What's important is that you find a partner with whom you have a match both in terms of frequency and composition of sexual practices. You only end up in trouble sexually when you have a *mismatch.*

RLM: So people reading this don't have to Google how many times a week or month or year they need to be making love in order to be "normal"?

LB: It is actually the opposite of that. As soon as you try to meet somebody else's needs or desires, you get away from your own. The whole object of sexuality is to be in *your* body—enjoying your pleasure, while at the same time intimately connecting with someone else. It doesn't matter what everybody else is doing. They're not in the room with you.

RLM: It sounds like a certain amount of luck is involved because two people could enjoy completely different things. So it's important that people find out their preferences before marriage. It reminds me of the famous split screen of Woody Allen and Diane Keaton, where she is saying he always wants sex, and he is saying she never does.

LB: Right.

RLM: So we best look for compatibility rather than for a number?

LB: Right, and you need to be compatible in many areas to have a good relationship. You may put more of a premium on having similar values, coming from a similar religion or background, or even wanting children versus not wanting children. That might make your relationship easier for you, and sex largely contributes to compatibility. If I see a couple that is having sexual issues, the first thing I'll ask them is how their relationship was in the beginning when they first started having sex. If they have had sexual difficulties from the beginning, then they probably weren't so compatible, or other issues were involved. If a couple began by enjoying each other, then we can usually get back to that place. If they never had that feeling, then it's difficult to fabricate. You can't fabricate chemistry. It's either there or it's not there.

RLM: Are people having more or less sex since the sexual revolution and the advent of the pill?

LB: I have no idea. Nobody was taking that many statistics. We have the Kinsey statistics, but who knows how many people lied when they were being asked questions? I personally don't care if people are having more or less sex. I want to make sure they're happy with the amount and quality of sex they're having. Often, quality is more important than quantity. Sometimes people will come in and say, "I need more sex. I want more sex." However, when their relationship gets better and their sexual experience gets more satisfying, they notice that the frequency wasn't as important as they thought it was.

THE EFFECTS OF PORNOGRAPHY

RLM: What kind of effect does pornography have on modern sexuality?

LB: It can have both a positive and a negative effect, depending on the people involved. For some couples, both people involved enjoy pornography. They watch it together as part of their sexual stimulation. Some people use it as an aide to communicate what they like sexually. For others, pornography gets in the way. They get so into it that they are no longer interested in their partner and it interferes with their sexual relationships. Pornography enables people to be inconsiderate to one another, so it can make some people more egocentric about sex.

Some women believe they are not as attractive as the women in porn and think their husband will not be turned on by them if he watches it. They may think of porn as an "either/or" type thing: "If you like porn, then I'm not enough." But porn can offer a different kind of satisfaction that doesn't have to affect them, so long as they're having a good and satisfying sexual relationship together.

RLM: Is pornography the taste of some people in a warehouse in LA, or something the public likes and wants? Is learning about sex from porn like learning how to ride a horse by watching a professional cowboy or learning how to play baseball by watching a professional baseball player? Pornography seems like a very distorted view of sex, because these are professionals chosen for certain physical attributes.

LB: Sex in an intimate relationship has to do with feelings. Pornography can tend toward the extremes. After you've seen people having oral sex, what will you want to see next? The relationship is absent; you need something else *visually,* and you move to more and more extreme images.

I'm specifically interested in the effect of porn on kids who aren't in a sexual relationship. This is their *introduction* to sex. They don't have the experience of what it's like to be involved with someone in a sexual relationship. Instead, they're being stimulated by something purely visual.

Oftentimes it's the case that you get hooked on what you see when you're young, because orgasm is a powerful reinforcer. You get connected to whatever the pornography you happened to tune in on was, and that may limit some people in terms of their exploration and ability to connect sexually. We don't know how that's going to play out yet.

RLM: Nancy Jo Sales has a book out titled *American Girls.* She argues that one of the consequences of pornography is that the self-concept of young girls is centered around being considered hot, so that boys want to "do" them. It's not that the girls want the sex so much as they want to be desired.

LB: That has always been true. One of the difficulties for young women all along has been having to please the guy through sex in order not to lose him. She wants him to find her desirable and attractive. Young women were often not having sex for their own pleasure. That has been an issue for as long as I've been working in the field and even longer.

RLM: In her book *Sex & Girls in America,* Peggy Orenstein discusses a dramatic increase in anal sex among young girls, where the incidence has gone from 16 percent in 1992 to 40 percent in 2015. They're attributing that in part to pornography, not to increasing enjoyment. As Orenstein says, many girls even find it painful.

LB: They do what they feel the guy wants. They are trying to do something to get accepted that gives somebody else pleasure. It's not about their pleasure. At the basis of it, we should be teaching young women not to be sexual until they're ready, and not to have sex until they want it with that person. They should be doing it for their own pleasure *as well as* because they want to express their desire and caring for the other person.

ANATOMY: A BRIEF VISIT

RLM: Orenstein mentions something else, which leads me into the next topic: In high school sexual education classes, they almost never mention the clitoris. In your book *For Each Other,* you explain how the clitoris and the penis develop in early stages.

LB: What you find out is that the outer lips of the vagina consist of the same tissue as the shaft of the penis. The clitoris and the head of the penis develop from the same tissue. So, men and women have an equivalent sensitivity. For women, the clitoris is not just on the outside of the body. The roots of the clitoris go into the interior, into the front vaginal wall.

RLM: Almost like a wishbone.

LB: Yes. For a lot of women, stimulating that area just under or above the pubic bone will be arousing. For other women, not so much. For some women, stimulation of the head of the clitoris is arousing. For some, that's too intense. They are more pleasured by a lighter stimulation. There is no one way. This can be difficult for male partners because they have to adjust to a specific partner.

It's about getting in sync with another individual: What kinds of things does she like? How does she like to be pleasured? Maybe she likes to start out with more subtle stimulation and then build up to something more intense. Maybe she likes to stay with more subtle stimulation. You have to know what's most pleasurable for the partner you're with.

HOW TO COMMUNICATE

RLM: You focus on *communication* in your book. You want to open the door for people to talk openly about their sexual likes and dislikes.

LB: It's difficult to know what people like without communication. How does your partner like her coffee? Black? With cream and sugar? At some point, you're going to have to communicate in order to find out. You're going to watch her, see what she's drinking, and learn from that, or you're going to ask her, "How do you want me to make your coffee?" Maybe she wanted it black today, but tomorrow she's going to want it with cream and sugar. It's important to ask that question.

Talking about sex should be a normal part of a relationship, but somehow, we put it outside of that. When the sexual relationship is not going well, the overall relationship often follows.

RLM: If I understand you correctly, you're advocating completely open and normal conversation about what feels good for each other?

LB: Absolutely, but you have to figure this out in the right way. A lot of discussion right after sex becomes an evaluation of how the sex went. You want to communicate without being *judgmental*.

RLM: That must be very challenging for couples, because I imagine when they're talking about what they like and don't like, such as "You did a little too much of this," it can feel like a criticism, correct?

LB: Right. It's important to be positive and say, "I'd like more of this, but I really like it when you do that," as opposed to, "I don't like it when you do this." It's more, "I'd really like it if you do more of this for me. My nipples are very sensitive and I like it when you stimulate them more. Spend more time over here." Also, in our culture, it's assumed that the man is born with sexual information and expertise.

RLM: As if we know what to do!

LB: You're supposed to know what to do and you're not supposed to have to ask. You shouldn't need to get any information, because you're supposed to know. You can't ask, because you're supposed to know. She can't tell you, because you're supposed to know. You get stuck. She can't tell you, you can't ask, and no information gets transmitted about an area that is totally personal and individual.

RLM: Somehow the man is supposed to know exactly what the woman wants in her coffee without ever having to discuss the coffee!

LB: Exactly.

RLM: It could be black, it could be a triple espresso, it could be cream or cream and sugar.

LB: He has no information except what he believed his last partner liked.

RLM: Or maybe what he saw in some pornographic movie. He could well have learned it that way. Since they're not teaching how to engage in sex in high school, and parents don't teach it, where else can a man learn what to do? He thinks, "Maybe what I see in porn is what I'm supposed to do."

LB: Exactly.

COMMUNICATING WITH YOURSELF FIRST

RLM: What a sad state of affairs—in your book, you also talked about something that is critically important regarding sexual activity, and that is: how you have to first explore yourself sexually in order to successfully communicate with a partner what you enjoy.

LB: Yes. For women, masturbation is the easiest way to learn to have orgasms. Women can learn about their own bodies. They can move at a pace that works for them, take as much time as they need, and not worry about pleasing somebody else. It has all of the attributes of a perfect environment for her to figure out what's going on sexually for herself.

It's a great environment for men to learn how to control their ejaculation. They can learn how to stop and to take their time. When most men masturbate, they do it as quickly as possible because they don't want to get caught. You don't want anybody to walk in on you. Men have learned how to have orgasms quickly and then often need to learn how to slow that down. Masturbation is a good way to do that.

RLM: What you say connects with some of my other guests describing masturbation as "making love to oneself." For the most part, men are just getting themselves off. They're not really making love to themselves.

LB: When people really are making love to themselves, it's a whole different experience, but most people don't do that. We've been taught that masturbation is shameful. It's not what you want to spend time doing. Something is wrong with you if you're doing it. Young women have a sex drive even when a partner is not there. It is important for people to own and understand their sexuality, explore it, and enjoy it.

RLM: Can you offer some guidance to women who have never done self-vaginal exploration? What do they do? Give us some guidelines.

LB: First, *relax*. Either take a nice bath or make sure that you're in a relaxed mood. Turn off your phone, and lock your door so you feel safe and private. Next, you need to get in an erotic frame of mind. For women, it's their partner that makes them feel turned on. Now, if their partner isn't there, they may need to fantasize about their partner or someone else, or maybe they're turned on by reading something erotic. When I started running my preorgasmic women's groups in the early seventies, one of the women said, "I don't feel that turned on by myself." I said, "Why don't you try to read something?" She said, "All of the stuff that was written turns me off."

This stuff is all written for men. That encouraged me to curate volumes of erotica written by women for women, so that women would have something arousing. Now, women can also read erotica to put themselves into the sexual mood. Then women need to follow their body, to find what feels good. When it feels good, keep doing it. If something starts not feeling so good, change it. It's about experimenting and trying to see what it feels like if they touch their breast, if they feel behind their knees, their vaginal area. Sometimes it's good to put something inside the vagina when masturbating in addition to clitoral stimulation. It's a matter of spending time at it and seeing what you like.

RLM: In a previous interview, you told me that it wasn't that long ago that a high percentage of women had never even *looked* at their vagina. I assume that's changed over the years, but now we're going beyond looking to touching. Women need to be able to say that touching, stimulating, and making love to themselves is okay.

LB: Nothing about it is bad. I'm a sexual being. Sex is healthy. It's a good part of a relationship. It's a positive part of who I am. I can feel good about it, enjoy it, and experience it with my partner or by myself in a way that makes me feel good.

RLM: There's really a male/female difference here. I've read the most recent research, and it appears that fifty years ago, Kinsey reported 50 to 60 percent of the men reported that they masturbate. The most recent report shows that, evidently, 99 percent of males—if not more—masturbate. But that's not true for females.

LB: That's correct, but I think it has increased for women. Today, women who have never had orgasms are a much lower population than when I first started doing sex therapy. Women know more about masturbation. They've gotten more positive messages about sex in terms of being sexual. I think that there has been a positive change. I'm not sure I believe all of the early research for men. I'm not sure how honest people were. You weren't supposed to masturbate. It was thought to make you blind and cause hair on the palm of your hands. I don't think people would have admitted it, but I suspect the large majority of people were doing it.

By the way, it's a really good way for adolescents to learn about their body in a safe way so that they get to focus on themselves. It's especially important for young women to learn about their bodies and to feel good about themselves. It serves a lot of purposes. We have our bodies for a reason.

RLM: Certainly two of the reasons that are obvious is that the female can have a pleasurable lovemaking experience for herself. The second is that she can tell the partner what feels good because she will have discovered this by herself.

LB: Yes, and sometimes in lesbian relationships, because there are two women with the same genitals, you expect one is going to know what the other one enjoys. However, it doesn't matter, because we're each so unique. Each person needs to be able to accept their uniqueness. This is crucial to enjoying your sexuality.

THE G-SPOT, THE KEGEL, AND THE FIVE STAGES

RLM: Some women reading this are going to do what you're suggesting, if they haven't already done it. Please tell them about the G-spot and the efficacy of the kegel exercise.

LB: What we call the "G-spot" is an area where the back side of the clitoris goes into the vagina, on the internal wall, just above the pubic bone. For some women, that's a very pleasurable area to have stimulated. For other women, it doesn't do much. As I've said, for some women having direct clitoral stimulation is an important part of their arousal process. For other women, it's too intense.

RLM: It's called the G-spot after a doctor—was it Grafenberg?

LB: Yes.

RLM: A male discovered the female G-spot. It's an interesting side headline. One would think that after all these hundreds of thousands of years, a woman would have figured that out rather than a man! Can you tell us about the Kegel and why it's worth doing?

LB: The Kegel is an exercise where you contract the vaginal opening. It's the muscle you contract if you were trying to stop the flow of urine. That muscle is strengthened both by contracting it as well as releasing it. The releasing is as important as the contraction. A lot of times, people are only contracting, but you want to switch between releasing and contracting it over and over. For a lot of women, that increases the sensation occurring inside the vagina. They get more sensitive. It also helps to foster more intense contractions during orgasm. It is also helpful in terms of urinary incontinence. As women age, doing their Kegel exercises means they will be less likely to lose little urine drops when they sneeze, cough, or laugh. It's a way of keeping the vaginal area healthy.

RLM: Would that be true for males as well in terms of later life incontinence?

LB: It could be.

RLM: I have been told it is good to hold a Kegel for fifteen seconds a certain number of times a day.

LB: Hold it for fifteen seconds or contract it continuously for fifteen seconds?

RLM: Tighten, then let go, tighten, let go, for about fifteen seconds. Don't make a lengthy thing of it, but do it frequently and make it part of your routine.

LB: Also, to hold the squeeze for three seconds for a number of times, a few times each day. Nobody knows you're doing it.

RLM: Your dear friend who passed away, Bernie Zilbergeld, talked about the "five stages of arousal." Is that a handy thing for us to be aware of?

LB: I really tried to get away from analyzing the sexual arousal process, to be honest with you, because if you are thinking to yourself, *Am I leaving desire and entering arousal? Let me see,* it's not useful to the experience of enjoying pleasure. It doesn't matter where you are in the arousal cycle. If you're enjoying the stimulation that you're getting, let your partner know to continue it rather than to change it. If that's the stimulation that you want, right then. I don't find the labeling useful.

RLM: That's helpful to know. As an aside, do you researchers know what the function of the clitoris is? Why does a woman have a clitoris?

LB: To provide sexual pleasure.

RLM: Is there a particular function of the orgasm for a female?

LB: Pleasure. The survival of the species depends upon sex. If it didn't feel good, it wouldn't be reinforced. We wouldn't want to do it very much and we'd all die out.

RLM: Dogs and cats don't seem to have a clitoris, though, do they?

LB: Actually, they do. I do know that if you didn't enjoy it, you wouldn't keep doing it.

RLM: It's positive reinforcement for reproductive purposes?

LB: Absolutely. We know that as you have an orgasm, oxytocin in your body is released, which is the "feeling-close" hormone, so you would feel more connected to your partner. The more connected you feel, the more likely you are to stay together, and that will help raise kids. These things are biologically built into us.

WHAT IS NORMAL?

RLM: When it comes to sexual activity, so long as there is sober mutual consent, are there any *no-nos*—things that people shouldn't do?

LB: As long as you're both enjoying it and nobody's getting hurt, then it's fine. I had one couple come into therapy who had a good sexual relationship. What turned him on was her walking around in high heels while he was in a chest.

RLM: Inside of a chest?

LB: He was inside a closed chest and she would be talking to him. Then they would have sex and he'd be very aroused. She was fine with it. It really turned him on. I said, "You have no issue, and if I were you I would be extremely nice to her." He said, "I am." Because it's rare to find somebody who is willing to have a sexual relationship in that particular form.

RLM: Was there something about hearing the clicking of the heels while he was in the box that excited him sexually? Was the clicking sound the sexual stimulant? After all, he couldn't see the heels.

LB: It must have been, or he knew it, or he saw it when he came out. I didn't go into all the details, because mostly I was concerned with whether or not they had a problem. I determined that they didn't, so there was no reason to go any further.

THE PROBLEMS

RLM: You've spent a lot of your career helping people with problems. Tell us about unhappy sexual relations, about typical obstacles and problems that people have and how to deal with it.

LB: Boy, this looks like the subject of a number of books of mine!

RLM: Yes, it does.

LB: Couples face all kinds of problems sexually. As I mentioned, they could have a discrepancy in desire where one partner comes into the relationship wanting sex three times a day and the other once a day— or, for a more extreme example, once a week. That's a hard difference to bridge for both parties to be satisfied. If it's three times a week versus once or twice a week, you can find a place to make it work, but if it's far apart, one person ends up feeling unloved and undesirable because their partner is not interested in making love with them. The other person feels that there's something wrong with them; they feel guilty and abnormal, and that leads to an even larger difference, as one person feels pursued and the other one feels rejected.

RLM: You are talking about something people can find out about earlier in the relationship before they get married.

LB: Some people feel that after they get married it will all change. Only it doesn't change. That difference becomes a problem. That's one kind of sexual problem. The most common sexual problem that I see in couples, maybe because I like working with it, is a lack of desire. Rather than a *difference* in desires, this couple isn't even *having* a sexual relationship. Neither one of them—or only one of them—desires sex. Then the issue is how to figure out what's going on. Sometimes it's something as simple as the woman going through menopause and being low on testosterone, or experiencing pain with intercourse because she needs some additional estrogen in her vaginal area. The most common case is a relationship that has atrophied over the years. They haven't put the time and energy into maintaining the intimate, caring part of the relationship. Maybe they've become a business partnership where they take care of the kids and the house, but they haven't been paying attention to each other's emotional needs. They don't feel connected and that lack of feeling connected leads to a lack of feeling sexual. Or they're feeling tired, exhausted, and overworked. It's too hard to find time—or to make time—in their busy life to be sexual.

Let's say you have a partnership where one person is angry at the other person. They feel hurt because they feel unimportant or unloved. Or they feel powerless in the relationship. Women sometimes use not having sex as a way to be powerful in a relationship. You have a partner who can tell you to do everything that he or she wants you to do, and the only power you have is in saying no. Saying no to sex can be a subconscious way for women to have power in the relationship.

My job is to figure out the problem in the dynamic between the two people. How can we unravel it and start a different kind of relationship so that both people feel important and cared about, safe, and respected? When that happens, then we can bring back a sexual relationship. For some people, if they don't feel safe in their relationship, they're not going to feel sexual.

BODY IMAGE
AND THE OBESITY EPIDEMIC

RLM: What about body image? Right now, 72 percent of the people in the United States are obese or overweight. A lot of those folks must feel badly about themselves.

LB: Some of them do, but some feel just fine about being overweight. You are looking at it from the dominant cultural perspective, which says that, "this is the way you ought to look." Some people buy into that and feel bad about themselves. If their partner desires them, then I have to work with the person who is not feeling good about their body so she starts to feel better about the body she *has,* as opposed to what the media says she *ought* to look like, which is a small percentage of what actual women look like.

RLM: Yes, a very small percentage.

LB: Part of the work is opening this up so that all of us can feel good about our bodies and enjoy the pleasure that we have. If the partner isn't finding her attractive because of her changing body, then it becomes more complicated, because if the partner isn't turned on, what can we do? As people age, their bodies change. For some people, that's a problem. Other people accept the body's changes. Our bodies may be different, but the fact that we can enjoy the pleasure of them even though they're changing can be a great gift.

RELIGION AND SEX

RLM: Is religion still a problem for a lot of people in terms of enjoying their sexuality? Does religion make sex life more difficult?

LB: Religion has been a huge problem. It was more so in the past, or at least it seemed to me that there were more women who felt religion told them sex was bad or wrong. So they've spent years turning off their sexual desire. Then one day, you're married and it's okay. You're in this relationship and you can feel sexual now. But they didn't because they learned to turn it off too well. When I did my first preorgasmic women's group, I had more ex-Catholics than any other religion. It was almost as if they had to give up being Catholic in order to be okay in terms of exploring their sexuality. It wasn't until they could give up their religion that they could feel free enough to explore themselves.

RLM: That's a heck of a conflict to be in.

LB: It was for a lot of people. I think when religion represses your sexuality, and if religion is important to you, you're in conflict. It can make your sexual experience difficult.

COMMUNICATION REVISITED

RLM: Before we conclude, I want to return to interpersonal communication, which is so important to you and all of us in our profession of psychology. Share with us some of the exercises that you suggest to couples to enhance their communication about sex and life in general.

LB: An intimate relationship is a lifelong conversation about feelings. Otherwise, you have a business partnership. Who is going to do the dishes and who is going to pick up the kids? How you have this conversation is important. First of all, you have to be willing to be vulnerable in order to share your feelings. All of us, but especially men, have been taught not to show feelings, to cover them up until they lash out angrily. You end up telling the person how bad and how wrong they are.

To let a person know that you're hurt in a vulnerable way means that it has to be safe for you to do that. This means that the partner, in order to hear about vulnerable feelings, cannot tell you that it is a stupid way to feel or deny your feelings. You can't dismiss feelings. You can't do that, because then it's not safe to come forward and share them. One has to feel safe to do that. Working with couples, my goal is to create safety so that they can share their vulnerable feelings and be able to let the other person know what's going on with them so they can be closer.

Another problem is that people are telling their partner how they're feeling rather than *asking* them how they are feeling. People regularly say to their partner, "You felt this way. You were angry at me when you came home. You didn't like this."

RLM: They tell the other person what they feel.

LB: Exactly. They say, "My experience of you is such that," and they believe that what *they* are seeing is the truth. That makes them an expert on their partner. Their partner is going to resist, get defensive and say, "I don't . . ." No one wants someone else to be the expert on them. Whereas if I were to ask you, "Were you angry when you came home yesterday? How did you feel when you said that? What did you mean by that?" I'm suddenly open to hearing what you have to say, and you're back to being the expert on yourself. You've been invited to tell me about your vulnerable feelings. This works like magic in a relationship. Communication is, in fact, the basis of a healthy relationship, in a sexual relationship as well as anywhere else.

RLM: Thank you, Lonnie.

4

Diana Richardson

Slow Sex: The Path to Fulfilling and Sustainable Sexuality

Diana Richardson is known as the pioneer of the Slow Sex movement and, along with her partner, Michael Richardson, is the creator of the life-changing weeklong Making Love Retreat, which they have been offering in Europe since 1995. She wrote her first book in 1996, published as *The Love Keys: The Art of Ecstatic Sex,* in 1999, and then later republished as *The Heart of Tantric Sex,* a bestseller. Since then, she has written a further seven books on the tantric approach to love and sex. These are translated into German, Spanish, and French, with certain books translated into Russian, Korean, Czech, and Estonian. Diana is now based in Switzerland with Michael, where they continue to guide couples in the art of slow, conscious sex in their highly successful Making Love Retreats. For more information about their backgrounds, retreats, and books, please visit their websites: *www.livinglove.com* or *www.love4couples.com.*

Dr. Richard L. Miller (RLM): Diana Richardson is the author of a long list of books on human sexuality. We've asked her to join us in our attempt to offset misguided attitudes towards human sexuality.

Diana Richardson (DR): Thank you so much, Richard. It's an honor to be here and be invited to speak about something as essential as the ground we walk on.

RLM: Let's begin by talking about one of your books, *Slow Sex*. You describe the various tactics to slow down human sexual activity and enjoy it even more. Let's go through the tactics so that our audience can hear what you're prescribing. Let's begin with slow-sex tactic number one: relaxation.

DR: Yes. To start with, I would like to say I'm not sharing a technique with people. It's a path to being more conscious, even in sex. If you look at how we behave, it's pretty mechanical and repetitive. We're lacking in awareness. We follow patterns. Another title for the book could be *Conscious Sex*.

RLM: What you're saying fits right in with current trends in the field of psychology because you're talking about presence, awareness, and expanding your consciousness.

DR: Absolutely. The beauty is, if you're more conscious, you slow down and become more sensitive. This enables you to feel more, perceive more—in the body, globally, and in the genitals. Relaxation is the keystone, because if we observe how we behave sexually, we're very tense. We compress our bodies and we tighten the musculature and the genitals. Then the energy gets compressed as well. So you can't have expanded experiences, which—energetically speaking—would lead to altered states or shifts in awareness and consciousness. So first, you should relax your jaw, shoulders, vagina—and, for men, the anus and perineum—all places where unconsciously and habitually, we tighten up that then limits our perception.

RLM: This muscle tightening regarding sex must be almost universal because we're uptight about sex as a nation. Males are literally uptight about their sexual performance: "Am I going to succeed? Am I going to get turned down? Am I going to get and maintain my erection? Am I going to *satisfy?*" There must be a lot of tension instead of relaxation.

DR: That's correct, Richard. Men, especially, feel a huge performance pressure around the erection issue. They go into sex with a lot of insecurity, which undermines them. Too much tension and anxiety is often the source of premature ejaculation. It's mostly not a psychological problem, although it can be. Generally, men are too tense. Women are part of the same picture.

TOXIC, PERFORMANCE-ORIENTED LANGUAGE USE

RLM: Even the language used by professional sexologists adds to the pressure on males because the experts talk about achieving an erection as if you go out, do something big, and achieve recognition. They portray an erection as something you have to work for.

DR: That's an astute observation of language usage. Sadly, men evaluate themselves according to their capacity to get erect and maintain an erection. They either feel like a man, or like less of a man. But the penis has its own life responses. For all of us, sex equals an entry into a woman, penetration with erection. But there are so many shades in between that—including non-erection, a relaxed penis. It's viable to make love without an erection. Of course, it does involve knowing how a woman or a man can insert the penis in its relaxed form. But because of this emphasis on erection, the pressure on men is undue.

RLM: Didn't we also create a huge distortion by teaching men that we needed to have an erection to enjoy sex itself? If we think about oral sex, the term *performing* becomes even more interesting. He's really not performing; he's licking and enjoying it. When a man engages in cunnilingus, he's most often focusing on the clitoris. If a woman reciprocates by licking and sucking on the man's soft penis, even a soft penis is much larger than the external clitoris. It is sort an unfair exchange. The woman has got plenty to suck on, even if it's a flaccid penis. Yet, if it's not erect, both parties are liable to create anxiety around the entire sexual adventure.

DR: That's because of the insecure sense that you're not exciting each other. Women, especially, feel the burden that they've got to be exciting for a man to respond with an erection. Everybody's focusing on somebody else, not on themselves.

SELF-AWARENESS TECHNIQUES

RLM: Talk to us about focusing on yourself.

DR: This is foundational if you want to set up a more nourishing style of sex because usually each person has got more attention placed on the other person than on themselves. All their attention is projected outwards. One can say that as a race of people, we have little body awareness. We're more into thinking and using the bodies as a vehicle to move the mind around. But few people have natural body awareness, and this has a lot to do with our upbringing. Many people follow practices to increase body awareness, which is a good thing. But in general, when two people come together for intimacy, it involves projection onto the other. Each one is "up-and-out" on their partner. I see it as nobody being home.

The first step is to get *home* inside your body and increase your body awareness, giving the body more space. The body knows timing, pace, and rhythm, but we don't trust our bodies because we've all been unconsciously imprinted, and that's affected the psyche. Whenever I've wanted to be with myself, I've looked around inside my body somewhere below the head for a place that I could easily perceive from the inside. That could be the vagina, the belly, the heart, the breasts, or the solar plexus. It can be anywhere, as long as it acts as an anchor point for your awareness. And if you can't find such a place, then just choose one and begin to tune in to it.

If you start there, you're much more inside yourself. I like to call it the inner home. When you do that, whatever you bring into the exchange is more authentic. It's more real—not the fantasy, projection, or ideas that many of us are acting out in sex. When you find your thoughts drifting, which inevitably happens, you re-anchor yourself in this inner home. You start an ongoing process to get closer to yourself. Strangely, we all want to be closer to somebody else, but we don't know how to be close to *ourselves*. When you're closer to yourself, a closeness to the other arises as a result. You can achieve this in simple ways: by relaxing your body, repeatedly using awareness, scanning your body for tensions, and softening them.

As soon as we relax areas of the body like the jaw, shoulders, solar plexus, belly, genital area, extremities, shoulders, and feet, we experience a global feeling of relaxation, even though they're not necessarily directly related to the genitals. While I might think my shoulder is not connected to my vagina, I do feel more in my vagina as soon as I relax my shoulder. We tend to divide the body up into parts. Meanwhile, the body itself is one complete organic unity. So, the first and fundamental shift is that you make your own body the priority. Find an anchoring in there, scan, and relax. Then, we add the breath, which is a natural bridge.

RLM: Breathing is my number one tool, Diana. I've saved my own life after a motorcycle accident by stabilizing myself and enduring the shock, with abdominal breathing.

DR: It's the fastest bridge between mind and body.

RLM: You seem to be close to the words of my old friend, Bernie Gunther, who liked to say, "lose your mind and come to your senses."

DR: You got it, Richard. That says it all.

RLM: It's important to understand that body awareness takes time. To achieve body awareness, it is necessary to take the time to focus, in, expand the awareness, and breathe, in and out, slowly. We're not talking about what another of my guests, Ayelet Waldman, happily pointed out the value of "embracing the quickie." We're talking about embracing the *slowie*.

DR: Yes, and developing body awareness also takes practice. It takes time to install in one lovemaking session, and more time to maintain and deepen that. That's why I suggest that people make time for love, and not leave it only to the quickie. We usually think sex is spontaneous, but so often it's just accidental. You disperse your energy. Whereas when you slow down and contain your energy, you can extend the love act for considerable periods of time.

RLM: I want to underline your words, "extend the love act," in bright red. Many people learn almost everything they know about sexuality from movies. We see from Hollywood a scene with two people alone in a room. All of a sudden, they're just hot for each other. They rip off each other's clothes. The man penetrates the woman. They go at it for ninety seconds, smoke a cigarette, and it's all over.

DR: Absolutely. Honestly, I watch movies sometimes, and it looks like the people are eating each other. They're so "on each other." There's no self-reflection, grace, or inwardness at all. It's highly unbalanced.

RLM: Hollywood is trying to teach us what real passion looks like, I suppose. And there is certainly nothing wrong with eating one another, but doing only that won't sustain a long relationship. That might be good for a quickie at a party. But if one wants a sustained, intimate sexual relationship, over time, we have to learn many other behaviors.

DIFFERENT GENDERS, DIFFERENT RHYTHMS

RLM: The next sex skill you talk about in your book is rhythm. Tell us about rhythm.

DR: I'm generalizing, so be aware that you'll always find shades to what I'm describing, but one major difference between male and female bodies is that the female system is much slower than the male one in terms of warming up and opening up to a sexual exchange. Generally speaking, men are ready quickly, meaning they soon get an erection and want to enter, whereas women need more time before they feel ready to take the penis into their bodies. But it's rare for a woman to say that openly. In fact, if she tells a man to slow down, the man will often be offended. Behind that is a fear of losing the erection. For sure, during the "honeymoon" phase of a sexual relationship, a woman will tend to be more immediately ready, but this tends to change after a while.

RLM: What you just said is critical. The man gets an erection, and because of his fear of losing it, he immediately wants to penetrate.

DR: That's right.

RLM: There's pressure on the man to move quickly, penetrate, and use that erection while he's has still "achieved it."

DR: Right—to maintain that erection, you need a lot of stimulation and excitement. This raises the sexual temperature, and that's the problem. As soon as the sexual temperature is raised, the man will be more likely to ejaculate. The prevalence of premature ejaculation is extremely high. But this really can be addressed by reducing the sexual temperature, by slowing down, being more cool and conscious.

RLM: Help me with this concept of premature ejaculation. I've never understood it, because it seems to me that the body ejaculates exactly when the body wants to ejaculate. The body doesn't pre-breathe, pre-defecate, or pre-urinate. How does it pre-ejaculate? Doesn't it ejaculate exactly on time for what the body wants to do?

DR: Many men ejaculate a lot sooner than they wish and this is usually to do with tension around sex and the resulting disturbances in our psyches. They come close to a woman or just enter her and will ejaculate. And this is premature in the sense that there isn't adequate time for an exchange of energy and love to happen.

RLM: Does the man have to quit after he ejaculates? Is there any rule in heaven that says he can't relax for a few minutes, brush his teeth, then come back and continue?

DR: We would hope so. But early ejaculation is undermining and leads to self-doubt in men. Often, men will even be reticent about approaching or being intimate with a woman because in the back of their minds they fear they will come too quickly.

RLM: Then he doesn't know how to continue because of that physiological refractory period where he feels temporarily complete.

DR: One can lose energy. So, one might not be in the position to get going again. Or one doesn't feel confident enough, or possibly the woman is upset because the exchange was so short. But, in theory, it's feasible to continue. And, the second time around, he's often more likely to be able to be inside the woman for a longer period. By then, that initial anxiety has passed.

RLM: In my experience, based on interviewing men for sixty years in my clinical practice—the sensation of the penis after ejaculation does decrease and how much it decreases varies as a function of age. Typically younger men have a shorter, after ejaculation, latency period than older men. By the same token a teenage male might get an erection from friction with his underpants while older men often require significantly greater stimulation.

However, while sensation post-orgasm decreases, it does not disappear. There's still plenty of penile sensation if both people are willing to continue rather than consider the orgasm the endpoint.

DR: Yes.

RLM: If the man, after the ejaculation, doesn't "achieve an erection again," soon enough, he's liable to feel let down.

DR: Absolutely. It's a known fact that a lot of men do lose energy once they have ejaculated. There's also something we don't pay much attention to, which is: How do we *feel* afterwards? Sex is all about the orgasm and building up sensation and intensity to a peak. But we don't consider the afterwards. We have this profound belief that sex equals having a peak. When you have a peak, a discharge follows, accompanied by a sense of disconnection. You were so involved, whether for thirty minutes or three minutes, and suddenly, this connection is gone, it's evaporated. It is a bit bizarre.

RLM: We certainly see the sense of disconnection you're describing in barnyard animals, because after they copulate, they immediately walk away from each other.

DR: It's a biological situation.

RLM: But we males can learn to stay connected—put our head on the other person's chest, embrace, savor, and perhaps enjoy mutual oral sex.

DR: Yes, absolutely. It is important to create an atmosphere afterwards, because we tend only to ask, "How was the peak? Was it great?" But we don't look at the aftereffects. It's crucial to be connected, lie together, breathe, or connect in some way, perhaps keeping eye contact. This simple being together is tremendously nourishing and healing.

CONNECTING THROUGH EYE CONTACT

RLM: Tell us about the importance of eye contact during sex.

DR: When the eyes are open, you know who you're with and what you're doing. Sex frequently happens in a dark room with closed eyes, and that has a place for sure. However, with closed eyes, you're not that present. Your mind can drift off into fantasy, which has become a tremendous fuel—especially for men—to get an erection or to come. Women often will have a little fantasy when they want to come. With eyes open, you're much more connected. The level of presence, awareness, and bonding is greatly enhanced.

When I started exploring eye contact, I found I had to change the way I looked, the way I used my eyes. Instead of looking out of my eyes, I started looking back into my eyes, into my body. I had to develop the capacity to *receive* through my eyes, not project out. That's how the eyes are designed. We don't have to do anything to see; we just see. However, we always look out through the eyes. When we look at something, we look at it, instead of letting it come to us. It's like inverting your vision. This also has a penetrating effect on the body's sensitivity and the level of intimacy.

RLM: Looking at the other person's eyes, during and after the sexual act, maintains that contact, doesn't it?

DR: Yes.

RLM: Where is it written up in the sky that sex needs to be something that takes place, at night, in the dark? It seems to be true for the entire world. Why? Is that another one of the terrible myths that are damaging us?

DR: Generally, some body shame is involved. People feel less self-conscious in the dark, and sex is usually associated with nighttime.

RLM: So, we're going back to the Garden of Eden and the shame over exposed genitals.

DR: Quite possibly. It's more comfortable. You lean over, switch off the light, and feel freer. But making love in the daytime is just as glorious—any time in the morning or afternoon. At nighttime, candlelight will do. It doesn't have to be full floodlights.

RLM: Sadly, I can tell you that many couples I've worked with have never seen each other naked.

DR: Well, Richard, I've heard that from a few people, and it is astounding.

RLM: It's the saddest thing. It comes from deeply misguided training, insecurity, and an unwillingness to show oneself to the other for fear that they'll find something wrong, which is a projection from the inner self. We're assuming the other person will find the same flaws we found. Such people remain in the dark, personally and interpersonally, for their entire married lives.

DR: There are so many layers. Women also get this beauty ideal of how they're meant to look. We enhance our bodies to be provocative, which is externally oriented. You've said we're *mis*guided, but sadly there's little-to-no *actual* guidance. The only "guidance" is through the movies—and pornography, which has skyrocketed since the age of the internet, especially in the case of young boys. They're starting to watch porno when really young, at eleven years old or even younger.

DISTORTED PORTRAYAL
OF SEXUALITY IN MOVIES

RLM: They're looking at pornography at the young age of eleven? Do you have information to share on the effect of watching pornography on their sex lives?

DR: The basic situation is that pornography is unrealistic. I've heard that erectile dysfunction in men is starting to happen in boys around the age of twenty. Classically, it was around the age of fifty. A lot of stimulation—either in masturbation or in actual sex—ultimately desensitizes the penis. Too much sensation for the penis is not good for the tissues and their erectile responses.

RLM: I have questions about that theory and would like to see more research. If you are accurate that sensation, in an of itself, has a negative effect on penile tissue, then men ought to begin wearing very carefully constructed penis protectors from a young age.

It sounds like you are saying that young boys might compare themselves, sexually, to Olympic sexual athletes. The boys are watching professional actors hired for the express purpose of having special sexual abilities, such as a woman having sex with ten men in a row or a male keeping a nine-inch erection for three hours. Given the bell curve, there are going to be men and women with extraordinary sexual abilities. Producers can advertise for these sexual athletes and put them in these movies. But that doesn't mean the average person can perform in the same way.

DR: That's correct. Pornography misleads both parties—girls because it makes them believe they need to allow what they see and have those bodily experiences, and boys because they have to live up to huge expectations. Nobody tells them what actually happens inside our bodies during sex. This is so sad because our body is relatively pure. Only our psyche has been disturbed through movies and unconscious sexual imprinting, and also the shame and guilt attached to openly talking about sex and pornography. The biggest problem with the imprinting is that we think it's all about the peak and building up sensation.

When we get together, we do everything we can to reach that peak, which involves raising the sexual temperature and intensity. People think sex has to be intense—the hotter the better—but sex can be very relaxed, languid, lovely, and sensuous. One becomes more sensitive. So, the real problem in sex is that peaking or the orgasm has become the goal. Having a goal puts us in the future, even if it's a millisecond. Before I changed the way I made love, I was only interested in the next penetration or thrust, not in this one, because that next thrust is another step up the ladder to the top of the mountain.

RLM: To the peak.

DR: Exactly. You got it. If we're in the future, it means we're fundamentally absent. The problem is not that we like peaks; the problem is that we go for a peak as the goal. We're ahead of ourselves, and we're absent. That absence makes a difference to the quality of the sexual exchange.

RLM: In your book's various chapters, you talk about relaxation, awareness, rhythm, pleasure, thought, the sacred, and the story. I gather from what you're saying that relaxation, awareness, and being present are the critical foundation.

DR: That's correct. From there, everything flows.

RLM: So, you're advising all of us to take time, relax, find our bodies, expand our awareness, and let our natural rhythms flow together. Sex shouldn't be a rushed job.

DR: Yes, Richard. As soon as one enters into the sexual exchange with more awareness and presence, it changes the constellation. The ingredients are the same—meaning we've got two bodies, a penis, and a vagina—but you feel entirely different during and afterwards. Having a peak is a choice.

RLM: We mentioned the impact of pornography in pushing, no pun intended, anal sex. Would you comment on anal sex for us?

DR: I need to say that my experience is heterosexual. So I teach heterosexuals. But any couple, regardless of the combination of genders, will change the quality of the entire sex act if they bring these inquiries in. Anal sex is an option. But from my vision, the penis and the vagina have a magnetic relationship. I don't know if that exists between a penis and an anus.

RLM: Is the anus an erogenous zone, Diana?

DR: Yes, it can be. It is used for stimulation, although not for everybody. I think it's become increasingly popular because it's not so personal, given that the partner is facing the other way. That might also be more stimulating and help to maintain an erection. I don't know.

VARIATION OF SEX POSITIONS

RLM: You mentioned the sexual position. Are there positions that you and your husband recommend for couples, or is that a matter of personal taste, so to speak. What do you want to say about positions during sex?

DR: I've got a whole chapter in most of my books about positions, and I call them "rotating positions." It's good to change positions because it can increase your presence. The idea is not so much that, say, you're doing the missionary position, and then disconnecting to get into another position. Instead, you let the bodies roll together. The penis stays inside; you roll around and adjust your positions. You can come to a whole range of different positions. In fact, every few millimeters is a new position. If by chance the penis slips out, then you put it back inside again.

There's a nice side position known as the scissors position, which is a good way to start. Both are lying down. Men are used to being on top, so we recommend that women go on top often, because, at that moment, a woman will observe that there is the feeling of pressure— you've got to do something.

So, it's a tremendous burden. I noticed that myself when I started to be more consciously on top. Imagine how the man feels. He's up there and feels he has to do something. So, in this scissors position, the man is lying on his back, almost on his side. The woman is on her back, and you can weave the legs in a scissor style. That's a handy position for entry if there is an erection or if you learn to put the penis in its relaxed state.

So, changing positions is good, especially because it raises your level of presence. If you get sleepy or fade out, you can change. You adjust, find a new position, and then you're back in the here-and-now again. The beauty of changing positions is that you're more present each time you make a shift.

TAKING EMPHASIS AWAY FROM THE CLITORIS

RLM: You wrote an entire book about the female orgasm. Let's hear what you have to say about the female orgasm.

DR: My book is called *Tantric Orgasm for Women*. The title is always a delicate thing. It doesn't say that women have to orgasm—as a goal—but many women don't have one. Many women struggle to have a vaginal orgasm for their whole life; they can get it more readily via the clitoris. In the female body, the clitoris is conventionally considered the center of female sexuality. It's how women get excited. But this is superficial excitement. In fact, it imbues the vagina with tension, hunger, and it becomes demanding. Sometimes, it almost gets achy because there's too much tension in the vagina. The real way women's bodies are deeply opened is through the breasts. In fact, the breasts are the key to accessing women's deeper orgasmic experiences.

When I talk about the breasts, I don't mean heavy-duty stimulation of the nipples, but caressing, loving, and consciously holding them. Especially women themselves should enter into their breasts with awareness. This opens up the female body on a deeper level. When the breasts are engaged, after a time the vagina resonates and turns into a receptive organ that can absorb the male energy. When the woman is receptive and able to take a man's energy into her, this elevates the quality of the exchange. So, it's advisable to take the emphasis away from the clitoris, and if it interests you, rather engage the clitoris at a later stage. But not as a starting point.

And as I've already mentioned, a woman's body requires *time*. Women need to ask for that, and men need to grant it. During that process, the man might lose his initial erection. But if a couple stays together in presence and connection through love, an erection will usually return. In my courses, I often ask who among the men has experienced an erection out of love and presence, and 99 percent of the men will raise their hands. So, men know that. If the atmosphere is right, the body will respond in this organic way, and that kind of erection becomes sustainable. That erection is coming from the inside out, through presence and awareness. It doesn't need so much stimulation to keep it going.

PATHOLOGICAL FOCUS ON THE ERECT PENIS IN LANGUAGE AND SELF-PERCEPTION

RLM: In my life, I have a hard time finding my keys and my glasses. Sometimes it can take what seems to be an inordinate amount of time to find them, especially if my wife and I are going somewhere. I would often get annoyed saying to my wife, damn it, I lost my glasses again.

Then one day it occurred to me that I haven't lost my glasses because they were in the house. I would be more accurate and more comfortable if I said, "Darling, I've misplaced my glasses."

By emphasizing "misplaced" instead of "lost," I feel better. Because if I misplaced them, that means they're around somewhere; if they're lost, I may never find them again. Losing my glasses is threatening because it's so inconvenient. I wonder if we may do the same thing with erection. Maybe we men do not lose our erections. Maybe we need another word that indicates we don't have it at the moment, but it will come back. We haven't lost it forever. It would sound funny to say I misplaced my erection. Perhaps temporarily soft is better.

DR: That's a beautiful analogy, and you're absolutely correct. I've also observed that men don't consider their penis a penis unless it's erect. When it's relaxed, they're always a bit ashamed.

RLM: There's a lot of wisdom and truth in what you're saying. We've become so identified with this phallus standing up, whether it be in sculpture, pictures, or pornography. Whereas a non-erect penis, or flaccid penis, is considered a hanging piece of flesh.

DR: Right, and valuing their penis as a penis, in whatever state, is an important shift for men because if you don't feel it as your penis when it's relaxed, there's this inner disconnect, which is disempowering. That's why the perineum area is so important and why men should keep focusing their awareness there while making love—but also as you stand, walk, drive, or talk to people. This awakens the whole pelvic floor. If you follow the muscle tissues back to the base of the penis, you'll see the penis arises from the perineum. The perineum is like the root of the penis. If men can start investing awareness in that area with loving attention or mindfulness, that will be a tremendous support. So, we haven't lost our erections or misplaced them, but our penis is relaxing.

RLM: Maybe *misplaced* wouldn't be the word. By the way, a little note for all of you bicycle riders: When you use the skinny bicycle seat on a modern, thin-tired bicycle, the pressure and vibration go right up into the perineum. So, when you go for a long ride, it can desensitize that area and has been known to do nerve damage. That's a word of caution for bicycle riders.

DR: Good point. I've also heard from women cyclists that these saddles are painful for the labia and the entrance to the vagina.

RLM: What do you glean from your studies regarding why women, more than men, have difficulty orgasming? How do you think this curse came about, and who put it on women?

DR: It's simply because women's bodies need more time to warm up. If a woman's body is given the space to relax and wait until there's the feeling that the woman wants to engage, this makes a huge difference. Many women are crossing their own boundaries, saying yes when they don't feel ready. In my seminars I always ask the women, "Who would like to ask their man for more time?" and every single woman will raise her hand. So, the time from initial contact to entry is simply too short for women to arrive fully inside their bodies. Another aspect is that the clitoris can give a superficial orgasm, but the deeper one comes through accessing the breasts and allowing this inner connection to open the body and vagina.

REDUCING THE SEXUAL TEMPERATURE

RLM: I want you to talk to us about your book *Cool Sex*.

DR: I wrote this book for younger adults recently. Essentially, it's the same material I use for adult books, only condensed. The idea of *Cool Sex* is about sexual temperature. We have this idea that sex has got to be hot—the hotter, the better. But to make each exchange last longer, we need to cool down and not push our bodies. As soon as we feel a little excitement, we tend to build on that until we reach a peak. So, the idea of *cooler* sex is about changing one's mind that sex doesn't need to be "hot." It's a matter of reducing sexual temperature: a little excitement followed by relaxation, then a little more excitement and then more relaxation. For young people, this is so helpful, especially since they're more impacted by pornography than you or I. I don't know how it was for you, but I *had* sex before *seeing* sex.

RLM: It was true for me.

DR: That's a huge difference from seeing sex and then having sex. There's a strong tendency to imitate what we see.

RLM: In fact, I had sex for decades before I saw sex because I'm eighty-four years old and, for most of us, there was no such thing as seeing sex when I was young. The closest I came to seeing sex, while growing up, were the underwear models in the Sears Roebuck catalog and the photos in my dad's anatomy books.

DR: I grew up on a farm. You see bulls and cows, but that's just nature. You don't relate that activity to human beings. It makes a huge difference not having preconceptions. Soon, there won't be any people in the Western world that have sex before they see sex. So, there's a tremendous loss of innocence around sex, which is so sad.

RLM: People are being influenced by pictures and movies rather than learning through education. As I'm listening to you, I think that the material in your books deserves to be taught in high school or even junior high school. You're teaching about an essential human function that's part of the entire world on a daily basis, and yet there's no guidebook. When you receive a television or a phone, it comes with a manual. Our amazing human sexuality arrives without any instruction.

DR: Absolutely. I would love that book to be included in school, but it hasn't been picked up in the school curriculum. Interestingly, some churches have started here in Europe, where I've been working for a long time. They have Sunday schools for younger people, using my books to teach them. I've had all kinds of diplomats in my groups, but I haven't gotten an education minister from any country yet. It needs to start in schools—the younger, the better. I've been waiting.

RLM: If I were looking to disseminate your books for early education, I would select the Scandinavian countries. They might be the best bet in secondary education, because they're an advanced culture. Are people around the world making an error by saving their sexual activity for when they get into bed at night?

DR: It's good to bring change into the situation and pick other times of the day.

RLM: I asked that because at the end of the day, after a full workday and dinner, people are tired.

DR: That's right, Richard. And sometimes we might have had a couple of glasses of wine. So, we are not at the optimum. We're digesting; our mind is full of the day. That's a good reason to make love early in the day, when your body is fresher, freer, and not impacted by the day's thoughts.

RLM: I appreciate your comment about having ministers of education become aware of real sex education, because youth is where the action is. We've got to get the educational people onboard to start teaching us about sex when we're young. Is there anything else you'd like to bring to our attention about the human sexual condition or sexual behavior?

DR: I feel we've covered a lot, and you've been so great in how you process things and bring in your own experience. I wanted to say one little thing earlier about the eyes, and that's not to try and look in both eyes simultaneously, but one eye at a time. So, you're not darting back and forth.

RLM: Thank you for that.

DR: Right. You can change which eye you connect with, but better not to flick back and forth. It's disconcerting for your partner. And another thing, if you try and look at both eyes at once, you get this mesmeric effect, which is not great. So choose one eye and stay with it. Of course, you can change to the other eye, but avoid flicking back and forth.

I'd also like to add one other thing about men and ejaculation. There's a popular notion that men should try to prolong the sexual act by "controlling" their ejaculation, meaning they build up the sensation and intensity, and just before the so-called point of no return, they stop, relax, and repress that tension and excitement. Then they build it up and repress it, over and over again. We don't recommend that because it creates a lot of heat, tension, and congestion in the genitals themselves.

It's a common approach, and many people do it. But in our view, it should be avoided. When we talk about relaxation and reducing the sexual temperature, it's more to stay in a cooler zone generally. That way, you don't arrive at the point that you're going to come.

RLM: So, you don't want us to practice retrograde ejaculation, where you supposedly start to ejaculate and then suck it back into your penis. I've never met anybody who's able to do it, but I've read about it. What you're saying is that holding back orgasm has a temperature effect on the testicles and the penis.

DR: A congesting effect. It creates heat and tension in the prostate area through building up intensity and then repressing it, trying to delay ejaculation for as long as possible. It's not healthy.

RLM: This is fascinating. I'm going to talk to some of my urology friends about that, because we do have a near epidemic of prostate cancer in this country.

DR: Right—although I can't say there's any relationship. But there is something going on with ejaculation, tension, and heat. Our approach teaches that you let the ejaculation through when it arises.

RLM: I wonder what I would have done had I known that sixty years ago when, during sex, I would start thinking about baseball games in order to go longer and longer, both to satisfy my partner and to extend the pleasure.

DR: Right. So, it's more about keeping the sexual temperature cooler so that you remain engaged, but you're not pushing it. If it goes over a certain temperature where you're going to come, please come. I would like to close on that, Richard. Bless you, Richard. Thank you so much.

5

Ogi Ogas

Data Science Uncovering
Our Sexual Desires

Ogi Ogas, Ph.D., dissects what data and statistics on popular internet searches on sex can reveal about our nature and our neighbors. Ogas, a computational neuroscientist, teamed up with another data-driven scientist, Dr. Sai Gaddam, to write the groundbreaking new book *A Billion Wicked Thoughts,* based on search data compiled over several years.

Ogas received his Ph.D. in computational neuroscience from Boston University, where he designed models of learning, memory, and vision. He was a Department of Homeland Security Fellow and a Research Fellow at the Harvard Graduate School of Education. He used cognitive techniques from his brain research to win half a million dollars on *Who Wants to Be a Millionaire.*

When Ogi Ogas and Dr. Gaddam studied human sexuality via the brain's software (how it *thinks*) rather than its hardware (the cells and neurons that enable thinking), they did not question actual people about their sex lives. They turned to the internet, which they used as the first new sex-study tool since Dr. Alfred Kinsey's frank studies of the 1950s. The web allowed them to examine a population of 1.5 billion subjects. What they found from their searches was a wealth of data on sexual behavior in terms of people's sexual identity, what they sought online, what they bought, watched, and downloaded.

In Ogi Ogas's words, you will find a report on sexual behavior "uncontaminated by human frailty and the tendency to forget and lie." This data shows wide differences in the sexuality of men and women, but it also reveals a seemingly universal that has been widely unrecognized. It may surprise you.

Dr. Richard L. Miller (RLM): Please tell our readers what a computational neuroscientist is.

Ogi Ogas (OO): Sure. Computational neuroscientists study the brain, but we look at the brain as software, so we rarely get our hands dirty with actual laboratory work. Instead of cutting into human or animal brains, we try to figure out the algorithms that operate in the human mind. This was important for our sexuality research because most people in my field study things like vision, memory, and language. They try to figure out the mental software behind those higher brain functions. But nobody had used the methods of computational neuroscience to study sexuality. So we thought if we approach the sexual brain in terms of algorithms—the processing in our sexual brain— that might open up new insights.

AVOIDING A CAREER KILLER

RLM: Being a computational neuroscientist and then studying what kind of porn people in the United States are browsing online is a tremendous risk for a university professor. You and I know the risks, but I don't know if our readers are aware. I'll tell a little story about that: When I was in graduate school, I attended a lecture by a famous Stanford professor named Ernest Hilgard, who had developed what he called the Hilgard Hypnotic Susceptibility Scale. He was giving our class a lecture on hypnosis. Later, after the lecture, I asked him how, after making his reputation for twenty years as a rat psychologist and becoming a full professor at Stanford, he was studying hypnosis.

RLM: Hilgard answered, "If I had gone into hypnosis early in my career, I never would have had a career. If you study certain topics in psychology, they can end your career. One of them is hypnosis; sexuality is another."

Yet, you took this risk, Ogi. Tell us about that. Is it still a risk to study sexuality? Did it get you in trouble? We know, for example, that Kinsey got in trouble for publishing his exhaustive research and books; he lost funding and was called a communist for studying sexuality. How has it been for you?

OO: You're absolutely right. Even today, Richard, there is tremendous prejudice toward doing research in sexuality. When Sai Gaddam and I first thought about this, we talked to a number of colleagues about approaching sexuality from the perspective of computational neuroscience; every single person told us not to do it. They said it would kill our careers, that we wouldn't find anything, or that there was no future in it. Not a single person encouraged me about the project, even though we felt sure there had to be some low-hanging fruit. There was much resistance, especially to studying it from a new point of view. Even today, it's challenging to get funding for basic sex research. You almost always have to frame it in terms of sexual health. We still live in an age that is extremely fearful and anxious about sex research.

PIONEERS OF DATA-DRIVEN NEUROSCIENCE

RLM: You and Sai went against the tide and researched human sexuality; tell us what you did.

OO: We knew that to study the brain's sexual software, we needed a lot of data; data drives our field. That opened this opportunity for us because we looked into ways of collecting data on sexual behavior. We immediately realized that the internet can provide a lot of detailed data about different kinds of people.

When we first set out to do this, we assumed many researchers were already doing it, so we weren't expecting to be pioneers. We thought we would use other people's data. We quickly discovered that nobody in sex research was yet mining internet data. Beyond that, we were shocked that nobody had done any systematic science on human sexual interest since Alfred Kinsey, which meant that the most comprehensive analysis of what turns men and women on was more than fifty years old. Since then, nobody has tried to replicate or extend Kinsey's research.

Getting funding or support to do raw research on what arouses men and women is still hard. Not only were we surprised to find that nobody was using internet data, but we were just as startled that there was little knowledge about the true distribution of sexual interest in the general population. There were guesses—but no study—for how many in any given thousand people were turned on by breasts versus by butts, for example. There was no rudimentary data like that, so we tried to get our hands on any internet data related to sexual behavior that we could.

Of more than a billion individual searches, we got about 650,000 personal search histories. We looked at the million most popular websites in the world, figured out which of those were erotic, and then looked at traffic patterns to those. We looked at purchases on more than a million erotic stories. We got more than 10,000 digitized romance novels and analyzed the text in those. We looked at downloads, clicks, tags—any kind of internet data we could get. We got our hands on a number of proprietary, commercial sites that were willing to share their internal data on user behavior.

A lot of people think all we did was look at searches—and we certainly did that—but our research went far beyond searches to look at all kinds of behavioral patterns online. Of all this data, we were the first researchers who looked at it. There was a moment when Sai and I were literally the first people to look at a detailed portrait of human sexuality. We could see—for the first time, across the entire planet, with clarity—the popularity of different sexual interests. That was an exciting, though disorienting and anxious, moment.

RLM: How long did your research take, and how many individual bits of behavior did you analyze?

OO: We spent roughly a year just getting data. Then we spent roughly another year analyzing it. Our data is accurate for the entire internet population, which at the time of our research amounted to about 1.5 billion people. Because some of our data was collected across the entire internet, the data on traffic patterns of popular erotic websites described the behavior of everybody on the Net. And we have data on different countries as well. Some people say that our data is limited to people looking at pornography in America, but that's not true. We do have a lot of data on that, but we also have data that reflects the entire internet population.

I would say our richest data is in the individual search histories. Those are primarily from people in North America, from America Online. They are one of the most notorious examples of a corporate blunder. AOL released the search histories for 650,000 individual users and made that information public. They tried to anonymize the data, but if you have extended search histories of individuals, you can figure out who they are. So it turned out to be not nearly as anonymous as everyone expected.

Today we have much higher expectations of privacy, and one of those reasons is because of the America Online blunder; but for us the blunder was wonderful because we got access to more than half a million people's specific sexual proclivities over a period of time. That's probably our single best data set, but we have plenty of other rich datasets.

THE U.S., APPLE, GOOGLE, MICROSOFT KNOW-IT-ALL

RLM: You weren't exaggerating when you titled your book *A Billion Wicked Thoughts*. You literally studied a billion wicked thoughts from all over the world.

Ogi, I'm focusing on the number of pieces of data you analyzed because of the politics involved. If two MIT scientists can spend two years on a research project and come up with results regarding what a billion and a half people are doing on the internet regarding sexuality, then it should be clear that our government, with huge computers and an army of scientists, can be analyzing everything we're saying in our tweets, emails, texts, and in every other aspect of our internet life.

Isn't that true?

OO: It is. Our research is a bit frightening because of the implications for someone who knows the identity of those people. We don't know people's identities in almost any case; but certainly for our government—or even for organizations like Google, Microsoft, or Apple—the amount of personal data they have is downright disconcerting.

RLM: What we look at on the internet is public information. Our web activity is not private; the process of utilizing the internet is *caveat emptor*—let the buyer beware—or, in this case, let the internet user beware.

Prior to your research, the limited amount of sexuality research that Krafft-Ebing did in 1886, Kinsey in the 1950s, Masters and Johnson, and everything since then has been done by interviewing people. Thereby we were dependent upon the interviewee's responses, whether honest or dishonest. You've taught us that people aren't necessarily forthcoming about sex; they're often embarrassed in front of the interviewer.

OO: That's an excellent and critical point. Until we did our research, virtually every bit of research on human sexuality had relied on self-reporting—a subject saying what they liked, did, or how they behaved. Not only are people embarrassed to admit to any of that in an interview, but they're willing to lie. They even lie to themselves.

Indeed, people might not be willing or able to analyze their own behavior honestly as to what truly turns them on. But our data described what people actually *did*—what they looked at, searched for, clicked on, read, rated, viewed, purchased, or downloaded. These are indisputable facts you can't explain away. Not only did we provide the most comprehensive snapshots of people's sexuality, but these were the first reliable, objective snapshots that didn't rely on people's willingness to disclose their intimate details.

AVOIDING WHAT'S WEIRD

RLM: You pointed out in your book that a great deal of research in psychology in this country is done on people in psychology classes because that's the cheapest and easiest way to get subjects. Otherwise, psychologists must get subjects from the general public, which is more time-consuming and expensive than simply walking through a class and telling the students what to do.

Tell us about the word *WEIRD* and what we know about it.

OO: *WEIRD* is a term that is not limited to sexual research but is relevant to research in psychology and all the social sciences. It uses convenience samples, or convenience populations, meaning people who are easily accessible. The most common example of this is surveying college students. This is particularly a problem in sex research because college students are in no way typical of human sexuality. They have complete freedom and little responsibility. They are at a time in their physical life when hormones are washing through them, so their sexual interests are at a peak. Yet much sex research is based on college students' choices, decisions, and behaviors.

WEIRD itself is an acronym that refers to people who are Western, Educated, Industrialized, Rich, and Democratic, which includes the populations that comprise about 95 percent of global research. Even though researchers tend to care the most about WEIRD people, these are not necessarily representative of humanity as a species. We can assume that our sexuality is deeply rooted, something biological. So focusing on rich, educated Western college students will not give us an accurate sense of the true nature of human sexuality.

RLM: Now we know why Ogas and Gaddam did not interview people. You didn't hand out questionnaires. You didn't study Western, educated, industrialized, rich, and democratic college students. Instead, you analyzed what people worldwide are actually doing on internet porn sites and what our erotic interests really are. Tell us about your findings.

OO: Our most important finding was that men's and women's sexual behavior and sexual interests are vastly different. We all know that men and women are different when it comes to sex, but Sai and I were surprised at how different they truly are. When we began our research, our background was not in sexuality, so we didn't know what to expect. If anything, going into it naively, we expected there would be a lot of overlap between male and female sexual behavior.

THE ONE SEXUAL INTEREST WE ALL SHARE

OO: Another surprise for us was that gay men and straight men are virtually identical regarding the form, content, and patterns of sexual behavior. The only difference is that gay men prefer to look at men and straight men prefer to look at women. The same holds for straight and lesbian women; both are much different than men but very similar to one another.

That's probably the single broadest finding, but our most important discovery relevant to almost everyone is that we all have one sexual interest in common, yet, this sexual interest is completely unacknowledged and unappreciated in the scientific literature. That interest is domination and submission—power themes relating to one person having power over the other. That is the one thing that we all share, the one place where our sexualities overlap. Besides those power themes, men and women have little in common sexually.

We found a considerable number of creative variations of domination and submission themes. You will find this running through every kind of erotica—both hardcore pornography for men, romance novels and erotic stories for women, plus gay content, and lesbian content. It runs through just about everything.

In our opinion, a person's preference and taste along the domination/submission axis is as fundamental to their sexual identity as their sexual orientation. We all understand the importance of sexual orientation—whether people are attracted to men, women, or both. Based on our research, a person's domination/submission orientation is fundamental and universal. And yet it is completely overlooked.

When we started our research, an interest in domination or submission was treated as an obscure, atypical fetish rather than a central part of human sexuality.

Those are the very broad top-level findings. Then, of course, we have many specific interesting results.

DIFFERENT GENDERS, DIFFERENT SEXUAL STIMULI

RLM: Listening to you talk about the role of dominance/submission in sexuality leads me to consider that the very act of what we call sexual intercourse, penile penetration of the vagina, is inherently a male dominated endeavor since the male is doing the penetration. If this be the case than the most egalitarian form of sexual activity is what the French call *soixante neuf.**

Moving on, how does sexuality become pornography? What is the relationship between those two?

OO: It's quite straightforward: Pornography is visual erotica, and it's the preferred form of erotica for men. By a huge margin, men much prefer to look at pictures and videos than any other form of sexual content. If we simply label visual erotica as pornography, then pornography is mostly the exclusive realm of men. There are exceptions, but for the most part, women are not interested in pornography; they tend to prefer textual content like stories and books—forms of erotica based on communication and interaction.

For men, when it comes to erotica, they want porn.

RLM: Prior to the internet, for a man to look at pornography, he would have to go someplace where people were performing sexual acts, which was rare, frequent a shady store, which showed films, or, possibly he could look at certain "girlie" magazines and see pictures. Kids, without access to porn, looked at medical books, *National Geographic,* or the Sears Roebuck underwear catalog. Eventually,

---

*69.

starting with *Playboy* in the United States, men could look at sex magazines and view naked breasts. But now, everyone can look at live sexual acts by pushing a button.

OO: If you had told Americans in the 1960s they would soon be able to watch free pornography twenty-four hours a day, in great diversity and in the comfort of their homes, many people might have considered that the signal for the end of civilization. The very fact that we have integrated this kind of immense access to pornography without much disruption to society is worth noting.

Men have always had an easier time than women, accessing pornography over the years, including before the internet. It's been a different story for women because most women aren't interested in looking at visual erotica. So there hasn't been much available erotica for women until recently. There have been romance novels, which took off in the 1970s, and those fulfilled some of the women's interests. But it took longer before women could finally access erotica in freedom, comfort, and security.

Keep in mind that going into a red-light-district movie theater would be downright dangerous for a single woman. Most women would feel embarrassed to go into the dirty section of a video or bookstore to get an erotic book or movie. When the internet came along, women could explore their erotic interests freely and comfortably for the first time. What did they do? A whole new form of erotic content sprung up—made by women, for women—and it's known as fan fiction. These are mostly short stories—created mainly by amateur women writers—based on popular books, TV shows, and movies. For a long time, the most popular fan fiction was built around *Harry Potter*, the *Twilight* series, and even *Buffy the Vampire Slayer*. A large portion of fan fiction is both sexual and romantic. It is almost exclusively the domain of women, and it has exploded on the internet.

One of the significant differences between the world of fan fiction and that of pornography is that pornography for men is a solitary experience. Men go online alone, look at what they want to look at, enjoy themselves, and get offline. They don't share their experiences with other men. They don't socialize over these experiences; they are private, isolated experiences.

All these years, women have been waiting for an opportunity to have a safe, comfortable way to indulge their sexual interests, which turned out to have an interactive textual base. For women, erotica is far more of a social experience than it ever was—and than it is right now for men.

DOES THE PORN INDUSTRY INFLUENCE EROTIC TASTE?

RLM: The films made for the internet are made chiefly, by men. A high percentage of all American porn production is done in Los Angeles. Are these men now directing people's sexual tastes? When we go to a clothing store, we can only choose from what the manufacturers and designers present us. By the same token, we can only look at the internet pornography, which a small group of men, mostly in Los Angeles, are producing. How much is that affecting not only what we look at, but our very taste?

Also, what do we know of pornographic movies being made by women, for women, that women are actually watching, in addition to reading stories?

OO: I think more research needs to be done on that, but I'm confident that these pornography producers do not influence taste. They are producing pornography for money. The people who run websites with erotic content want to be successful. They are sensitive to what people want to look at, so they're putting up on their sites the very material that people want to click on the most.

We've seen relative stability in terms of the most popular kinds of topics for male pornography. These topics, of which we see examples repeatedly, are pornography with young women, including teenage women. These remain extremely popular because youth and sex are very popular in every culture in every country.

Sometimes producers make new material that caters to an unusual sexual interest, and if it doesn't get a lot of clicks, they don't push it anymore. Like any commercial enterprise on the internet, they try to give people what they want to see. They're not trying to influence taste as much as react to taste.

RLM: You're saying that the porn producers might float several balloons: people having sex with flagpoles, with women, dogs, automobiles; they then analyze what people click on and then generate more movies of that genre. Is that how it works?

OO: That's basically it—and the things that have always been popular continue to be popular now. Any kind of pornography you can think of is available; if there were a bigger audience for different tastes, there's no shortage of people who would rush to cash in.

RLM: I think I read in your book that you said, "If you can think of it, somebody has already made a pornographic movie about it."

OO: Since we've done our research, there's been a narrowing. There was a greater variety of sexual content available when we started. These days, because websites cater to growing audiences, they need increasingly popular material. They're like network TV shows, which don't like to take risks. They want to develop new TV shows that cater to as broad a segment of the population as possible.

Many people think the internet is pushing men to more and more deviant tastes, whereas, if anything, the internet keeps pushing towards the same taste they've always had. I'm confident that the internet *reflects* taste rather than influencing it. Once again, it has to do with women; women have created the greatest concentration of new content for women by women.

Fanfiction virtually didn't even exist before the internet existed. Only a tiny portion of the population even knew about it. Now it's exploded on the internet, and that's because it's the content women responded to. It didn't exist until they started to create it. The more they created, the more popular it became. So watching women's erotic content come online and develop into large, global communities, we could see that there was, in fact, an opening. A taste was not being fulfilled, and tens of thousands of websites quickly arose to cater to female taste.

You asked about pornographic movies by women, for women. Actually, there is no shortage of such erotic movies. There is plenty of female-friendly porn, but most women are not interested in it.

DIFFERENCES IN PORNOGRAPHIC PREFERENCES OF MEN AND WOMEN

OO: A lot of people have suggested that women don't like pornography because it caters to men's tastes. That is true; whenever women create pornography that does cater to women's tastes, the movies are typically more character-driven, emphasizing emotions, which many people might consider a softer kind of pornographic relationship.

Women are not much interested in looking at that either. More women are looking at hardcore male-targeted pornography than so-called female-friendly pornography. Both audiences aren't huge, but if a woman does like pornography, she's more likely to like the same stuff that men do than to like female-friendly pornography. That was a real surprise.

RLM: You said in your book that a percentage of women do like to watch pornography.

OO: Correct. It's hard to get an exact number on that, but our best guess would be that somewhere between 20 percent and 35 percent of women do enjoy looking at visual erotica.

RLM: So what kind of porn do you think men are most interested in?

OO: Let me just say a general thing about doing research on sexual behavior and sexual tastes: from a methodological, data-crunching point of view, men are easy to study—unlike women. Men are easy because they search for the same things over and over, and they have consistent behavioral patterns. For example, the single most common sexual interest for men is young women—or young men, in the case of gay men.

But even more broadly than that, men are interested in age. Men use age as the broadest category to qualify their searches. Even though teenagers and young women are the most popular, there is a great deal of interest in middle-aged and older women. It's often called "granny porn." There seems to be a small, significant, and consistent level of interest in granny porn in every culture we studied. So it's very easy to track men's interests in age.

By contrast, women's searches and behavior are more open-ended and harder to figure out. Where a man might repeatedly search for young teens, a woman will search for stories about cowboys set in the nineteenth century, or naked pictures of Brad Pitt, but they're not very consistent. They don't search for the same thing over and over. A lot of their searches are elaborate sentences where it's challenging to decode exactly what they're looking for. We can tell they're looking for a story, but what is their interest? Is it cowboys? Is it historical drama? Or is it the relationship? It's harder to simplify, so women are harder to study from a methodological point of view.

Another interest that surprised us, in terms of men's taste, was weight. Men are very focused on women's weight, and even though the number one interest for men is women of a healthy weight, it turns out that men are far more interested in overweight than underweight women. In fact, we found there are three times as many searches for fat women than for skinny women when it comes to pornography. There are plenty of sites devoted to heavier women—sometimes called "BBW" (for "big, beautiful women")—popular in every culture that we looked at all around the world.

So even though women tend to think that men are mostly interested in looking at the skinny models they often see in women's fashion magazines, in the privacy of their laptops, some look at heavier women. That, too, was a big surprise.

THE EVOLUTIONARY LOGIC BEHIND
INTEREST IN OVERWEIGHT WOMEN

RLM: When I read in your book that men are interested in overweight women, it gave me a whole new slant on what I've been talking about on the radio for at least fifteen years, which is a deep concern for the fact that presently 72 percent of our American public is obese or overweight. I never thought of being overweight as a way to be more sexually attractive.

OO: Yet it makes sense from an evolutionary point of view: for most of the history of our species, a woman with a few extra pounds was more likely to be healthier and fertile than a woman with fewer pounds. That's probably where this is rooted.

RLM: What else are men interested in? Straight and gay men are interested in youth; you say many straight men are interested in women who are overweight—are there particular behaviors that men watch more than other behaviors?

OO: As we looked at the body parts men were most interested in looking at, it was easy to analyze. The number one piece of anatomy for men is breasts, which is probably not too big of a surprise, though it was consistent across cultures, which might be more surprising. Some people think that an interest in breasts is exclusively a Western cultural phenomenon, but we found it everywhere—including South America, Asian countries, and Middle Eastern countries. Any place that has the internet, they're looking at breasts.

WHY MEN WATCH WOMEN
REACTING TO PENISES

OO: The real surprise was men's interest in looking at penises, particularly among straight men. I don't think it's any surprise that gay men are going to look at penises, but many heterosexual men do as well. When we first saw this, we were surprised. When we looked closer, we found that men are not only interested in looking at penises; they're interested in looking at penises as large as possible.

When we first shared this with other people, most women we heard from would say, "That's because men want to check out the size of what they've got compared to other men." That's not it, although I think many women might check other women's bodies to compare to their own, so they imagine men doing the same. When we talked to gay men about it, they said, "It's because even straight men secretly have some suppressed homosexuality, and you're finding that most men have a gay side."

We don't think it's that either. When you look at the actual erotica men are looking at, it always involves the woman's reaction to the large penis. You rarely see a penis without a woman's face nearby. The emphasis is on the woman's response: whether she's scared, surprised, amazed, dazzled, or excited. Why might that be?

We think the answer to this also comes from our evolutionary past. With all the other primates—chimpanzees, gorillas, bonobos, all of our primate cousins—the males focus on other males' penises, and the penises are prominent tools to exchange information about social rank, aggression, marking territory, and of course about sexuality. All primates use the penis as a sign for all of these things. It's not surprising that human males are also looking at it and showing it.

This explains why exhibitionism, which is considered a psychological problem or deviant behavior, is more widespread than people believe. We see this on the internet; you find that vast numbers of men are constantly pointing their webcams at their penis. We think that showing their penises and looking at other men's penises, particularly with an emotional reaction associated, is probably a vestigial primate behavior that we've been oblivious to.

FEAR OF HAVING ABNORMAL PROCLIVITIES

RLM: In my clinical practice, I learned that when some people reveal things they look at or do, regarding sex, they have a deep concern that these things are somehow abnormal, aberrant, or morally wrong. Your book brings out that these behaviors are part of the human condition. Whether it's looking at penises, looking at breasts, or women sharing stories—this is part of who we are—neither good nor bad, and not sick, crazy, or stupid.

OO: There's an immense gap between what we think we know about sexual tastes and the truth about sexual tastes: what society tells us are normal, typical tastes versus what the data shows are the actual prevalence of sexual preferences. We hope the most significant contribution of our research is to narrow that gap.

People feel shame, guilt, and anxiety over their sexual interests, as you pointed out, because they don't have access to accurate knowledge about how common, natural, or normal these are. Time and again, when we found sexual interests in our data, they turned out to be common universals in every culture. These interests are considered rare, abnormal, or atypical in public perception. Unfortunately, even many professional clinicians, sex therapists, and sex scientists have been promoting wrong notions about sexual interests, which has made things worse. I hope the data in my book goes a long way to comfort people about their sexual interests.

People often write me emails asking about this or that sexual interest they have, asking whether it's unusual or normal; almost always, it's one of the most common interests in our data. It's simply not widely known because it's hard to find information about sexual interests outside of our research.

HOW MUCH PORN IS REALLY ONLINE?

RLM: Can you give us an idea of what percent of internet traffic is sexual?

OO: It's much lower than people might think. Of the million most popular websites globally, only 4 percent of 40,000 are sexual. In terms of the number of sex searches, we looked at a half-billion searches on one search engine; only 11 percent of those searches, around 55,000, were for sexual content. That's a relatively small percentage, although it's still big in terms of absolute numbers. But you often see online numbers bandied about that claim half of all internet traffic is porn, and it's not even close to those numbers.

Gender Identity & Non-monogamy

We get hope and inspiration when we witness cultural change, that we perceive as positive. But cultural change takes time, and our lives are relatively short. The Earth has been here for billions of years, and we humans exist for a mere hundred years or fewer. And yet sometimes we get the chance to experience cultural change. When I was in college, "homosexuality" was a diagnosis of pathology and gay men were arrested for simply being gay. During that same era, a man in NYC, Ralph Gleason, was jailed for showing a Black hand holding a white hand on the cover of his magazine.

There are still battles ahead for equality, dignity, and respect for people of all colors and sexual preferences—in fact, for all people—but we can take hope and inspiration in the direction of our progress, which we can see by looking backward to norms that are now understood to be, well, backward.

In our puritanical society, a relatively small minority of people have the emotional wherewithal to be open about their sexuality when they engage in alternate forms of sexual activity than those that are permitted in mainstream white Anglo-Saxon culture. These people persist even though they're frequently looked down upon, stigmatized, and demonized if their sexual lifestyles are revealed.

By observing and learning about alternate forms of sexuality, we find a lot of commonalities with our own life experiences. In discussing real-life examples of alternate forms of sexuality, I hope to shed light on what we share, as well as what we can still learn from our differences.

We all get jealous from time to time, but people living in a ménage à trois may offer us a different perspective on our jealousy. We all deal with problems like sharing expenses or complex issues like the sexual mores in our society.

What can we gather from those among us who don't find themselves represented in a heterosexual life? Which problems arise when we try to understand in fixed terms, the complex spectrum that is our sexuality?

And what about gender? Where does the analytical approach of statistics not meet the subjective experience of being a gender-fluid person? What we learned from Dr. Alfred Kinsey is that hetero- and homosexuality are not either-or categories but rather they exist on a continuum with 100 percent heterosexuals on one end of the spectrum, 100 percent homosexuals on the other end, and everyone else in between. Perhaps we will discover that this continuum also best describes gender fluidity.

Having a gender identity that doesn't match your biological sex is the foundation for the experience of being transgender. But who among us is 100 percent male or female in their heart of hearts?

In this section, we will discuss the alternative experiences and expressions of gender identity, non-monogamy aka polyamory and ménage à trois, in which the threesome may or may not be fidelitous to one another. In polyamorous arrangements, there can be loving, affectionate, and sexual relationships among any number of consenting adults occurring simultaneously. Of course, many so-called monogamous people live polyamorously, but they are cheating. Approximately 5 percent of the population are polyamorous and 10 percent have engaged in polyamory.

A gender-fluid person is flexible regarding the sex with which they identify. They believe gender is non-binary, meaning that not all humans fit squarely into either the male or female category. Gender, then, differs from biological sex, which refers to the genitalia with which you are born. Gender-fluid people can be gay, straight, bisexual, and transgender, as gender identity is separate from sexual attraction.

I would like to invite you to learn along with me as we embark on the endless journey of discovering the universe of alternate ways of experiencing ourselves and each other.

6

Ritch Savin-Williams

Sexual Identification and Gender Fluidity

Despite the increasing visibility of LGBTQ people in American culture, our understanding of bisexuality remains superficial at best. Ritch Savin-Williams, Ph.D., provides an important new understanding of bisexuality as an orientation, behavior, and identity in his book titled *Bi: Bisexual, Pansexual, Fluid, and Nonbinary Youth*. As the book reveals, bisexuality is seen and embraced as a valid sexual identity more than ever before, giving us timely and much-needed insight into the complex, fascinating experiences of bisexual youth.

JUMPING INTO THE FRAY

Dr. Richard L. Miller (RLM): How did you have the nerve to conduct a study of human sexuality and not get drummed out of the corps of academia the way Dr. Alfred Kinsey did?

Ritch Savin-Williams (RSW): I came along just in the right time frame. There had been quite a few recent initial studies of sexuality—though not great ones—and I was bored with my previous topic and decided, "Why not?" There was a great need for understanding. I was appalled by a lot of what I'd read, and I have this missionary zeal to correct false beliefs.

RLM: You certainly jumped right into the fray. As you and I know as former academicians, certain topics are dangerous to study—human sexuality is certainly one of them.

RSW: Cornell hired me as a social-personality psychologist. I had done no sex research at all. I decided to switch the year that I came up for tenure. Maybe I was stupid, but I think part of it was that I did not want to be known for something that would not be my future. Fortunately for me, I was in a great department in a great college at a great university, which said, "Well, of course, do what you want to do."

RLM: Very fortunate.

RSW: Very.

KINSEY REVISITED

RLM: Your most recent book is called *Bi: Bisexual, Pansexual, Fluid, and Nonbinary Youth.* Tell us what each of those words mean.

RSW: That's what the book is about to a large extent. In a very foundational way, we've created these historical categories of sexuality. But when I interview young people, many don't identify with them. One of those sexual categories is called *bisexual,* which is supposed to mean "attracted to multiple sexes." But when you look at it from the eyes of young people, you see that it is also beginning to apply to different genders—which is where the pansexual comes in. It doesn't matter to which gender or sex you are attracted; it's the person that matters most. The idea that the person matters the most in our romantic and sexual attractions sounds revolutionary.

Fluidity simply refers to you changing over time. It could be day-to-day, which might seem strange, or maybe over the course of your life, month to month, or year to year. The term *nonbinary,* then, attempts to capture that gender is not limited to masculine and feminine, but that, like sexuality, it exists along a spectrum. This makes it difficult for traditional researchers because it's so much easier to put people in these categories. But when you find out that young people don't identify with those—they don't like them, they think they're inappropriate, or they believe they don't capture the essence of their lives—then I think we need to reexamine our conceptions—our understandings—of what sex and gender are all about.

RLM: You remind me of myself as a young person reading Kinsey. Kinsey described a continuum of sexual preference. If you were at one far end of the continuum, you were very heterosexual, and if you were far at the other end, you were totally homosexual. Most everybody was in between. If somebody was relatively in the middle, they were bisexual. That was understandable to me, and I bought into it. Are the young people coming back to that notion now, seventy years after Kinsey?

RSW: Yes. I think the development since Kinsey, which he would not be happy with, is that we began grouping people. He would've found that unusual and not true to the experience of real people. I even get emails from non-young people who say, "Great. Finally, we can begin to discuss these things—not in terms of categories, but along the spectrum," which Kinsey was all about. I consider this his most important revolutionary idea—maybe second only to the fact that we can study sex and still be legitimate scientists.

In some ways, young people are going back to that idea of a spectrum. I don't think it was ever gone; only scientists and a lot of common people ignored it in saying, "Are you gay or straight? Maybe you're bi. If you're male—maybe bi—you identify that way because you're on your way to being gay. Or, if you're female—well, aren't all females bisexual?"

We get into these strange conceptions, and the reason why we can't fight our way out is that we don't listen. We don't go back to the source. It's strange to me that psychology is supposedly a behavioral discipline based on the human experience. Yet, over the last fifty years or more, it has in many ways gone away from that foundational idea.

ENFORCING SEXUAL IDENTIFICATION

RLM: It sounds to me like crazy-making. Why are we putting young people, or any people, in this position of having to identify their sexuality as if it's a static point on a chart? We don't go around asking people how much money they make; everybody accepts that's a fluid and private matter. Not that it ought to be, in my opinion, but we accept it as private. How did we get into a situation where people have to identify as bi or pan? Isn't it enough just to be sexual?

RSW: I would hope so, and I think young people are way beyond us. A lot of them would read my book and not even question it. Bisexual includes this large group of people. But you can look at many national statistics, which ask, "Are you gay, bi, or straight?" Basically, they forget the Kinsey spectrum. If they keep it, they put it back together again into three, even though they may have measured it along a five-point continuum. They go, "Well, the mostly straights are really straight, the mostly gays are really gay, and bisexuals are those in the middle because they have equal attractions." Very few people have equal attractions. That doesn't mean they're not bisexual; it simply means that they're somewhere on that spectrum.

I think that we got lost somehow. I hear young people saying to me, "I don't know, does it matter? Why does it matter what I am? If you want a term, you can use this." When you look at the full spectrum of humans and see the number who are dually-attracted or attracted to multiple sexes, I'm proposing it's not the 3 percent that national surveys register. Once again, they're only looking at this narrow equal attraction. It's more like 25 percent of the population, from my estimation, based on looking at the research and including people that we formally kicked out of it because they didn't conform to one of our categories.

Think about it: If people don't respond in the way we want, we delete them. Then we think of everyone we've included who's left and say, "Ah, these are the true ones." We do that because we've deleted all the people that mess up our categories. We don't know what to do with them. Is that a justifiable reason to exclude them? Think about this: a lot of young people decide not to answer the sex question. We don't know why. Are they afraid of being persecuted, or that it's going to be reported to the federal government? Did they simply not understand the question? They might say, "It's none of your business." They might not see themselves in the listed terms.

We don't usually ask them about pansexuals, and yet, there are probably as many who identify as pansexual as there are who identify as bisexual. At least it's moving in that direction. What do we do with pansexuals? We kick them out of our research. They're not important enough. If we were to take another look at the data that already exist, we would have a substantial bisexual group of 25 percent, and I'm being conservative with that estimate.

RLM: I think you're being very conservative, because if we use the bell curve on the Kinsey continuum line, one standard deviation on either side indicates 68 percent of the population is bisexual.

But there's a question here I need your help with.

RSW: Sure.

DIFFERENTIATING PANSEXUALITY FROM BISEXUALITY

RLM: If *bisexual* means "attracted to either sex" and *pansexual* "is attracted across sexes," then how does *pansexual* differ from *bisexual* if there are only two sexes?

RSW: The standard definition could change, of course. The people who identify as bisexual are supposedly attracted to both sexes. Pansexuals are the same, but they add one other dimension: they're attracted to people regardless of their gender expression. For example, a pansexual could say, "I don't care if they're male or female, masculine or feminine. That's not relevant to me. It's the person." Whether that person would rate high on masculinity or femininity is of no interest to me.

But bisexuals might say, "I'm attracted to masculine girls and feminine boys."

That would be bisexual because bisexuals make a distinction on gender expression, but pansexuals don't. "I like masculine boys. I like feminine boys. I like feminine girls. I like masculine girls." They're more inclusive. The umbrella should be larger for pansexuals. That gets messy because a lot of people know what bisexual is, but not pansexual. Does it mean you have sex with anyone?

RLM: Isn't that close to what they mean?

RSW: No, because it's the person that matters to them.

RLM: It's not anyone. It's very personal. That's very helpful because I really didn't understand the difference between a pansexual and bisexual and you've clarified the difference.

RSW: In the past, when you studied fluidity, it was almost entirely limited to girls or women. We thought that fluidity—the fluctuation in attractions to males or females, exclusively one, or to both—can change over time or context. The context aspect is a bit fuzzy. In a group setting, you might be attracted to one sex, on a one-to-one basis maybe to the other sex. It's easier to understand over time. The problem here is what you mean by *time*. What causes the shift is not in the definition of fluidity. It only states that there's change over time.

We've missed out on the fact that men are also capable of being fluid, and I want to emphasize that. It's not just a female thing. It's not just a male thing. However, women seem to feel more comfortable saying they're fluid. It's more acceptable for women. Men are usually raised under the idea that you've got to make a decision and stay with it. That's masculinity—staying firm, staying even, staying the same. Men have been reticent to say that they're fluid in their sexuality. But the reality is, they can be just as fluid as women. I'm trying to emphasize in my book that both sexes can be fluid, and we shouldn't assume that, once we've assessed the sexuality that's our interest, that's the way it's going to be for the rest of that person's life.

RLM: You're making an extremely important point because of the effect of culture on how we behave. If we start with a belief system that our sexual preferences are set for life, then we're going to behave differently than if we start with a belief system that we're fluid for life.

RSW: It would also help us be more tolerant and accept people who are different from us. Once we realize that that friend or family member could be us, then I think we could say, "That's within the normal range of sexuality and romantic attractions." That's important. We need to get rid of these often undefined and strict categories we've used for way too long.

This is true not just among scientists but also media experts. They look to science to decide how they're going to report on sexuality and romantic attractions. In a larger cultural sense, I would love for us to widen the boundaries and allow more fluidity in treating sexuality and romance.

HOMOPHOBIA'S EFFECTS ON SEXUALITY

RLM: When you talked about the differences between males and females on fluidity, I started to wonder about the effect of homophobia on people's willingness to state where they are regarding fluidity. I understand that there's more homophobia about males than females in our culture.

RSW: Very much true.

RLM: Talk to us about how that homophobia is affecting these categories of sexuality and our belief systems.

RSW: There's a men's movement that attempts to undo some of the homophobia to which men appear to be sensitive, and other researchers have noted this. As boys grow up, their best friends, their group of friends, are traditionally male, at least in many cases. At a certain point during adolescence, they learn that it's okay to be with males, but that you can't be romantically or emotionally available to them. You've got to keep them at a distance. Otherwise, people will think you're gay or call you gay, fag, or some other horrible name we use to put people down.

Females, on the other hand, can walk down the sidewalk holding hands, arm in arm, and few people would assume that they're lesbians. If two guys did that, we know we would assume they're gay. It's interesting to me that we wouldn't say in either case that they're bisexual, which could be the case. That's part of biphobia, which is like homophobia, only it's against bisexuals. We assume they're either lesbian, gay, or straight. But two guys could hold hands and not be gay. They could be straight, bi, or somewhere along the spectrum.

I know from growing up in the Midwest, where ideas and messages for guys are very standard, that it's a challenging task. Here in California, it's not nearly as consequential to have same-sex attractions, regardless of how you identify.

RLM: Is it worse to be homosexual, or worse to be bisexual in the eyes of our homophobic country?

RSW: For women, it seems to be worse to identify as lesbian because being around or dating a bisexual woman is a turn-on for some straight men. For guys, it's clearly a detriment to be bisexual because the assumption is that they're really gay, that they're just holding out the olive branch to straightness and saying, "I could be in your camp. I'll take the middle road and say I'm bisexual." If you're going to come out to your parents, most parents would rather hear that you're bisexual rather than gay because their attitude is that there's still hope for you. I've heard parents say, "If you're bisexual, then go the straight route. Marry a member of the opposite sex. If you're attracted to them, take the easy road. Don't take the tough road of marrying or dating a member of the same sex."

RLM: I interviewed Letha Hadady on her book *Three In Love,* where she talks about ménages à trois. Is there any hope in the future for people living together in small groups and having children, or is that a fantasy of sexual idealists?

RSW: I hope it can occur because I've interviewed young people who would love to have that grouping. But they realize that the culture isn't going to accept it. There's only some hope that maybe they'll put themselves in an environment in which that's considered okay.

I don't know the data because it's not my major area of research, but at least the straight men I talked with were okay with the idea of the threesome, as long as it's two women and a man. If you've got two straight men and a woman, or if one of them was straight, the other one bi or gay, that would be uncomfortable for the straight guy, except with unusual individuals. I also know some guys wouldn't mind seeing an erect penis. But if you were to ask them, many would say, "As long as there are two women, I would *love* to be in a threesome."

SEXUAL IDENTIFICATION—BUREAUCRACY AND PREJUDICES RUN INTO SELF-EXPRESSION

RLM: Let's talk about the effect of identifying one's sexuality or having one's sexuality identified for us by others based on their preoccupations or biases. How do young people see this affecting their careers? You did mention filling out forms and fears of the government spying, which got my antenna waving.

RSW: Both young people and older adults seem to be clear that some professions are more open and accommodating. In some cases, it doesn't really matter. In fact, it could be an advantage. When you watch some of the shows on cooking or design—*Project Runway,* for example, then it would seem to be an advantage not to be straight. Drag shows are sort of a unique recent exception. So it's more acceptable in some professions.

But when you come to hardcore masculine careers such as football, hockey, baseball, or basketball, it becomes difficult. A few stars who are gay who play those traditionally masculine sports are starting to come out, which is a great sign. I didn't think I'd ever experience that during my lifetime. A lot of them previously only came out after their career had been over because they thought others would take aim at them on the football field, hit them harder, ignore them in the locker room, or whatever happens in locker rooms that would frighten them. I'm pleased to see openings. People are showing the ability and willingness to open up careers to anyone, regardless of their sexuality. But some footholds would still be difficult to gain. That certainly is true for men. I'm not so convinced that it would be equally true for women, or that it would be such a negative factor in their career choice.

RLM: You mentioned the locker room, and I'm going to take us on a brief aside and tell you a story about Norma Jean Almodovar, who is currently the president of COYOTE, Call Off Your Old Tired Ethics, the women's prostitute union. She told me on air that she was a policewoman in Los Angeles for many years before she became a prostitute. The policemen in the locker room were pressuring her to give them blowjobs so often that she decided to charge for them. When she started making money, she thought, *I don't need to be a cop anymore, and I'm going to go into this full time.* There is that locker-room effect.*

Talk to us about the United States government. How do people's careers get affected? Are they blackmailed if they're bisexual or homosexual? Is that used against them if they're going to run for office?

RSW: I've heard very few horror stories lately, and I think that's because of recent laws that are attempting to eliminate such discrimination. There's still subtle discrimination, which cannot be overt because people might fear the consequences. Clearly, some religious leaders are set on hiding their sexuality because they think that will have a negative impact on their careers. But I think the government is staying out of it, which I'm happy to see. That wasn't always the case, but at least we've made great strides. It's hard to know exactly what causes what, but clearly, the movement for same-sex marriage did a tremendous amount for our culture in seeing that people with same-sex attractions weren't perceived as weirdos anymore. They also wanted love, marriage, children, a future, and to be themselves. The vast majority of Americans—much more true of younger than older

---

*See chapter 12.

people—support same-sex marriage. Many people know someone who is gay, lesbian, or bisexual.*

Being familiar and having that personal experience, which is clearly the best way to get rid of homophobia, biphobia, or any kind of phobia, is best achieved by having personal relationships with people identifying with those who are not straight. As more and more people come out—which has always been a priority for many, if you want to call it that—you help get rid of a lot of negativity and discrimination.

RLM: You're accurate in saying that most of the country is now in favor of same-sex marriage, and that our laws are demonstrating that. However, "most" doesn't mean "all." Most can mean 52 percent, as we well know. Even if 55 percent favor same-sex marriage, that means 45 percent are still opposed. We do know of an estimated 30 percent of the country who are evangelicals and who are strongly opposed to same-sex marriage, and homosexuality, based on their religious beliefs. How does that large percentage of homophobic people affect the mental health of young children and adolescents who are growing up, uncertain about their feelings towards people of the same sex?

RSW: I'm happy to say it feels much less so than it used to. As the culture changes, you get approval ratings in the younger generations approaching 70 to 80 percent. Once you go back to the silent generation, those percentages begin to drop to 52 to 55 percent.

To be blunt about it, those people will be dying before long. They had these views from day one, and unless their favorite grandchild comes out to them, they likely aren't going to change.

Youth will tell their parents, but not their grandparents because they know the grandparents are solid in this antigay stance, but they perceive their parents as more flexible because a lot of them might have friends who are on the spectrum. So youths hope their parents are more accepting and understanding if they have gay friends.

That doesn't mean that some young people aren't terrified to

*Editor's note: On December 13, 2022, the Respect for Marriage Act was signed into law by President Joe Biden, requiring the U.S. government, and all states to respect the validity of same-sex marriages.

come out. They can face a wide range of issues: the desire not to disappoint their parents, being very religious, and fear for their income or their career. Obviously, holding it back is not good for mental health. Nowadays, they can find a fairly large amount of support from friends or elsewhere.

So, they need not hide in silence. They may have to be selective in who they come out to because some families do cut them off. They say, "Get out of the house. We're not going to pay for your college."

I don't know the research, but I would expect right-wing extremists to be less negative about homosexuality than abortion rights. A lot of extremists on the right have begun to shift, whereas, in an earlier time, one could imagine the Supreme Court overturning same-sex marriage. I hope I'm not proven wrong, but even with the current conservative majority, I doubt they would have enough support. I think they're aware that the culture has changed, and they don't want to disrupt it. With abortion and gun rights, the culture is fifty-fifty. But when you look at the data and poll numbers, I'm not sure the Supreme Court would overturn same-sex marriage.*

HOMOPHOBIA AND PREJUDICES IN STATISTICS: GEOGRAPHY & AFFECTED ETHNIC GROUPS

RLM: What struck home for me is how having someone who's not straight heterosexual in your family affects your outlook. Thus, when a Dick Cheney has a gay daughter, it's most likely going to affect his earlier extreme homophobic position.

RSW: Yes.

RLM: I want to move on to the effect on different ethnic and racial groups of being other than straight heterosexual.

---

*Editor's note: Much has changed since this interview was conducted. As we mentioned, the Respect for Marriage Act was codified into law, validating same-sex marriage federally. On June 24, 2022, Roe v. Wade was overturned, which eliminated federal protection for the legal right to abortion in the U.S.

RSW: This is the weakest area in the research that I've seen; I'm not sure why. When the total percentage of your population that is not straight is 5 or 6 percent, and you try to parse that into ethnicity, it becomes so small that a lot of researchers aren't willing to make much of it.

I don't share that view. We should look at ethnic, racial, and social class differences, but we can't go with numbers alone. At this point, we need to talk with people and find out what it's like.

There are classic cases, like a lot of Americans with an Asian background who find it difficult to tell their parents about their sexuality. It doesn't mean they wouldn't be out about it with their friends, but they fear for the family because of the collective view of Asian communities. The idea being, "You may be that, but don't talk about it because we're responsible to this larger culture."

A lot of Black adolescents are also concerned because of their religion, which tends to be fairly conservative. On the other hand, there is a very strong ethic of loving and supporting your family within the Black community. You might not like what your family does, but you're going to be there because it's your family. They might come out later to their family, or they're fearful of what's going to happen in their church, but on the other hand, they are able to come out and develop their friendships. We need more information about their unique struggles, especially with black churches, because they seem to prevent a lot of Black youths from coming out.

RLM: Are there studies about people who are other than very heterosexual migrating from the center of the country towards more permissive areas? Have we seen sexual population migration?

RSW: There's definitely the image that that's the case. I have not come across what I consider a good study that explores that issue.

However, there's an interesting contradiction here. The usual sense is that people who aren't straight move from rural, conservative areas to liberal places on the East or West Coast because the acceptance rate is higher. Then you begin to read stories where lesbian and bisexual women who have children will return to the rural farm area to raise their children because they don't threaten the men as much as gay men moving back into the rural community would.* They find support among other women who may be lesbian or bisexual.

We need to be aware that migration may look one way for men and a different way for women. Plus, that migration pattern may be changing, especially as more men raise children. That's because many people, regardless of their sexuality, believe that urban communities might not be the best place to raise young children. I think same-sex-attracted people are the same ilk. They also prefer to get away from the big cities in order to raise their family. I wouldn't be surprised, because I don't think anything about their sexuality would prevent that same value system from kicking in.

RLM: You've been saying that—regardless of your skin color and where in the United States you live, if you're other than straight—it's easier for you to be female than male.

RSW: That's probably true. The research seems to be somewhat unresolved because we haven't done a good job of parsing people on the spectrum to see how they relate to each other. It may be that urban areas are better for gay guys and rural areas are better for lesbian women. I don't know.

HOW DOES SEXUAL IDENTIFICATION WORK FOR THE INDIVIDUAL?

RLM: Somebody is reading our interview, and they're saying to themselves, "How do I know what category I fall in? I don't want to be in these categories, and I think these two doctors are right that maybe they ought not exist. But the fact is there are these categories, and somebody is going to ask me about them on some form." In fact, I was recently asked about my sexual preference on a form

---

*Editor's note: Queer migration studies research these trends.

for a medical examination. I had never seen anything like that, have you?

RSW: I don't think I have. I'd probably cross it out and correct it.

RLM: I filled out a form, which no less than a half-dozen prominent medical doctors had seen before I consulted with them. Every time I filled out the form, separately for each of doctor, I checked off lesbian for my sexual preference. None of them has ever mentioned it to me.

RSW: I'm surprised that those are still legal.

RLM: So a person of any age is reading this, and they're saying, "I shouldn't have to identify my sexual preference, but I do. So how do I know what to say? What does it take to make me a bisexual? Do I need to think of a penis? Do I need to suck on a penis? Do I need to date men as well as women? How does this work out for me? If I'm forced to fill out one of these forms for a doctor, how do I know what to check? What are the rules for identifying as bisexual?"

RSW: I would advise that if you don't want to answer the question, then don't. I don't even know what reason there would be to force someone to fill it out. If I were in control of assessing sexuality, I would put an open box and say, "How would you describe your sexuality? How would you describe your romantic attractions?" Then, I would allow people to tell me. Interpreting what they mean might burden a researcher, but that's okay because it's real. I once asked someone to describe their sexuality, and they wrote in "happy." I'm not quite sure what to do with "happy," but it's there.

If that's how they want to do it, I can live with it. It's their decision, not mine. I developed a nine-scale to assess sexual and romantic attractions as a child, as an adolescent, and as an adult. I included two more points than Kinsey, so that you had more options along the spectrum. Youth appeared to appreciate this modification to better represent themselves in greater nuance. For example, you could say "exclusively," "primarily," or "mostly straight"—with the same on the gay/lesbian end. That way, you give more options and then ask for greater details or meaning if you're interviewing them. In addition, the key for me is that I also ask them not just about their sexuality but also about their romantic orientation. Using a continuum, "Do you fall in love only with women or only with men, or somewhere between those extremes?"

It's important to assess romantic as well as sexual attractions. They're usually congruent and usually, the people we fall in love with are those we have sex with, or at least they share the same gender. But that's not always the case. I interviewed a young man who watches gay porn to masturbate, and yet he falls in love with women. The question is, should he tell the women that he goes to gay porn in order to get off? When he is having sex with them, should he say that he's imagining gay sex? Mind you, *he* wasn't confused. He knew what he was and what attracted him, and he just felt like there was no one else in the world like him. He shouldn't feel alone, and he wouldn't if we talked to more people and got their stories.

I wanted to say, "You may be unique, but there are other people like you"—along the same continuum. These men might only fall in love with women, but if the right guy came along, they might have sex. It's not always congruent between sex and love, and the scale items aren't always identical. We don't know that because we don't measure it. Yet it would seem to be a major issue in young people's lives. How do I cope with this discrepancy? How do I measure a woman who loves her best friend and says, "If I could just find a guy like her, I'd marry him"? Does she want to interact with this best friend sexually? Maybe, maybe not. What do I do with that, and how do you tackle these discrepancies? That's where textbook research has failed us tremendously.

RLM: I remember reading in your book about the man who was sexual with a woman but who couldn't orgasm unless he thought about gay sex. I found myself wondering why he didn't try gay sex and see if that worked for him. But that was a silly thought because he was both attracted to this woman and having that particular sensitivity.

RSW: He did try sex with men. He felt just what you were saying, actually: "Well, maybe I should try sex with men." So he did, with the help of Grindr. For him, it was kind of boring. He said, "I'd take sex with a woman anytime." My problem with this is that he's normal—he's not *typical,* but he is normal. We're built to be able to have these discrepancies. It simply means we're built differently, but it doesn't mean that one is right and one is wrong, or one is better and one is worse. We have got to get out of that mindset, that judging syndrome.

RLM: I believe that years ago, our profession came to the agreement that anything two consenting adults do together sexually is normal. Do you agree with that?

RSW: No. I think we widen the boundaries, but extreme cases mean we might not be normal.

RLM: You mean, if you hang upside down in the bedroom while the other person is whistling Dixie, that's not normal? Why not? No one is being harmed.

RSW: Right. But they have the right to do that as long as no one is hurt. They wouldn't call it typical, but they would say, "That doesn't sound very healthy," or they would still judge it, even as they allow it. The problem is, they hesitate to allow that same freedom to young people because somehow they think it will ruin them for life.

RLM: So if young people have to do the missionary position, in order to be normal, they can then start experimenting with doing it on the pool table or in the kitchen after they get to a certain age?

RSW: That's right.

RLM: In that case we will have an age for going into the army, an age for driving, an age for drinking, and an age to graduate from the missionary position!

THE INFLUENCE OF GENETICS AND CULTURE ON OUR SEXUALITY

RLM: At the bottom line, isn't most—if not all—of what we're saying about sexuality cultural and not inherited, or genetic? Aren't we talking about nurture, not nature? Does not nature make us all simply sexual?

RSW: I cannot say yes because, for example, there are asexual individuals. Whatever nature does, it doesn't do it to everyone. In most situations, there seems to be room for nature—that is: I do think we're born with one of a variety of orientations. I would even say that fluidity could be an orientation, that we are born with the capacity to be fluid.

Still, it's key to ask what culture does. That's also what we've been talking about here. What does culture do with the biology that's already in place? Everything is biological: we exist; we have biological systems; we have genetic codes; we have hormones. That's why I think discussing biology and nature is important because it increases people's willingness to accept things they might not otherwise.

This is one of the reasons that a lot of antigay movements have faltered. As the evidence began to build that there was a genetic or biological component to our sexual and romantic orientation, they would aim at changing one's sexual desires. They tried many things, all of which were unsuccessful. So there are limitations—as well as opportunities. I would argue that a good culture helps us to understand the real world without judgment calls. I don't want to get anti-religious about it, but there are real things in the real world, and I think we ought not be so judgmental.

RLM: Not to be argumentative but I think being asexual is a form of sexual.

What have we not talked about that you would like us to know from your vast experience studying human sexuality?

RSW: I think what we've missed is trying to understand the way people actually live their sexual and romantic lives in a way that would help us understand those aspects of our development. We should quit making assumptions and just go with it. Talk with people. Don't treat people as if they were code, or a line of data. Sexologists and a lot of other scientists have neglected that—whether in the push for publications, or to get on various kinds of social media. I think that's a big mistake.

7

Letha Hadady

Ménage à Trois

Letha Hadady is one of the nation's leading experts on natural Chinese remedies and the author of books on health and beauty. She has led stress management workshops and acted as a natural product consultant for Sony Entertainment Inc., Dreyfus, Ogilvy & Mather, and Consumer Eyes, Inc. in New York. In 1980 Letha became involved with novelist Michael Foster and librarian and poet Barbara Foster, in a ménage à trois of writers. Together, they researched and wrote two biographies of Alexandra David-Neel: *Forbidden Journey* and *The Secret Lives of Alexandra David-Neel*. Their book *Three in Love: Ménages à Trois from Ancient to Modern Times* has been called "racy and engaging" by *Entertainment Weekly*. The three have been featured in television and radio interviews and a European documentary, *Ménage à Trois*, in 2008 by Catherina Klusemann. Hadady has also authored *Tea for Three: The Other Woman*, as well as coauthored *Outlaws of Love: A History of Forbidden Desire*.

Dr. Richard L. Miller (RLM): Welcome, Letha. About a quarter century ago, I read a review of a book titled *Three in Love*. I heard that one of the authors was coming to a nearby bookstore to give a talk. The bookstore, A Clean Well-Lighted Place for Books, was in Marin County, California, where I lived part time. I attended the lecture, and I listened to your coauthor Barbara Foster talk.

Letha Hadady (LH): How nice!

RLM: The book impacted me greatly, and I've referred many people to it over the past twenty-five years.

LH: Thank you.

THE HISTORY OF MÉNAGE À TROIS

RLM: For those who don't know, what is a ménage à trois?

LH: That's a good question because the French has been translated into English, but it's lost its original meaning. Originally, in French, *ménage à trois* meant "a household of three." It's when three people can work together, associate with each other, or even harmoniously live together as a family. That's the ideal presented in the book. If you imagine a continuum, a horizontal line drawn, one end of it is three people who cooperate, who have managed to overcome the most devilish of human emotions—jealousy, hatred, envy. They've formed a coordinating and compromising harmonious family of three. On the other end of the line is a triangle, which can become a bloody triangle when one picks up a gun and shoots the other two.

The idea behind the book is that we're on that continuum. A family of three can become a triangle and vice versa because we're all evolving human beings. The relationships described in this book are the history we're not taught in school. The sexual history of individuals who have impacted our lives—who have made decisions and created great works of art—has been important in politics and history. This is not a book about your neighbor who had an affair with the milkman or your cousin who is dallying with someone and keeping it secret from their husband or wife. It's about people who've made a real impact in the world. And the three of us have all made contributions to literature and the arts.

Michael Foster, who I describe as the author of this book, was a historian and biographer. He specialized in early American history and wrote two novels about early American history and several celebrated biographies—including, for example, the biography of Alexandra David-Neel, the explorer of Tibet. He was the great artistic and aesthetic creator of this book. Barbara Foster was a librarian at City College, and she helped with the research. I was the youngster—much younger, and greatly influenced by them. Michael took me to my first yoga class, encouraged me to study Chinese medicine, and insisted that I write books. I've written six natural health books and four novels because of him.

The tone of the book is very literate. It's not about how you can get together with two other people and have a good time; it's a history of many love affairs among people who chose a lifestyle beyond coupledom.

RLM: How does a ménage à trois differ from polygamy or polyandry?

LH: There's an overlap. The book does not deal with polygamy, a man with several wives, which is the modus operandi in the Arab world, for example. That's a religious choice. We chose to talk about people in history who chose consciously, without religious concerns. Polyandry was traditional in Tibet, where one woman married a man and his brothers. That could be a household of three to five. But the book dealt with people we all know from history and our lifetime, but whose sexual lives, we in the public didn't know.

For example, there's the Kennedys or Franklin and Eleanor Roosevelt, along with her lover, Earl Miller. They cooperated to the extent that the government ran smoothly. We had a president who had polio and kept it secret, and his wife went out campaigning and forming the United Nations. *His* lover, social secretary, and junior wife was Missy LeHand, who lived with them. Eleanor knew and liked Missy. The difference between a ménage à trois and a triangle is that everybody knows about everybody. Everybody knows who's sleeping with whom—and they approve. Whereas a triangle or an affair is often kept secret from the spouse.

RLM: Because we have monumental hypocrisy about human sexuality in the United States, secrecy is en vogue. You're talking about something different: the opposite of secrecy. You're saying that, in a real ménage à trois, there's transparency rather than secrecy.

LH: You got it exactly right. It takes great courage to have that level of transparency because it's required for us to look at ourselves, see our weaknesses, try to overcome them, and be generous and compassionate with the other people involved.

LIVING TOGETHER AS A THREESOME

RLM: When the three people get together and decide to form not a triangle but a threesome and they're banding together, do they typically live together, or might they live in separate places? How does it work in terms of cohabitation?

LH: That's a good question. The answer is: the total spectrum. They can live together or separately. In a positive ménage à trois, or threesome, they can live in separate places but work together. There can be a working ménage. Michael even invented the terminology for a *metaphysical ménage,* which means that one of the people is not present; one person is an influence and not involved romantically or sexually with the others. For example, Clara and Robert Schumann were a couple. Brahms never slept with Clara Schumann, but their love and respect for each other are celebrated in the music of Robert Schumann.

You had Nietzsche, Freud, and the first major woman psychoanalyst, Lou Salome. She respected Freud; Freud respected Nietzsche. A metaphysical ménage is not necessarily a physical ménage, but the people influence each other. So a threesome contains the whole spectrum. It's people who either live together or don't live together, sleep together or don't sleep together, but they impact each other.

RLM: Let's focus on the ménage where people either live together or live close enough to get together often so that they act as a trio the way we're used to people acting as pairs. We know how couples typically act: they're likely to go to dinner together; they might go to the theater. If they're athletic, they might play sports. Couples do things together as a pair. We see couples walking down the street as pairs; we call that being "coupled." In what you're calling a real ménage à trois, it's a threesome, and the vectors are going in every direction with equality and transparency. When I first heard of you back in 1997, you and the Fosters were an active and successful ménage at the time.

LH: Yes. We encouraged each other, and we all wrote books.

RLM: Together, yes.

LH: Together and separately. Before I ever met them—for 20 years— they had an open marriage. She dated men simultaneously while being married to Michael, and Michael and I lived like a married couple. We were exclusive with each other sexually.

RLM: But not exclusive of Barbara?

LH: Exclusive of Barbara, sexually, yes. We worked together, but we didn't sleep together. We're not lesbians. Her book about her sexual adventures around the world is called *Confessions of a Librarian*.

RLM: I'll have to interview her about that. It sounds fun.

LH: If you can find her. Threesomes and ménages à trois stay together while the energy is alive and cohesive. Michael kept us together. Now, since Michael passed on in 2016, Barbara and I are not in touch with each other.

RLM: In a classic ménage à trois, are the three people all making love with one another, or not necessarily?

LH: Not necessarily.

RLM: Two of them might be making love, but the third one doesn't join in.

LH: Not necessarily. People are individual. Ménages à trois, threesomes, or triangles are individual as well. We see this in literature and movies.

One of my favorite examples is *Design for Living,* a delightful movie with Miriam Hopkins, who is in love with two men, Gary Cooper and Fredric March. She can't decide which one she loves most, so she loves both. You can also find threesomes in other movies we know and love, like *Paint Your Wagon* and *Butch Cassidy and the Sundance Kid.* These are people who live together and cooperate as three.

RLM: Typically, when a couple gets together, be it same-sex or opposite-sex, they get a government contract called a marriage license. When they do that, most of the time, they also share finances. How does that work in a ménage à trois?

LH: There has to be some manner of cooperation. FDR was born into wealth, and his mother was a worse-than-usual mother-in-law who insisted he marry his cousin Eleanor and forbid him from getting involved with Lucy Mercer, who was of the same social class as the Roosevelts. Missy LeHand, who took over the pleasures and duties of a wife, was also an employee. But she was supported financially by the Roosevelts. There has to be some equality. What works best, in my opinion, is if there's an equality of spirit, education, development, and some sharing of finances. It's inevitable—you can't have someone poor plus a rich couple. For example, the great French writers had a mistress and a *maison secondaire,* a secondary home. They provided for their children with the second woman, and they kept their wives. That happened with Victor Hugo, with Dumas père. It was a French tradition, and that's why we have the French term *ménage à trois.*

DEALING WITH JEALOUSY

RLM: Everyone knows that coupling—same or different sex—is hard to sustain over a period of time. Our divorce rate in the United States is over 50 percent, which is a testament to the difficulty of marriage. It would seem to me, a priori, that a threesome would be even more difficult than a twosome because now you've got all these additional vectors of relationships. Tell us something about your experience, not just about the famous people in your book. It is a wonderful book, but what is the actual *experience* of a threesome like? How do you deal with jealousy or insecurity?

LH: Before I do that, I want to read one lovely sentence from the book, which will give you an idea of its tone. Michael wrote, "The ménage plays out in exaggerated form the repertoire of romance, from infatuation to quarrel." It runs the whole gamut.

RLM: That's a beautiful sentence.

LH: Michael was a poet as well as a biographer.

RLM: What's it like on a daily basis to live in a threesome, especially in the beginning when you're ironing out the jealousy and the quarrels?

LH: It's hard. It requires courage, devotion, and generosity more than anything. It's a struggle with oneself. We were together 40 years as a working ménage à trois. As a daily relationship, it was probably easier because we didn't live together. Michael had a home with her for several years and visited me during the week and the weekend. Later he moved in with me and visited her. Throughout that time, they worked together as best they could as a writing team, with her doing research at the library while he did the writing.

I think their background and age created a special relationship. They were close in age and both Jewish. She was from Philadelphia and he was from Brooklyn. Michael's idea of an ideal ménage à trois was based on his background, which was communist, Jewish from Brooklyn: from each according to their talent and to each according to their needs. His talent was writing; hers was researching and bringing in money. He stayed home and wrote books. Mine was evolving. I was younger than them, and I became a writer and an editor.

RLM: How many years younger?

LH: Ten. I did the final edit to his books because he couldn't cut his own writing. I gave it the final polish. There's a sequel to *Three in Love*, and it's called *Outlaws of Love: A History of Forbidden Desire*.

The author is Michael Foster. He asked me to finish it. The book took at least a dozen years of research. They were researching it and writing it while writing others. But when he knew he was going to die, he told me to finish the book. I added the last half-dozen chapters and published it.

RLM: Is the book by Foster and Hadady?

LH: No, it's his book.

RLM: The way you described the three of you, no offense meant, but it sounds polygamous, where Michael was with Barbara and then with you. I don't get the sense of the three of you together.

LH: I understand.

RLM: I don't get a picture of the three of you walking down the street, going to the theater, or getting into bed together.

LH: We did. In New York, we went to theater, concerts, and dance performances together because that's what we do in New York. In winter, we would go to Miami, and she would join us for a couple of weeks. We would rendezvous in Vermont in the summer and rent a big ski condo. We also cooperated with our writing, in the editorial and writing process. We would read to each other. When we would go off to Vermont or Miami, expenses were shared.

RLM: Expenses were shared. If people read about this and want to experiment, could you comment on raising children in a ménage à trois?

LH: I would say that's more possible than it used to be since we acknowledge that gay people can get married or that relationships can be open.

RLM: Can you see a situation where children have three parents right in the house?

LH: It's called a *kibbutz*.

RLM: It's a mini-kibbutz, isn't it?

LH: Yes, it's very traditional. The kids from that environment grow up socialized with other kids who grow up in the same structure. They don't play one parent against another because they're going to get called on that.

RLM: Couples in our country claim monogamy and fidelity, though we know the reality is often not what they claim—another piece of hypocrisy.

LH: In rare cases, I think it's true.

RLM: You're saying there's monogamy in rare cases.

LH: Sure. I've known couples who've been together for a lifetime, and it's beautiful. I'm not against that. I was the most conservative of the three of us because I had been married for ten years before I got together with the Fosters, and I was devoted to Michael like a wife. I acknowledged Barbara's preference for having many lovers.

RLM: But no children were involved?

LH: No. In New York, our apartments were so small that we were forced to live separately.

RLM: You had the option to make one apartment out of the two, and you would've saved some money on the second apartment.

LH: It was a twenty-minute walk between them. But we did share space when we went off on vacations together.

RLM: Yes. And, as I was getting at, couples make claims for monogamy and fidelity, and we know that's not what they're actually doing a significant percentage of the time. In a ménage, is there an agreement for fidelity, or is a ménage by definition an open marriage?

LH: It's too variable to make a rule.

RLM: I see.

LH: It's whatever the group decides on, and there's usually a fourth as an observer. In the book, there's Henry Miller, June Miller, and Anaïs Nin. Anaïs Nin was encouraged to write because she idolized Henry Miller, and June supported Henry's writing. But the fourth, who observed, was Nin's husband, a conservative banker. He became a photographer and filmmaker because he started filming her. He was involved vicariously and excited by reading her diaries.

RLM: We know historically that the aristocracy, Bohemians, and artists engage in many behaviors that the rest of us don't do. But what impressed me about Barbara's talk was that when she traveled across the United States, regular, everyday people came out of the woodwork to tell her they were living in a ménage à trois.

LH: Exactly. It's the unrecognized relationship on which many people spend a certain amount of time, maybe as part of their maturing process. Many go through it and don't acknowledge it other than thinking they hate their mother-in-law or spend more time with their husband, wife, or interfering relative. That's a triangle. If the interfering relative is helpful, it could be a ménage à trois, even though it's not sexual. You asked me about my experience, and I wrote about that in a novel. I think the novel is another valid description of the problem, which is asking whether a given situation constitutes a ménage à trois or a triangle. It could be one or the other, and it could change. So I wrote about it in a novel called *Tea for Three: The Other Woman*.

In the novel, a young Chinese girl grows up in Thailand. Her father is European. She gets involved with a sophisticated New York couple who have a love/hate relationship. This is autobiographical in some sense. It was my opportunity to express the various dimensions of love, including jealousy, hatred, and cooperation. At the end of the novel, each of the three lives out their karma—whether a grabbing, selfish karma; idealistic, self-sacrificing karma; or mystical love karma of devotion. In all three cases, each has expressed their life to the fullest.

RLM: In your case with Michael and Barbara, if this was a ménage emotionally, then what happened after he died that you and Barbara seemed to have gone separate ways? I would think that after you were so close for forty years you would remain close. Are you disappointed about losing her friendship?

LH: We were always so different that it seemed a natural progression. She always had a separate life. It was more comfortable for us. When you lose someone, the memories and experiences are there. We became more evolved people. We've gone our separate ways and stayed strong. Now, she might have a different view of that.

RLM: Do you think you'll find another couple of people to ménage à trois with again?

LH: No, I don't think so. I'm not looking for a relationship, and I don't think you can go into such a relationship with an expectation. I don't think you can tell yourself you're going out to find two people.

RLM: I was thinking people are going to read this and say, "That sounds like a great idea. My parents and everybody I know are divorced. I'm going to go find two people." Do you think that's likely?

LH: It's possible, but you asked about me. It's certainly possible with younger people because they might be more open and are more financially dependent on each other. It might happen with a bunch of older women who move in together to share expenses and cooking privileges in the kitchen. We're social beings and need to interact with other people and share.

SEXUAL MORES IN AMERICA

RLM: Do you think, in the twenty-five years since you've written *Three in Love,* that the sexual mores in our country have changed significantly?

LH: It's a battleground politically. The Trump years brought it out, but it was always there. On one side, you have the conservative people who say a woman's place is in the home—carrying her pregnancy or being punished—as Trump said. On the other side, you have people who say we have to take care of those who are less fortunate and adopt and care for the entire spectrum of people, not just the rich being richer and the poor being poorer. It's a battleground, and it's being fought on a sexual terrain. As a historian, Michael Foster looked at what was going on in America when he was alive, before Trump's presidency, and he said, "The civil war has never ended; it's turned into a sexual war."

When Trump took over, he started limiting the freedoms of women and the LBGTQ community with judges, legislation, and presidential proclamations. I treat that in the book *Outlaws of Love* because I added a chapter on Trump. He was most influenced not by his wives but by his religious teacher, an evangelist woman who said you could do anything because God has given you the right. God said, "Be anything you want and do anything you want without reservation," and he listened to that.

That's why we have people like Trump, Bolsonaro, and Orban, who are idealizing authoritarianism. That is the battleground of who controls our life, sexuality, social exchanges, and finances. This was meant as a political book because Michael never lost sight of that. We did many radio and TV interviews in the 1990s. One of them was with Geraldo Rivera, but it was never aired because Michael made his grandstand statement: "Don't listen to the church, your parents, or the government. Decide for yourself what your life and sexuality are going to be."

RLM: So you're saying that the sexuality struggle is just one aspect of the planetary struggle between what I call the Social Humanists or Gaiaists—those of us who believe that the planet is a living, breathing organism, and that all of us are part of it—and the others, whom I call Social Darwinists, who believe we live on the surface of the planet and it is ours to plunder and extract from. These people would have the rest of us be subjects rather than citizens.

LH: Beautiful. That's very California. I love it.

RLM: The Social Darwinists believe life is about the survival of the fittest—whoever gets the most "deserves" it. In their view, the fittest live at the top, and everybody else lives at the bottom because that's how it's supposed to be. If the less fit all die, it's because they're supposed to die.

LH: It sounds like Calvinism. Go back in history, and that speaks to the philosophy of the chosen: "We're the chosen, and you're not. Too bad for you."

RLM: Yes. As opposed to, "We're all in this together, and let's make the best we can of it."

LH: Yes.

RLM: The Social Humanists and the Social Darwinists are engaging in the planetary struggle. I view the major cancer at the root of the planetary struggle as capitalism. Because I believe it's inherent to the structure of the capitalistic system that some people will be at the top and everybody else will be below. The socioeconomic stratification is not because anybody is bad, irresponsible, or malicious. The danger of capitalism is personified by the boardgame Monopoly. If you play Monopoly with your friends for four days, a couple of people end up with all the money while everybody else has nothing. That is capitalism, which I see as a species-wide autoimmune disease.

LH: It starts with an attitude of, *Me first. I'm the most important,* and it's a shame.

RLM: Getting back to sexual customs in the United States. Do you think young people nowadays are freer to engage in sexual activity than twenty-five years ago? Or is it still the same where women are slut-shamed and men are considered studs if they go out and have a lot of sexual encounters?

LH: No, things have radically changed since the sixties since unisex* men have become more gentle and possibly more threatened. We're

---

*Hadady is referring to unisex presenting.

talking about America in 2021. What troubles me is looking at the young people who are about to enter puberty. Instead of looking for a love relationship, they either commit suicide or pick up a gun because they feel hopeless. They've been raised to be hopeless instead of to feel loved and be loving. It's troubling, and I think it has been since drugs have become everyday occurrences, not just for kids but for everybody. The internet has given us a good means of immediate communication, but it has blurred the difference between reality and fantasy. If you see it on the internet, it must be true, even if it's ridiculous.

They've never learned critical thinking. When he said goodbye to CBS, Walter Cronkite said, "The worst problem in this country is poor education." We can back that up with the loss of cohesiveness in the family. The conservative Christian family is based on their practices and religion. That has kept that group conservative; they know exactly what's right and wrong but only according to their definition.

RLM: You were going to say something about Eric Fromm's book *The Art of Loving*.

LH: Yes, the kernel sentence of that book is, "It is better to be loving than to be loved." For someone to say, "I'm going out to find two people," or, "I'm going to find one person," is an approach, but it might end up in sadness, disappointment, or tragedy. Because we should develop ourselves when we can. I don't mean just, *love yourself.* That idea has been cheapened. When we develop a love for ourselves, our health, and the planet, we will be more generous and evolved.

RLM: I'd like to end with you telling a story from your book. Which one jumps out at you as a favorite?

LH: There are many. *Design for Living*—a favorite ménage à trois of mine. There's Fredric March, Miriam Hopkins, and Gary Cooper. Gary Cooper plays a painter; Fredric March plays a writer. Miriam Hopkins plays a wannabe artist, but she knows that her talent isn't the equal of those two men. They are two giants, but she has to develop them personally because their egos are so big it's interfering with their art. So she adopts both of them. There's a gentleman's agreement in the movie, which is funny. They agree to have no sex whatsoever.

She prods them to excel in their work. She marries a wonderful comedian, Edward Everett Horton, in the movie. But she can't stand conservative married life because it's too constrained for her. At the end, the threesome get together in a taxi and go back to their apartment in Paris, where they had this gentleman's agreement. They all agree that it'll be a gentleman's agreement, but they all smile because we know as viewers they're all going to have sex together. The 1933 play *Design for Living* by Noël Coward resembles the loving, working relationship Coward had with the married actors Alfred Lunt and Lynn Fontanne.

RLM: It's fitting that our interview ends with an example of everybody having sex together, since that's the theme of the book. *Three in Love* is the book, and the sequel you want to read is called *Outlaws of Love: A History of Hidden Desire,* credited to Michael Foster.

8

Sumati Sparks

Open Relationships and Polyamory

Sumati Sparks has been a personal- and spiritual-growth junkie her entire life. Her training includes having attended over forty workshops with the Human Awareness Institute. She is a trained Zegg Forum Facilitator and part of the Network for a New Culture, has studied Nonviolent Communication (or NVC) with Marshall Rosenberg, has been practicing 12-step work in the areas of relationship and addiction since 1985, is a trained PSYCH-K Facilitator (a process used to remove limiting beliefs), has a Yoga & Meditation teacher certification through the Sivananda school, and has studied sacred sexuality with Evalena Rose, Baba Dez, and other prominent teachers. Since 2000, she has been coaching people in the areas of relationship and sexuality and now specializes in helping people create successful open relationships.

Sumati's first name—which means pure essence—was given to her by the "living saint," Amma (Mata Amritananda Mayi).

WHAT IS MODERN POLYAMORY?

Dr. Richard L. Miller (RLM): Sumati Sparks is a polyamory and relationships coach. Sumati coaches people of all relationship configurations, gender expressions, sexual orientations, and cultures to create successful consensual, ethical, non-monogamous love and intimate connections.

Let's start with you telling us how you define polyamory in the modern era.

Sumati Sparks (SS): The term *polyamory* was invented in the nineties, and it takes the root of two different languages. *Poly* means "many" and *amory* means "love." So it refers to somebody who wants to have the freedom to love more than one person, whether it be sexually, romantically, or just emotionally. It can mean "love more than one person," which may not be accepted in our default culture. Certainly, you can love your children and family members, but there are barriers to who you can love. Polyamory sets you free. Everybody involved knows about it and consents to it. It doesn't mean there aren't going to be feelings, but at least everyone is aware that there's more than one love relationship. I also coach people who are swingers or have open relationships, which doesn't necessarily mean they're having regular, romantic, ongoing connections with people. It could mean they have friends with benefits. People have non-monogamous connections in a variety of ways, but polyamory tends to refer to those involving love and ongoing connection.

RLM: Is it correct that you differentiate between an open relationship and a polyamorous one depending on the level of intimacy involved?

SS: It's a good question because people who practice this love style tend to be rebellious types in the first place who don't want to go along with the mainstream. So any person you ask might have a slightly different definition. From what I've seen, it's most common to use *ethical non-monogamy* as an umbrella term. On one extreme, you can have swingers who go to parties and for whom sex is recreational. There's a fun Netflix movie about that called *The More the Merrier*. It's based in Spain and way sexier than any American TV production could be. I highly recommend it.

RLM: Can Americans get the film *The More the Merrier* on Netflix?

SS: Yes, it's dubbed. It's funny and super-sexy. One of the things they say in that movie when going into the swinger club is, "Leave your emotions outside." That's the typical swinger mentality. Cut off your emotions—just bring your body in for pleasure only.

I'll give you an example of the other extreme. I went to a polyamory conference years ago. A group of us was sitting around the lunch table and somebody said, "Let's go around and share how we do polyamory." One woman in her fifties said, "It bugs me when people think polyamorous folks are promiscuous because I've only been with four men in my life and three of them are here with me at the conference."

In other words, she'd only had sex with four men and three of them stayed in her life long term. That's an extreme example of somebody who's more on the polyamorous end of the spectrum, where they're not into play parties or casual sex. They just "love big"—as in: when they love somebody, they stay in their life forever. But there's an enormous gray area in between.

I would say *open relationship* is a loose term for somebody in a non-monogamous relationship. They may not even have a primary partner because *open relationship* doesn't necessarily mean you have a husband, wife, or someone you live with. There's also something called *solo polyamory,* where you treat every relationship as an equal. There's no hierarchy. It doesn't necessarily mean you're a couple opening your relationship. It can also be that you practice open relationships in general. There's so much variety within those two extremes.

POLYAMORY VERSUS OPEN RELATIONSHIPS

RLM: It's confusing. I'm trying to get a handle on some principles to differentiate polyamory from open relationships. So not everybody who's in an open relationship is necessarily polyamorous?

SS: Correct. *Polyamory* as an umbrella term has been replaced by *ethical non-monogamy.* We even use the acronym ENM.

RLM: I have a hard time with groups and concepts described as *non.* In psychology, people talk about non-dual psychology and nondualism, and I wish there were a way of putting that in the positive. It's one thing to describe something as non-something, but please also tell me what it actually *is?* You can tell a person where not to cross the street fifty times and they still won't know where to cross. Tell them once where to cross the street and they know where to cross safely.

SS: I agree. I wish there was a term that describes what we are rather than what we aren't.

RLM: When you say *non-monogamous,* you're being described as what you're not rather than what you are.

SS: To take it a step further, putting the term *ethical* in front implies that most non-monogamous people are unethical, whereas you don't say, "I'm ethically monogamous."

RLM: Yes.

SS: Often, I've dropped the term *ethical. Non-monogamous* has almost become a word. See how fast I say it, as if it's not even in opposition to monogamy.

RLM: Saying "ethical" almost implies there's a reason to be defensive and justify oneself.

SS: Exactly.

RLM: One place where I thought the use of the word *ethical* fits regarding sex is in Dr. Janet Hardy's book *The Ethical Slut* because there, the word modifies the sex-shaming word *slut.*

SS: They're reclaiming that word because it only refers to somebody who is consensually choosing to have sex frequently with more than one person.

RLM: If I understand correctly, you are a spokesperson for people who are polyamorous.

SS: No. I support people in all forms of non-monogamy. In my personal life and relationship practice, I do fall under the spectrum's poly-amory part.

RLM: You're saying that people involved in a polyamorous relationship aren't necessarily in an open relationship.

SS: I'm not right now. I don't live with a husband, wife, or *nesting partner*—which is a term we use. I don't even have an anchor partner right now. My whole life, I've had a primary partner. I've been poly-amorous for twenty-five years. All that time, I had a primary partner, and my last primary partnership ended when the pandemic started—horrible timing.

RLM: Terrible timing.

SS: I've been dating online, and have met sweet people, but haven't met somebody like a life-partner type. However, here in Hawaii, I'm in a relationship with a couple. They've been together for three years before and are primary partners. We have slowly fallen in love since I moved here over the past year. I loved them as friends before, but we've moved into romantic love; mostly with the man because I'm primarily heterosexual. But I have a deep love for the woman as well. That has evolved into a romantic sexual connection.

RLM: But you're not living with them.

SS: No, but they're vagabonds. They go here and there. Oftentimes, they stay with me, but I wouldn't say this is their home.

RLM: Is that a situation where eventually, the three of you would live together as a ménage à trois?

SS: No, there's another term called *relationship escalator*. In the default world, if you start dating somebody and you have sex with them regularly, there's an expectation that you'll eventually live together. If you're younger, maybe there's an assumption you're going to start a family. Whereas here, there's no such assumption or expectation—no relationship escalator. It's us, sharing love while acknowledging this is an unusual time in the world. I may find a life partner and things may shift between the three of us, but we're enjoying it now for what it is.

RLM: You just mentioned that you've been practicing, if you will, polyamory for twenty-five years.

SS: Correct.

RLM: That means you started quite young. How did you start out on something so unconventional at such an early age?

SS: It wasn't an early age. You're looking at me on Zoom and I've mastered the art of lighting. I'm sixty-one. So I started in my late thirties.

RLM: (laughing) I see what you mean.

SS: I had always cheated in my relationships. I would be able to stay monogamous for two to three years, and then I would end up fooling around and hating myself.

RLM: Hating yourself because you were breaking a deal?

SS: Yes, I was lying. I was hiding it from my primary partner.

RLM: Why?

SS: I thought that's the only option available. I didn't know you could talk to your partner and agree to it. It was a new concept to me. So when I went to a workshop and I saw other people who were polyamorous, only then did I understand I don't have to cheat anymore. I can talk about it.

RLM: You went to this workshop when you were thirty-five years old.

SS: Yes. Then, I learned that I can be honest, talk about this, and tell my partner what I want. Now, just because I learned about it, that didn't mean I could immediately *do* it. All of us have this monogamous programming. In our culture, that's the default assumption, and you're bad if you don't do it. A lot of us have religious programming or strict parents who have shamed us about our sexuality. There's a lot to untangle and overcome before you can change the way you communicate.

I was afraid if I told my partner I wanted to see other people that he would then do the same. So I could see other people. But when my partner did, that's where the rubber meets the road and you have to manage your jealousy. I was afraid I couldn't handle my jealousy. Some polyamorous people aren't jealous, but some are, and I'm as jealous as anyone else. I've had to learn to dance with my jealousy and transform it into something I can play with, live with, learn from, dance with.

MANAGING JEALOUSY IN POLYAMOROUS RELATIONSHIPS

RLM: I've got to hear more from you about "dancing with" jealousy.

SS: Okay. It probably took me ten years out of the twenty-five years to not be susceptible to complete meltdowns. For example, I was ten years into practicing polyamory and my five-year partner decided he wanted to go back to a former partner and treat us both equally. It felt like a demotion to me. I had been his primary partner for three years. Now he wanted to see us an equal amount. He wasn't even demoting me below her; he wanted more equality in how often he saw the two of us and how much devotion he gave us in his life.

RLM: What did he want the living arrangement to look like?

SS: He was already living with her. They had become roommates for a while and she was in another relationship. When her relationship ended, they looked at each other and went, "I like you after all." So they wanted to start reconnecting again.

RLM: At the beginning of your relationship with him, was he still living with her?

SS: Correct. So I saw this man for five years. The first year I assumed he was a polyamorous man in an open marriage. I dated him as if I were a secondary partner. Then she got into a new relationship, fell madly in love with somebody, and started traveling with this other man. She was hardly ever home and they rarely saw each other. They were ships passing in the night. For three years, they would have a date two or three times a month to spend any time at all together. By default, I guess, we became primary partners for each other.

RLM: Even though you were not living together?

SS: Correct. We would still spend four or five nights a week together, either at his house or my house. So we spent a lot of time together— every weekend, every vacation—even though his residence was at this other place. For three years, I felt like his primary. Then she ended her other relationship and decided she wanted to spend more time with him again. I had a meltdown because they wouldn't talk to me about it. Here's another term for you: *kitchen-table polyamory*. That's where you can sit around the table and make sure everybody's needs are met. They wouldn't do that.

I kept asking them if we could talk about this change and how we can all get our needs met, but they weren't willing to give me the time to do that. I couldn't handle watching them reconnect in their romantic love in front of my face without me getting a chance to process my feelings. So I tried to do the work on my own without getting to talk to them, but it was too much for me. Then I stepped away because it was too painful.

RLM: From the way you're describing it, you were squeezed out.

SS: It felt that way, even though they wouldn't say it. He said he still wanted me, but he wasn't willing to involve her. He even went to therapy with me alone, but he wouldn't facilitate the three of us talking about it. He said he only did separate dyads.

RLM: So what he wanted, in effect, was a variation of polygamy.

SS: Maybe, but he's used to doing separate dyads. The only time the three of us ever sat down and talked together in those five years was when he had engaged in risky sexual behavior and we had to have a conversation about the potential exposure to an STI. There was none, but the three of us sat down to talk about it and he was sweating bullets. He was so uncomfortable being with the two of us at the same time. We'd been in groups together, but never the three of us alone except that one time. That's what I was asking for and it was way out of his comfort zone.

RLM: I made the comment about polygamy because, from my perspective, in polyamory, everyone in the group talks to one another. There's open communication, not a squeezing out of people at "lower" levels. As soon as you described it, it did sound like a guy that wanted to have two separate women and call it a day.

SS: I want to own that this is my side of the story. As a relationship coach, I know there are always two sides to every story.

RLM: Yes, indeed.

SS: But the point is that that experience led to me diving into my work as a coach, because I had to figure out how to get into a relationship that's right for me. Look at all the nuances of non-monogamy— sometimes you don't even know what you want until you get out there and try things. So I got clear that I need kitchen-table polyamory. I need all of us to be able to talk and feel comfortable when we're together. I call myself *tribal-amorous* sometimes, because I love when I'm in a whole community of polyamorous folks where there's enough for everyone. We're all loving each other, holding space for each other's jealousy and feelings.

Back to your question about jealousy. I've created a workshop called *Transforming Jealousy into Love* that's based on how I learned to overcome the jealousy that led to that meltdown about fifteen years ago. I've learned to work with jealousy. So if you want, I can go into that a little bit more.

RLM: My question is: How do you *dance* in jealousy? The situation you describe was not a classic polyamorous situation and I cannot understand if you were experiencing jealousy or feeling some other emotion related to getting squeezed out. So what are some of the things you suggest to people as a way of dealing with their emotions when there's actual jealousy involved? Let's say you're in a three and you're living together, but one person feels the other two are giving each other more attention. So you're jealous of that attention and want to be part of it.

SS: That's a good example. The most common example I get with people I coach is: they're an existing couple newly opening their relationship. One of them meets another person first before the other and the one who hasn't met anyone yet is jealous. Or they've already fallen in love with somebody and say, "Now, what do we do? I've met this person and my partner's jealous."

It could be the case that people are living together, but it's less likely. Usually, they're dating outside their couple.

RLM: Your examples are good. Let's explore them.

SS: The main thing is to reframe jealousy so it's not something to be avoided. It's so common in the default culture. We assume we're supposed to do whatever it takes to keep our partner from feeling jealous. If we do anything that might make them feel jealous, we lie. So we avoid it like the plague. You can reframe that by saying, "Jealousy isn't going to kill you. It can be painful, but it can also be a great sign of something that needs to grow or evolve within you." It's funny. When people say they're going to open their marriage, the first thing on their mind is all this sex with new people. But before you can get to the fun sex, you have to prioritize your personal growth. You can reframe it: "When I feel jealousy, it's about me. It's not my partner's fault. They're just living their life and I got a button pushed. So what is that button? Is it insecurity? Do I need to look at why I feel less than somebody else? Is it scarcity? Do I feel like there's not enough time for me? Do I need to ask for more attention and time?"

In your example of people living together, it might be that they're feeling scarcity. They want more time or affection, more sex from their partner. They get to learn how to ask for that. If they still can't get it after they've clearly asked for it, then it might be time to change the relationship. Other questions to ask yourself when you're feeling jealous are, "Are you enmeshed with your partner? Are you codependent? Are you making your life all about them? Is there a way that you can disentangle that enmeshment and be more sovereign, making more friends and intimate partners?" They don't even have to be sexual. Have somebody you can cuddle with and watch a movie—get your affection needs met somewhere else. Do you have a hobby that you're passionate about? Get more of life so that you're not so wrapped up in everything your partner does.

How is your spiritual life? Who *are* you really? Are you this person who needs attention from your partner all the time, or are you bigger than that? When we practice our spirituality, most people eventually come to the place where we are all infinite love. So when you can tap into that fact, there's no room for jealousy. I encourage my clients to develop a spiritual practice.

FEAR OF LOSING YOUR
PARTNER TO POLYAMORY

RLM: To what extent is fear of loss part of jealousy? In the example you gave, a couple, A and B are living together and they then open up their relationship. Then person A finds somebody else, person C, and starts having a relationship with them. To what extent is person B simply afraid of losing their partner?

SS: That's a really good question. The feeling in the one who's not dating and who fears losing their partner is very common. The first thing I say is, would monogamy solve that? Would monogamy guarantee that your partner is never going to leave you?

RLM: There's no guarantee of anything in life.

SS: Right. What I've learned is that the more you can set your partner free to express themselves, the more likely they'll want to stay with you. Why would they let you go if you're celebrating their full expression in life? Sure, it's possible that your partner could meet somebody monogamous, convince them to leave their partner, and stay monogamous with them. But that points to a weakness in the original relationship.

RLM: Let's say Fred and Ellen are living together as a couple. Fred meets Harriet and starts having a relationship with her. They're dating and having sex. Now, Harriet offers something to Fred that Ellen can't offer, which is all the excitement, romance, and sex of a date. Whereas Ellen is involved with the sharing of the chores of living such as taking out the garbage, paying the bills, cleaning the house, and walking the dog—all the stuff that comes with cohabiting. There's a lot that has to be done when actually living together.

SS: I get it.

RLM: The other person—the date, so to speak—has all the glamour—a dinner out, sex afterwards—without any of the chores. How do you beat that?

SS: You're touching on all the common things, which is why people need me. We have a term for that, too. We call his new relationship *NRE,* which stands for "new relationship energy." It's that honeymoon phase when you're almost drugged. Your serotonin and dopamine are going. An experienced person with an open relationship will know that's a temporary state. When I coach people who are new, I just say, "You're in NRE. That never lasts. In the history of humankind, nobody has ever stayed in NRE forever."

One thing that the partner who's not in NRE can do is practice letting them have that experience. They may not immediately feel happy for them, which we call *compersion.* That's when you feel happy that your partner is having this awesome time. It would be great if you could feel compersion for them, saying, "We've been married for thirty years and I'm so happy you get to have this exciting new love affair. At the same time, I'm feeling insecure because I can't make you feel that way anymore. But I know that's my insecurity. So I'm going to work on that with my therapist, continue to find another partner myself, or tend to the art that I've ignored for the last twenty years."

Whatever it is, they don't take it personally. They notice the feelings within themselves and let their partner go have that experience. If the original relationship is strong, that man is not going to just bolt on his wife to go be with this new love because they have a commitment that they're going to open their relationship, but not leave each other. So if he leaves her for this other person, that speaks to their original relationship. They didn't have the commitment and the tools to manage this open love style.

RLM: Talk to us about how people make a commitment to purposefully get involved with people, other than their primary partner, while consciously not letting their feelings and thoughts carry them into going off with that other person.

SS: Let me answer the second part first. With time and practice, you can own your feelings and not blame the other person. No matter how hard it may be, it's *my* work. If my partner goes off to have amazing sex with a new love, swinging from the chandeliers, and I'm feeling like I'm not enough, there are things I can do. I can say, "Sweetie, I want you to give me a little more attention than usual so that I don't feel replaced by your new sweetie."

Most people will feel so enlivened by their new sweetie that they have more juice to bring home, so it overflows. When it comes to sex and love, I say: "the more, the more." It's not a pie, where you take one piece out and there's less for everyone else. The energy of sex and love is ever-expanding.

I'm not talking about *anatomically* having sex, especially if you're an older person. You might not be able, technically speaking, to have *intercourse* all the time. But the partner who's got the new love can bring that energy back home and make their sex life with the original partner even better. I've seen that happen over and over again.

RLM: I interviewed a retired courtesan named Veronica Monet recently.* She has a great book out called *Sex Secrets of Escorts*. Veronica tells a story about being in a marriage relationship while

---

*See chapter 13.

working as a courtesan. Her husband said, "You can do anything you want, but don't have orgasms." What that meant was she would go out, do her sex work all day, and when she came home, she was hot to trot because she wanted to finally have that orgasm. She came home to him prepped. I thought that was a creative way to handle that particular situation.

SS: Exactly. The main thing I want to mention is that, sometimes the feelings that come up from jealousy can trigger serious old trauma. It can be more than, "I'm feeling insecure and need to work on that," or, "Can you spend more time with me if you're going to see a new partner? Can we make sure we have sex before you go on the date?" You can make requests of your partner so that you're not feeling neglected when they have a new sweetie.

But for other people, it can trigger old trauma. You feel like you're insane and don't know why. You can't manage your feelings. You're feeling horrible all the time, even if you're telling yourself, "This makes sense to me. I agreed to an open relationship. I've read all the books. I understand. It doesn't mean I'm less, and yet I feel horrible." Maybe they even start saying mean things to their partner or doing self-harm because their old traumas are triggered.

I work with people with inner-child healing processes to go back to that stuck place within them that got frozen in time in their youth and that wasn't ever dealt with. If it's significant trauma, I might refer them to a trauma-informed therapist for EMDR* or a more advanced practice around healing trauma. But I do want to stress that old trauma can come up from this love style.

IS AN OPEN RELATIONSHIP ALWAYS SEXUALLY OPEN?

RLM: To what extent is an open relationship always open sexually? How much does sex play a part in an open relationship?

---

*Eye movement desensitization and reprocessing, a therapeutic modality used to treat trauma.

SS: There's no relationship police that are going to come to knock on your door and say, "You're not doing it right." We live in a free country. It's illegal to be married to more than one person, but outside of that, nobody is telling us how to do it. So the foundation of any open relationship is getting the communication down. One of the first things I teach my couples is how to have weekly conversations to attune to each other—to connect, to feel safe. Only then can you make requests and be able to hear each other's requests without getting defensive and be someone that your partner can tell things to. Once my couples have learned that, they can design the kind of relationship they want.

Maybe one person wants to have a love partner that they date and never have sex with. That could make their partner jealous because it involves love, connection, and late nights of talking. Another couple might feel okay with the sex but don't want the late-night talking. Everyone has got different needs and boundaries. You have to get the communication down so that you can be honest about what you want and work that out with your partner.

RLM: How do children fit into this picture?

SS: I don't have children myself, but I've worked with clients who do and I read a lot about it on the forums that I'm on. A lot depends on whether the parents have careers or other factors in their lives where they could be significantly harmed if people knew they weren't monogamous. If they're school teachers or a pillar in their community and church—meaning they can't afford to be outed—then they have to keep it from small children because you can't ask them to hold this in confidence. That's not fair to a small child, nor do they know how. If the children are older, they can usually keep confidence.

I work with many mature couples whose kids are grown. Their kids' careers are already established, and they don't care what anyone thinks of them. But if you have small children and you have a career that can be affected by being outed, that's different. You know how children are. If you're intense about something and you feel like it's a big deal, they'll pick up on that energy. But if you're matter-of-fact about it, then they take it as a matter of fact. Having extra lovers around is like having extra aunties and uncles. Obviously, you're not going to tell children what you do in the bedroom. You don't even do that when you're monogamous. If they see you being affectionate with other people and you normalize that, then children will feel normal about it. It depends on the other factors in your life.

RLM: I would think that having unconventional sex lives is even more challenging with teenagers.

SS: Yes, that "ick factor" is there for teenagers, and even young adults can think it's weird, but it depends on each situation. Not everybody engages in kitchen-table polyamory. But I know lots of people who have children that are involved—not sexually but in terms of knowing what's going on. It's such a bonus for children. As they say, it takes a village to raise a child. They've got lots of adults loving them, extra people who care. When a child or another adult is sick, there are more people around to help. Having that community is a huge bonus. But a lot of people practice open relationships outside of their homes. It's a separate thing, sometimes part of their entertainment.

RLM: If you don't mind using yourself—or one of your clients—as an example, how does the family of the polyamorous person relate to the unconventional lifestyle?

SS: It's similar to being gay. There's a point where you start to consider coming out to your family. That's an individual choice for everyone, and it's often a scary moment because they're not sure how the family's going to react.

For some people, just like being gay, you get to a point where you can't stand hiding who you are. Let's say that I'm married and I've had a new lover for five years. My husband knows about him. It's a deep love connection. He's not going anywhere, and I'm tired of not being able to bring him to Thanksgiving. Or I've been bringing him and acting like he's just a friend. I eventually want to tell my family, "Hey, Buster and I are more than friends. I'm tired of having to hide that." But I did something many years ago—do you remember the book *Radical Honesty?*

RLM: Yes. Written by Brad Blanton.

SS: I was three-quarters through that book, and I blurted it out to my mom. It probably wasn't the best way or timing to do it. But that book influenced me immensely, so I had to tell her. She comes from a Catholic background and she was older. She only said, "I don't understand." She was upset and it felt selfish, like it didn't do me any good to tell her. I wasn't even living in the same city as her. But what was good about that is, when I became a professional open relationship coach later, she already knew. So she had many years to get used to it. But again, it's similar to being gay. You have to measure whether it's worth it to you. Sometimes family members will cut you off, at least for a while, and you have to learn to make a choice. "Is this way of relating more important to me than my family? Is my family so screwed up that I don't care what they say?" Every situation is different.

RLM: To what extent are open relationships and polyamory sex-driven, and to what extent are they driven by other factors?

SS: I would say an open relationship is more driven by sex, but polyamory is not. I've been throwing all my terms at you, so here's one more—

RLM: Good.

SS: I have a *post-romantic partner.* I was in a primary partnership for eight years and sex became problematic between us, but everything else was great. We decided to take that off the table so we'd stop fighting. Eventually, we both started seeing other people. We already had other lovers, but eventually, we stopped talking multiple times a day. We never lived together so we didn't have to move out. Over time, we would talk every other day and then a couple of times a week. Then one of us would go on vacation and not call for the whole week.

Now, we're not so connected as we were, but we still have the same love and feeling of life partnership. We're going to be in each other's live for as long as we're both alive. We call each other when we want to celebrate an important moment, or to get support in difficult times. We still have that intimacy, but without the sexuality. I think polyamory is a great way to stay connected with all of the people you've ever loved. You don't have to cut them off because your next partner doesn't want you talking to your ex. The design of the relationship can shift and change, but the love is still there.

TRIBAL-AMOROUS LIVING ARRANGEMENTS

RLM: Letha Hadady says in her book *Three in Love* that polyamorous people living together is more like the basic family group because so many of us grow up in a household with at least three people. I say "so many of us" because a number of us nowadays are growing up with one parent and I don't want to be disrespectful of that group by implying there are always two parents. Hadady is talking about what we consider the basic family unit, which is two people and one or more children.

She says polyamory feels emotionally comfortable because you have at least three adults living together and thus you re-create the original family unit. She makes a strong case that polyamory—rather than being about more sex—is about the basic unit living together in a small tribe. Are there polyamorous communities? Is that what you meant by polyamorous groups?

SS: As I mentioned, I use the term *tribal-amorous*. Yes, there are many communities. A few of them live together and most of them that I've been involved with come together for temporary living situations, evening events, or retreats. It's a loose-knit community where it's not always the same people every time. Let's say there's a community of a hundred people. At any given event, you'll see some subset of them. You may not have dates with them outside of the events, but you're seeing the same people over and over, so you begin to have lighter relationships with them. You may have a physical, romantic, or sexual connection with them at the event.

We used to call them swinger parties, but now they're called play parties because *swinger parties* implies that there are couples playing together with other couples, whereas this could be couples who go—but don't play—together. They go their separate ways at the party and then drive back home together. It could be singles open to meeting a partner. Or it could be somebody whose partner doesn't like play parties so they go without them. Play parties tend to bring together people in all different relationship configurations and they need strong consent education. A lot of the communities I'm in make you go through an orientation where you learn how to say no, negotiate boundaries, and talk about the risks of STIs. You need a lot of education to make a good play party community. That's happening right under our noses.

As far as the communities that live together, I know of one on the big island of Hawaii, where I'm taking a retreat next month. They started as a polyamorous community together. There are about twelve adults in the community. They're not all lovers with each other, but each person has between one and three other lovers. They live together in a permaculture village off the grid, and they host one or two retreats a year for other like-minded, free-love individuals.

RLM: Are they open to the public? Do they have a website?

SS: They're pretty open because they do host events and that's part of how they make their living. You can find them at *permaculturehawaii.com*.

ARE OPEN RELATIONSHIPS STRONGER?

RLM: The divorce rate in the United States is almost 50 percent, which indicates that marriage coupling in itself—at least in the ways that we're doing it—is a difficult endeavor.

SS: Yes.

RLM: Does opening the relationship—whether open relationship or polyamory—make life more difficult because of the complexities of all the different relationships? If so, does the polyamorous or open-relationship person more likely find themselves in a series of short-term relationships rather than going the distance, as do the 50 percent of marriages, which are successful?

SS: I thought you were going to ask me whether open relationships last longer and are less likely to end in divorce than monogamous relationships.

RLM: You can answer that question also, if you like.

SS: There's a researcher on polyamory named Elisabeth Sheff. Her studies have shown that people in open relationships are happier by a few percentage points. At least they *claim* to be happier more than monogamous people do. This is not an easy endeavor. It takes a lot of work on yourself, as you can gather from my meltdown.

I was just listening to an interview with two people who are fairly big names in this subculture. Both of them remembered having difficult experiences ten years into being polyamorous. So it's not something you can learn overnight. You have to take it on as a life-long practice, continually work on the monogamy programming, and look for ways to shift your paradigm.

I'm polyamorous because it's an identity for me—like being gay. As I said, I always cheated. I can't thrive in a long-term monogamous relationship. Other people can choose to be polyamorous or not. We call that being ambi-amorous. It's not part of their identity, whereas I don't have a choice. If I want to have a fulfilling, thriving life, I've got to figure this out. So it's going to be a way that I practice relationships for the rest of my life.

I also know lots of couples that have been married a long time and have successful open relationships. Sometimes they have partners that come and go, but their primary relationship is strong and they've figured it out over the years. They've worked through the jealousy, insecurities, and communication issues, and they've gotten to a place where they're solid, committed, and they know how to roll with it. It takes some practice, but I think it can strengthen relationships.

RLM: Letha Hadady told me that when she went on a lecture tour, people all over the country came to her and told her they were in various forms of ménages à trois, which falls under polyamory. She said she was surprised at how many people came out of the woodwork to tell her about their lives. Do we have any way of knowing what percentage of the population falls into one of these two categories, open or polyamorous?

SS: I've seen some statistics; it's still in the 1 percent or 2 percent, maybe under 5 percent. I don't remember exactly, but it's getting more and more common. Even celebrities are practicing it. There's Will and Jada Smith, and their daughter also came out as saying that she's bisexual and polyamorous. So more and more celebrities are coming out about it.

RLM: They lead the way, I guess.

SS: It's becoming more normalized. People often want to be polyamorous because they want more of something they're not getting, or they want something different than what they're getting. They may want a different gender because they're bisexual, or they may be pansexual and want to date genderqueer people. Or they may want a different kind of sex than they're getting. They may want more kink than their partners. So they get tied up with their partner, but then they come home to their spouse.

RLM: The person who ties them up unties them.

SS: Exactly. That can be an additive in a relationship. The other person can let them go get what they need outside. If the other person doesn't want to give it to them, or if they *can't*—you can't, for example be the opposite gender than what you are—they only have to accept that, "I can't be everything to all people."

We're asking a lot of each other in the modern era. We're hoping to find *one* person who exists as our lover, our best friend, co-parent—and maybe even a business partner—who supports us in our careers and makes us the best version of us we can be. Even being a bed partner alone is challenging. I know a lot of people that don't sleep in the same rooms because their sleeping styles are so different.

So we're asking this one person to be everything to us, and it's a big burden to put on someone. If you can step back and say, "It's unrealistic to expect this one person to be my everything," then you can open up to other people. You can get your needs met from a variety of people and not be so frustrated and angry at your partner for not meeting all those needs. You can accept them for who they are.

When I teach classes to mature folks, like *Polyamory Over 50*. I say, "Stop looking for 'the one.' Because how has that been working for you so far?" Giving up looking for *the* one doesn't mean you're never going to find that ideal life partner. Just stop *looking* for them. Instead, look for a few—and be open-minded because you never know. People you normally wouldn't choose could suddenly become your partner, if you cast a wider net.

Most people have time in their life for a maximum of three partners, and maybe more on occasion. If you go out there looking for three partners, maybe one will end up being special. But you're opening your vision to looking past the physical traits, the checklist you're trying to check off, and just being open to connecting with different people in a range of capacities. One of them may surprise you and turn out to be an incredible life partner.

COMPLEXITY

RLM: Is it accurate to say that when you add people to the basic relationship, you add complexity? Is that the tuition you pay for the benefits?

SS: Yes, definitely.

RLM: In addition to the fun of the expanded sexual opportunities, there's more processing when adding an additional person to a dyad—more material to process, more emotional ups and downs.

SS: Right, but it's not like we have to process; instead, we get to get "naked" with each other, to get real and share who we are, be vulnerable, and go deep. We *get* to do that; we don't *have* to.

RLM: We've got a great question here from one of our team, our sound engineer, David Springer, and he wants to know how you deal with various sexual diseases when people are open or in polyamory.

SS: Thank you. That's a common fear. Studies have shown that people who are ethically non-monogamous have less incidences of STIs than the greater population of single people because they know how to talk about it. We don't have shame around letting others know if we tested positive. So we have what we call "safer-sex conversations."

No sex is 100 percent safe. Even if you're monogamous, somebody could be cheating and not telling you. Unless you're having no sex at all, there's no sex that's 100 percent safe. We talk about it. For example, just when you're about to have sex, maybe you've started to get into some heavy petting, and then you pull back and say, "Would this be a good time to have a safer-sex conversation?"

You've got to stop what you're doing and just share: "What have you been tested for recently? What were the results? What are your practices with other people? Who are you fluid-bonded with?"—meaning, Who do you not use condoms with?—"What are your agreements with your partner? What do *we* want to do together? What kind of barriers do we want to use or not?"

You're making a conscious decision based on knowing what the other person has tested for, what their practices are. Then you can make a conscious consensual decision about being willing to take the risk or using barriers. So you make an agreement and then you move forward.

RLM: Thank you. I have one last question. If a person or a couple comes to you and they're traditionally partnering, monogamous, or a traditional single, and they want to get involved in an open or poly-amorous relationship—what do you tell them? What are the first baby steps?

SS: I have a quiz on the home page of my website that goes into how suited you are for ethical non-monogamy. I would start there and see how you score. If you score low, then you're probably not well suited for it. But if you still want to do it and you want to commit to your personal growth no matter what, do whatever it takes to get past your traumas, get to where you can love someone freely, I believe anyone can do it.

Somebody who scores high on the scale might already be well suited for it and not become jealous easily. They may have a certain confidence in themselves. So it depends on where they are on the scale, how much support they need from me. It could be that they need some tweaking, to read a few books, and they're on their way. Other people have to do a lot of deep inner-child work.

I'm sorry I can't give you a definitive answer. It depends on where the person is on that scale with regard to how much support they need.

9

Janet Hardy

The Ethical Slut: A Practical Guide to Polyamory, Open Relationships & Other Adventures

Janet Hardy is an award-winning best-selling author and educator. She has an AB with honors from UC Davis and a master of fine arts in creative nonfiction. Her best-known of more than a dozen books, *The Ethical Slut,* coauthored with Dossie Easton, has sold more than 500,000 copies and has been translated into several languages. Janet is also an activist championing the cause of positive attitudes toward all forms of consensual sexual behavior.

Dr. Richard L. Miller (RLM): Politics so invades our entire culture that, even if one lives off the land in a remote area, one is affected by political realities and decisions. Politicians decide upon the quality of the air we breathe, the quality of the water we drink, and the level of ambient sound in our environment. Hospital care, education, housing, and even the quality of the food we eat are influenced by political decisions.

We the people have created and formed a government which involves itself in almost every aspect of our daily lives. Notice I said *we* because we are the ones who form the government. This is not about us being victims of the government. This is about us *creating* a government and living within the government we form. Allowing the government great power gives us citizens safety and security. We pay for safety and security with our freedom and liberty.

Governing ourselves, as we do, is a balancing act between freedom and security. The more security a government provides by policing, the less freedom we, the people, have. By the same token, if we're free to do whatever we want, our world is not safe for our kids, or for us. This is a tough balancing act. The danger of the tradeoff is that, if we give the government too much of our freedom, the government may not be willing to relinquish its hold on us.

Difficult economic times are fertile ground for a strongman dictator type who tells the people, "Your government has failed you. I can fix all of your problems." Although strongmen are sometimes initially elected, like Hitler, there are only two successful strongmen in all of recorded history who voluntarily gave up their leadership positions. The first was the Roman general Cincinnatus. You may remember that he had retired, was called out to become dictator, won the war, and then went back to farming.

The other was our general and founding father, George Washington. After the Revolutionary War, he likewise turned in his sword to Congress and went back to his farm, Mount Vernon. He stayed there for five years until we formed the Constitution, and then he was duly elected president.

Since our country's formation, we have continuously striven to broaden our democracy to provide all citizens with equal constitutional rights. From a country, which allowed slavery, we have become a country with a Black president. From a country in which women were chattel, we nominated a woman for president, we elected a Black female vice president, and we now have a Black female on our Supreme Court.

From a puritanical country that looked down upon dancing, we became the country of rock and roll. From a country in which homosexuality was a clinical diagnosis, we have become a country in which same-sex people can obtain a marriage license.

Given the level of political influence in decision-making on almost every aspect of our minds, bodies, and health, it is in all of our self-interests to be informed, active in our communities, and to vote.

Today's guest, Janet Hardy, is a political leader who has taken sexual freedom as her political cause. Janet's mission is to change our sexual attitudes from being looked down upon to being accepted. She is particularly interested in sexual freedom for females who have long suffered when expressing themselves sexually.

Janet, I'm going to start with page 226 of your book *The Ethical Slut,* from the chapter titled, "Sex and Pleasure":

> Sex is nice and pleasure is good for you. We've said this before and it bears repeating. In our present lives your authors enjoy sex for its own sake and it feels natural and comfortable, but we want you to know that it wasn't always this easy for us. In a culture that teaches that sex is sleazy, nasty, dirty and dangerous, a path to a free sexuality can be hard to find and fraught with perils while you walk it. If you choose to walk this path, we congratulate you and offer you support, encouragement, and, most important of all, information. Start with the knowledge that we and just about everybody else who enjoys sex without strictures learned how to be this way in spite of the society we grew up in, and that means you can learn too.

Janet Hardy (JH): That sounds about right to me. We've heard a bit from the growing community of people who identify as asexual that the "sex is nice and pleasure is good for you" doesn't apply to them, because to them sex is not nice. I think we're softening that to something along the lines of sex can be nice and pleasure can be good for you because that's unquestionably true for everybody.

RLM: Very interesting. You have information that says a growing percentage of people identify as asexual.

JH: It's a new identity, Richard. There's a group online called the Asexual Visibility and Education Network. When we wrote the edition you're holding in your hands, we weren't aware of asexuality. It is becoming a more visible identity and we want to address the concerns of those people as well. I think a lot more young people are finding that identity to be their best fit.

SOLO AND CONSENSUAL

RLM: I'd like you to talk about *solo and consensual sex.*

JH: Absolutely. I think solo sex is an important skill for anybody who wants to enter into a nontraditional relationship, in particular any kind of polyamorous or open relationship, which sounds contradictory. You're going to have more sex with more people, so in order to learn that you have to have more sex with yourself. This is important because if you cannot be sexually satisfied with your own company, you're always going to be desperate and it's going to be difficult for you to hold relationships loosely enough to be comfortable with polyamory. It's a little bit like being financially dependent. If you're financially dependent, it can be difficult to let go of your relationships.

The greater culture still tends to define the fundamental sexual unit as two people. That means that people who don't fit into those tidy couples often think of themselves as broken. I redefine the fundamental human sexual unit as one person, so that you can be a complete sexual unit unto yourself. Once you have that, you can be free to open it to other people and welcome them in without holding desperately to them.

RLM: You're differentiating between sexual behavior for pleasure and for procreation, correct? Because obviously, you need another person for procreation.

JH: At least another person as seen through a turkey baster or a syringe, but you need at least two people involved in the process.

RLM: I love the way you said that, because you're absolutely accurate. Two people must be involved in the procreative act, even though one of them may be represented through a turkey baster or a syringe. Procreation doesn't have to be the result of intercourse.

JH: We all know a lot of possibilities are opening up for people for whom heterosexual intercourse doesn't work but who nonetheless want to be parents. There are all kinds of options that didn't exist when you and I were younger, and I think that's marvelous.

RLM: You talked about *solo sex* and the importance of getting to know oneself to bring more into consensual sex. Tell us about what you mean by consensual sex.

JH: *Consensual sex* is sex in which everybody gets a vote—not necessarily just the people who are having it, but the people who are connected through relationship commitments. They may not have a veto, depending on what arrangements have been made, but they get a chance to speak their minds. If anybody does say "no," it's respected. If there is a "yes," then the one, two, or three people involved do their best to fulfill that person's "yes."

THE ETHICAL SLUT

RLM: Let's go back to the beginning. What is an *ethical slut?* Why did you name your book this way?

JH: When Dossie and I were working on the first edition, that was a joke between us. Dossie came up with the phrase. We went, "Very funny. We'll call it that for now but before it goes to print we're going to have to think of a real title." Fast-forward a year when it was going to print, we still hadn't thought of a real title. We had told our friends about it, and they were all telling us, "No, you have to call it that." I published the first edition through my little publishing company, and I had considerable qualms about that title, but boy, did it ever work! I don't think anybody involved expected it to take off the way it has.

If you search "ethical slut" now, hundreds of thousands of hits show up, many of which turn out to be personal ads from people who are either looking for ethical sluts or saying, "No ethical sluts" in their ad.

RLM: So, what *is* an ethical slut?

JH: An ethical slut is a person who believes that any sexual pathway that is consensual and mindful can be a force for good both in the person's life and in the greater world.

RLM: Does this change the way we understand the word *slut?* How did the word come about? It sounds like a nasty word for a woman who enjoys herself sexually.

JH: Yes, and it's significant that you immediately tagged it as a woman. The words we use for men who have a lot of sex with a lot of people are generally approving. We call them *studs* or *players,* things that men want to be called. When we describe the same thing for a woman, it becomes a negative. Let's just say that, as female-bodied persons, Dossie and I have a problem with that. We used the word for our book very consciously, and it's caught on in the language since we wrote the first edition. *Slut-shaming* has become a topic of discourse, and there are slut walks in many cities. These are walks to protest the idea that an overtly sexual woman is asking to be raped. There's no telling whether that was due to us or somebody else, but it has become more prominent in the intervening twenty years than it was in 1997 when we wrote the first edition. In today's world, it's more of a possibility to be both a slut and ethical.

RLM: Is this slut walk growing around the country?

JH: I believe so. The "slut-walks" draw thousands of people. You could do a search on the phrase *slut-shaming* and it would turn up all over the place. There is greater visibility for the possibilities of slutdom for people of all genders who simply think that sex is not necessarily a negative thing in their lives.

RLM: You're putting forth an amazingly sex-positive attitude.

JH: We try.

RLM: Do you get a lot of blowback?

JH: Not as much these days. We did when the book first came out. Back in 1997, through a concatenation of circumstances, we wound up doing many interviews with Howard Stern wannabes and we got the usual teasing you would expect; but we were also doing a lot of radio talk shows. Some of the call-ins on those were very hostile.

RLM: As we were talking about the importance of getting to know oneself alone sexually, I immediately thought about people who might see your book—people whose religion is against masturbation—and whether they might come to attack you.

JH: I think they understand that we're not speaking the same language, so there's not as much blowback from the religious right as you would expect. We do get blowback from people who I suspect are in unhappy monogamous relationships and who have stayed in them because they've been taught that that is the only moral way. So when some lady comes on the radio and says, "There are plenty of ways to be ethical that work out fine, don't harm anybody, and don't conform to the standard monogamous relationship," they get angry. And I don't blame them. It would probably take me more than the duration of a radio show to figure out that I shouldn't be angry with the people on the radio, but those who told me about monogamy in the first place.

THE MYTH OF SUCCESSFUL RELATIONSHIPS

RLM: Tell us more about your "myth number one"—that long-term monogamous relationships are the only real relationships.

JH: We still see that everywhere. I get gasps from audiences when I talk about my first marriage, which lasted from when I was twenty-one until my early thirties. We had two marvelous children of whom we maintained joint physical and legal custody. We remain friends. We email often. We're both in other relationships now, but I consider him one of my closest friends. When I tell people I consider that to have been a successful relationship, they're startled. The fact that it ended does not make it unsuccessful. The fact that it ended with the two of us still friends, co-parents, and colleagues—with mutual respect and affection for each other—is what makes it successful.

RLM: The fact that a relationship can have a solid beginning, a decent, realistic middle, and an unsuccessful end is not part of our culture. Our culture wants success until you die. Isn't that right?

JH: When my mom was a therapist, she used to tell the story about a couple in her practice who had recently celebrated their sixtieth wedding anniversary. She spent weeks trying to get each of them to pay the other one a compliment. The furthest she could ever get was for him to tell her, "That was a pretty good dinner you cooked last night. Too bad the beans were burnt." *That* is what a culture that considers duration the only criterion for success sees as a successful relationship; but duration is not the only criterion.

RLM: That reminds me of a couple I counseled where the wife was complaining that the husband never said "I love you." I looked at him and asked if that was true, and he said, "I don't know what she's talking about. When we got together, I told her I love her—doesn't she remember?"

JH: Exactly.

SUCCESSFUL NON-MONOGAMOUS RELATIONSHIPS

RLM: Tell us about legal marriage relationships that are not monogamous.

JH: There are statistics showing that non-monogamous marriages are growing rapidly, as people are seeing—from our book and the other excellent books about polyamory—that it's possible to have a successful relationship that's not necessarily either sexually or affectionately monogamous.

RLM: Another one of your described myths is that jealousy is inevitable and impossible to overcome. Tell us about how you get around jealousy when you know your guy or your woman is with somebody else?

JH: What you don't do is expect jealousy to disappear because it doesn't. Some people are more prone to jealousy and some less, but we all have it at some point in our lives. I tend not to get jealous over sexual or romantic things, but I get very jealous of my friends whose writing success is greater than mine. That's the way I'm wired. What makes you jealous is usually a good clue about where you feel less secure. So you can tell a lot about me from what I just told you. I feel more secure in my relationship life than in my writing life.

RLM: Are you saying that, after that initial marriage, you've been able to engage in relationships in which your partner was having sex with other people—and you were cool with it?

JH: Yes. I have not been "monogamous" since leaving that marriage, and in my current relationship, my spouse and I have been together for ten years now. Agreement-wise, we're in an open relationship; but because of some health issues and living in a smaller town than we did when we first met, neither of us has acted on that in a while. But it's there for us if we want to. I don't think I would have issues if he were to find a squeeze, and I know he doesn't have issues with it when I do, because it has happened.

RLM: When you were living in the larger community, were the two of you sexually active with other people so that you could test out your theory?

JH: Yes. Both of us.

RLM: How did it go?

JH: Fine. He was in a previous relationship with someone who was not always honest about their sluthood. So when he and I became a couple, it was an adjustment period to start trusting that I would tell him. It happened a few times; I told him, and he relaxed. He wasn't so much concerned that I was having fun with someone else as much as he was concerned that I was going to lie about it.

RLM: When you lived in the larger city where you had an open relationship, did you tend to travel in the circles of people who shared this open relationship philosophy with you?

JH: Yes.

RLM: Did it make life easier?

JH: It does because you don't have to hide anything. If you run into a glitch of the kind that all couples do, you can talk about it to people who are not immediately going to say, "Of *course* you're running into problems—you're doing this weird open-relationship thing. What did you expect?" If you're with other people who have the same values, you can talk about the actual problem instead of blaming it all on non-monogamy.

RLM: Now, Dossie Easton, with whom you wrote the book *The Ethical Slut,* is a therapist, is that correct?

JH: That's correct. I should mention here that Dossie and I are long-time lovers as well. We are each other's preexisting condition. Any other relationships we get into have to acknowledge that this partnership of ours is terribly important and that we're not going to give it up because we've fallen in love with someone else.

RLM: The writing partnership, the sexual partnership, or both?

JH: All of the above.

RLM: So when you said that you and your partner in the small town hadn't tested the openness, that doesn't count Dossie?

JH: No, it doesn't. That's so much a part of my reality that I didn't even think of it.

RLM: Fair enough. So from time to time, when you and Dossie are consensual and want to make love or engage in sexual behavior, you do.

JH: Yes.

RLM: This is cool with your spouse.

JH: Yes.

RLM: He knows Dossie well, I'm sure.

JH: Actually, he knew her for longer than I did.

RLM: Okay. If Dossie has a partner. . .

JH: She doesn't at this time, but she has had a partner at times during the twenty-five years we've been working together.

RLM: So, at those times, her partner would know about you?

JH: Yes.

RLM: This is part of what you mean by "ethicality" in sluttiness, if I understand you—you're completely transparent.

JH: Yes. Different partnerships make different decisions about how much to tell. Some couples want to hear absolutely everything and some want to hear nothing. Others just want, "I'm spending the night with Dossie. I'll see you tomorrow." They don't want the nitty-gritty of what happens, and any of that can be accommodated as long as people are clear about their desires.

RLM: When you and Dossie talk about this—and you've been working together as a team for twenty-five years in studying various forms of human sexuality—do both transparency and agreed-upon secrecy work?

JH: Fully agreed-upon secrecy gets called "don't ask, don't tell" in poly circles. A lot of poly people think it never works. I don't believe that it *never* works. I believe it's an accommodation that a lot of couples make. It can work, but we don't recommend it. When you don't have much information about another person, that might feel like a threat to you. Your brain is going to fill that in with whatever scares you the most. In general, we advise that at least meeting the other partner is a good idea. That way, you know they're not this sexual superstar that's going to take your partner away from you. You can see that they're a plain, schlubby person like everybody else you know.

Beyond that, you may not want to know the specifics of what your sweetie and their squeeze are doing in bed together at any given time. Some people do want to know that and others don't. Either one is fine.

WHY A BOOK ON POLYAMORY?

RLM: I want to read something again from your book. This is from chapter three:

> Our Beliefs: We are ethical people, ethical sluts. It is very important for us to treat people well and to do our best not to hurt anyone. Our ethics come from our own sense of rightness and from the empathy and love we hold for those around us. It's not okay to hurt another person because then we hurt too, and we don't feel good about ourselves. Ethical slutdom can be a challenging path. We don't have a polyamorous Miss Manners telling us how to do our thing courteously and respectfully, so we have to make it up as we go along

You've had to make up a lot over these twenty-five years.

JH: We have. It's easier now than twenty years ago when we wrote the book. At that time, there was only one other book about polyamory, and it dealt with a specific type of polyamory, which is the long-term multi-partner relationship, the triad, or quad. We wanted to write more broadly about open relationships, sex parties, and all the different ways people can connect emotionally and sexually. My colleague, Franklin Veaux—who has also written an excellent poly book—keeps count of the number of polyamory books on his website More Than Two. The last time I looked, it was up to about thirty-seven.

Back when we first wrote this, readers would comment that most of the skills we teach work for any relationship, not just poly relationships. So why did we position this as a polyamory book? The reason is that if you browse the bookstore for a book about how to improve your monogamous relationship, there are three shelves. There just isn't as much about how to make a non-monogamous relationship work better, so we felt we needed to address that. That's the bulk of the people Dossie sees in her practice—and the bulk of our friends—so we were in a position to teach those skills.

RLM: I was reminded of the book *Three in Love*. It was eye-opening for me to hear that when the author, Letha Hadady, went around the country on her book tour, people told her about their undercover triadic experiences. It was fascinating to hear about a "straight and narrow" college professor living her life in a ménage à trois.

I view her as being part of normality rather than pathologizing it—which is what, sadly, my profession of psychology so often does when they hear of something sexually unusual. You're aware of that, of course.

JH: Of course. It's not like we invented polyamory. The term was coined in the seventies or early eighties* by Morning Glory Zell-Ravenheart. The idea goes back through human history, but we're certainly aware of it in the writings of the Bloomsbury Group in the early twentieth century or the Oneida Colony in the late nineteenth and early twentieth century. There have been all sorts of experiments with radical families, open relationships, and different ways of relating. We only get to know about the ones someone wrote about, but I think your college professor was right that when someone starts talking about their experience, other people will rise and share their own.

RLM: By the way, is the Oneida community the one that was in Pennsylvania?

JH: Yes.

RLM: I didn't know they were a polyamory community. I do know that they gained fame because they were one of the few communities

---

*In fact, it was coined by Zell-Ravenheart in 1990.

that lasted and withstood the test of time, and I believe they started a silver company, didn't they?

JH: You can still buy Oneida silverware.

RLM: That's how they supported themselves.

JH: Yes. It was a polyamorous community that practiced *karezza* from "caress"—a form of intercourse that does not lead to orgasm.

THE DANGERS OF THE SLUT WORLD

RLM: You have a chapter titled "Battling Sex Negativity," where you say that from the slut's point of view, the world can be a dangerous place. Talk to us about that.

JH: There have been numerous stories about people who've lost jobs, friends, connections to families of origin, and even the custody of children because of their lifestyle. It's not a safe world yet for people whose sexual path is not heterosexual monogamy.

RLM: You're an educator. Have you lost teaching positions as a result of what you did in the privacy of your home?

JH: No. But I used to be an advertising copywriter before I got into running a publishing company and being an educator, and I lost my last job in advertising because of it. People were listening in to my personal phone calls.

RLM: So you lost that advertising job based on what the bosses heard about your personal life.

JH: Yes.

RLM: Do you have advice for people who are engaging in some alternative to mainstream sexual behavior?

JH: If you are fortunate enough to have a life where you can come out as being whatever you are, please do. The more people do that, the more visible it becomes, and the easier it gets for everyone else. Once people see that it's possible to be an ethical person who raises good kids and contributes to the community, it becomes more accepted. A lot of studies during the fight for same-sex marriage showed that the single factor that most dictated whether a person accepted same-sex marriage or not was whether they knew gay people. So it'll be the same with us.

If you work with children, the elderly, or the disabled—and if you're a politician or someone whose life could be ruined by public knowledge of being sexually unusual—then it's best to stay closeted because you have a lot at risk.

RLM: Hear this, gentle readers and friends, our author of *The Ethical Slut,* Janet Hardy, is saying openly there are circumstances in which you need to stay closeted to protect yourself. That is how life is, and we have to deal with it.

JH: We're doing our best to make it not be that way anymore, and we're making progress, but I would hate for anybody to lose a job because they heard Janet Hardy say they should be out.

BISEXUALS' BAD REPUTATION

RLM: Let's talk about bisexuality, and then I want to ask you about the sexual exercises you prescribe in your book. What is bisexuality? Is it real, or is it just heterosexuals playing around?

JH: Speaking as a longtime bisexual, I assure you I am neither hetero nor playing around. The current definition of bisexuality acknowledges the capacity to be sexually and/or romantically attracted to at least one gender. A lot of people have issues with the word *bisexuality* because they think it posits that there are only two genders, and we're sure that there are more. Rather than choosing *pansexual* or another alternative, though, I'm sticking with bisexuality. I am a visible person, and I think it's important for us to stand up and be counted; but you could equally well describe me as pansexual. A lot of people think women are bisexual and men are not. I'm married to a longtime bisexual man who would be happy to assure you that he is truly bisexual.

RLM: Why do you think bisexuals get a bad reputation?

JH: I think the whole idea of sexual orientation does not hold up well to close examination on a personal level. It is important on a cultural level. But a lot of people who are stuck in binary gender and sexual orientation feel that the existence of bisexuality loosens their hold on things they consider important. That's why we get a lot of blowback. If you've built your life around the idea that you're born gay—that there's nothing you can do about it—and you suddenly fall in love with a woman, what does that mean to your worldview? It can be challenging.

RLM: Very challenging indeed. Woody Allen has a line about bisexuality. I'm sure you know it: "Gee, I wish I were bisexual; it would double my chances for a date on Saturday night."

JH: It doesn't really, but it's a funny line.

RLM: It's a great line. Tell us why it doesn't double your chances.

JH: Because a great many monosexual people—which is to say, people who are not bisexual—are turned off by the idea of dating a bisexual.

RLM: Do they hold moral judgment?

JH: They do. They think we're untrustworthy and promiscuous. A lot of women think that dating a bisexual man is putting them at risk for disease. Self-identifying homosexuals, on the other hand believe that if a bisexual partner can retreat into heterosexual privilege, they will. So there's a lot of judgment about bisexuals.

RLM: Do you agree with Kinsey, Pomeroy, and Martin—probably the most well-known sex researchers since Krafft-Ebing in the nineteenth century—that human sexual behavior is on a continuum? One end being people who are 100 percent hetero, and on the other end we have people who are 100 percent homosexual. Everybody else is somewhere in the middle. Are we a mix of both? Does how much of a mix we are tell you where we are on that scale? Do you agree with that theory?

JH: It's better than anything before it, and I think it holds up statistically. Many people have had fantasies and/or experiences that don't fit in with a monosexual preference, but it's more nuanced than that. We relate to people on many levels. The person to whom we feel sexually attracted may not be the person with whom we want to form a domestic relationship, which in turn may not be the person with whom we want to form a romantic relationship. You might fantasize about things you don't want to do in reality. By the time you build all these vectors into a model, it becomes difficult to print a theory on a piece of paper. I think all of these things have spectrums. By the time you get all the spectrums interacting, you've got a wibbly-wobbly, gendery-bendery ball of stuff.

RLM: So you can't quite put yourself somewhere on a scale that way.

JH: Yes.

RLM: Interesting.

JH: I typically form domestic relationships with men—at least statistically. I've been in three long-term domestic relationships, and they've all been with men. Sexually, however, I tend to connect better with women.

THE MECHANICS OF SEXUALITY
AND THE TYRANNY OF HYDRAULICS

RLM: You talk about penetration versus non-penetration and how both can be enjoyable. Sexuality between a man and a woman doesn't have to be about penetration, which is typically the way it's seen in our culture.

JH: Sadly, yes. The main problem with that is that you and I are both of an age where that might not be the best fit for people anymore.

RLM: So to speak.

JH: So to speak. I wasn't going to go there, but since you did—if you haven't spent your life learning other ways of connecting sexually, then at fifty-five, seventy-five, or eighty-five, you will feel like you can't have sex anymore because you don't know any other ways of having it. That's too bad. Leaving aside the issue of safer sex, which encourages people to learn different modes of connecting sexually, it behooves us to get good at all kinds of ways of connecting physically and sexually so that we don't get into a rut.

RLM: This is so important as the population ages and women are experiencing vaginal dryness or a lack of elasticity in the vaginal canal, and as men are experiencing problems with erections, or what we call erectile dysfunction.

JH: Dossie calls it "the tyranny of hydraulics."

RLM: That's a great one. You're putting forth important information about what can be done if we allow ourselves to get off the track of what we've been taught, which is penetration exclusively. According to our Kinsey friends, it's penetration for ninety seconds and goodbye.

JH: There was a study a few months back showing that lesbians are likelier to have orgasms during any particular sexual session than women in heterosexual relationships. We learn from this that penetration with an organic penis is not essential to female pleasure. There are lots of alternatives. If people wanted to learn ways to have sexual pleasure without relying on penetration, they could do worse than looking at how lesbians connect.

RLM: Do sex toys have a bad reputation in our country?

JH: It's getting better. All of this is getting better. Joani Blank, who founded the first feminist sex toy store, Good Vibrations, died several years ago. That was the first store that brought sex toys into the sexual mainstream. Now towns of any size will have a clean, well-lighted sex store where a woman can come in by herself and not feel like she's going to get assaulted, or where a couple can go together. There will be knowledgeable staff to guide them to the toys that do what they want. That has become huge, and Good Vibrations started it. Sex toys have gotten much better.

I'm on the mailing list for a lot of catalogs that carry clothing for older women, and most of them now have a little section for vibrators and lubes. The first time one of those came, my mouth fell open. I couldn't believe it. But now they all do. It's gotten that easy.

RLM: I've read that there are now sexual Tupperware parties around the country.

JH: Pleasure parties. Absolutely.

RLM: Tell us what a pleasure party is.

JH: I can't use the word that the people running them call them. Imagine Tupperware turned into another word, and you get the idea. It works like a Tupperware party. A knowledgeable representative shows up with a briefcase full of sex toys. Everybody has drinks, snacks, and chats, gets to hold things in their hands, and compares notes about what might or might not work for them. They get to experiment with them if they feel safe doing that. It's a great way to buy sex toys for people who feel shy about walking into a shop. It's certainly better than choosing them online where you can't hold them in your hands and see if it feels good or triggers your arthritis.

RLM: You get to kick the tires. Might we call them humperware parties?

JH: Exactly right.

THE BATTLE OF WORDS

RLM: Janet, you knew you couldn't mention the seven dirty words on this radio program, because we all know the government will fine us, or take us off the airwaves if we say certain proscribed words on the radio. Isn't this language suppression connected to your concept of sexual negativity? After all, most of the forbidden words have to do with sex.

JH: Yes and no, Richard. I think it's more complex than that. If you listen to the old Lenny Bruce routines—and he was a foul-mouthed, brilliant comic—we're not shocked by sex words but by race words. Those still land hard.

RLM: I'm not sure race words are one of the seven dirty words we're not supposed to say on the radio, but I think we know enough not to say them.

JH: I don't know what the effect would be of saying one of those words on the radio, but it wouldn't be good. It might not lead to the station getting shut down, but it might. I'm not a lawyer. I don't know what would happen.

RLM: I'm talking about it having to do with a morality play being placed upon our sexuality. It's so pervasive that even vernacular words describing sexual parts or acts are not allowed.

JH: Yes. As a writer, I use words as my tools, and I get testy about having my tools taken away, just as a carpenter would.

RLM: I enjoy your putting it that way. I love the George Carlin joke regarding the seven taboo words. He says "you can say I pricked my finger but you can't say I fingered my prick."

JH: They're just a series of phonemes. It is what it is. I do think that the more forbidden they are, the harder they land when they get out. Again, for those of us who are not on the radio and don't have to deal with fines, it's not a bad idea to use those words. If you hear them on the street today, it's not like you would have had to go home with smelling salts.

RLM: No. The forbidden words are now appearing on television.

JH: Exactly. I've watched the series *Deadwood* through at least three times, so it's going to be tough to shock me with words anymore, and yet the government hasn't caught up with that. I think a lot of older people haven't caught up.

AN EXERCISE FOR SEXUAL EXPLORATION

RLM: I want you to talk about putting lists up on the fridge. Tell us about that.

JH: The "Yes-No-Maybe Exercise."

RLM: "Once you've made a list," you say in the book, "you can do lots of further activities with it. Put your lists on the fridge." What kind of lists should they put on the fridge or in the bathroom?

JH: I encourage all of your readers to do it. The way "yes, no, maybe" works is: you sit down with a person with whom you are sexual or considering being sexual with. Together, you brainstorm everything you can imagine that two people could do together sexually—even what you think is gross or weird. Just spit it all out and get it down on paper. Then each of you takes a different colored marker and next to each item, put a *Y* for yes, *N* for no, or an *M* for maybe. Then you have your list of what's possible for you. If any activity gets an *N* from each of you, it goes off the list. It's not under consideration because there's no consent.

RLM: That's your concept of consensual sex.

JH: Yes. You're probably already doing the ones with two *Y* answers, but if you're not, you should be. The ones with a yes and a maybe— or two maybes—let you talk about what would make you feel okay doing them. What would the circumstances be that would make me want that? It might be that I might want to if I felt safe enough, if I was turned on enough, or if I knew I wasn't going to hear about it afterwards, or that we did another thing first. I don't know what any individual's conditions might be, but you can talk about those and work out ways to get them met to expand your horizons.

RLM: I love the concept. I hope all our readers are willing to try it out. I love your exercises so much that I want to talk about another one. Tell us about your concept of "getting loud."

JH: I was just working on that section for the new edition. Most of us have inhibitions about being loud when we're sexual.

RLM: That is the truth.

JH: But it opens it up. If you open up your throat, you're opening up your whole body, and when you let the noise out, you're freeing yourself. Even if it means you have to go someplace that doesn't have paper-thin walls like your regular apartment does, it's a good idea to try being loud during sex. Then your neighbors might feel safe to be loud too, and you'll have a neighborhood with lots of loud sex, which sounds like an excellent neighborhood to me.

RLM: Express the energy as you do when you're excited.

JH: Absolutely.

RLM: I've wondered what it does to us to keep that energy in. We are all concerned about who can hear us emote, and from how far away. I've wondered about how that self-consciousness inhibits our sexuality.

JH: All of your readers can try this at home. If you're tightening your throat, you're tightening your body and sexual parts, which will inhibit you from being relaxed and having wonderful sex.

RLM: Outstanding exercise. There are so many more in this book. It's called *The Ethical Slut.* It's written by Dossie Easton and our guest today, Janet Hardy. The book is by Celestial Arts. This is a book to read because it's like nothing you've ever read before.

10

Annie Sprinkle &
Beth Stephens

Assuming the Ecosexual Position

Beth Stephens and Annie Sprinkle have been pollinating the ecosex movement through art, theory, practice, and activism since 2004.
They've produced numerous performance artworks, ecosex symposiums,
weddings to nature entities, workshops, walking tours, and art exhibits. Their award-winning documentary, *Goodbye Gauley Mountain: An
Ecosexual Love Story,* played many film festivals and is on iTunes. Beth
is an art professor at UC Santa Cruz; Annie earned her Ph.D. in human
sexuality. Their new film, *Water Makes Us Wet,* is about the pleasures
and politics of water. They aim to make the environmental movement
a little more sexy, fun, and diverse. You can find out more about Beth's
and Annie's work at *sprinklestephens.org.*

Dr. Richard L. Miller (RLM): Today, we have an exciting and educational interview with Drs. Annie Sprinkle and Beth Stephens. Annie
Sprinkle has been creating multimedia projects about sexuality for
four decades. She was the first adult film star to earn a Ph.D. She
then bridged into art and toured her one-woman theater pieces all
over the country and all over the world. Annie's new book, which
she co-authored with Beth Stephens, is titled *The Explorer's Guide
to Planet Orgasm.* It's all about the orgasm. Beth Stephens, Annie's
longtime collaborator and spouse, has been a filmmaker, performance

artist, activist, and educator for three decades. Beth is the founding director of E.A.R.T.H. Lab at UC Santa Cruz, where she is a professor and former Art Department Chair. In the last five years, Beth has produced two new feature documentary films and has shown many video installations in galleries and museums.

Together, Beth and Annie are founders of the ecosex movement, where they aim to make the environmental movement sexier, fun, and more diverse. They were selected as *documenta 14** artists with their new film, *Water Makes Us Wet: An Ecosexual Adventure.** They're now also completing a book about their work, *Assuming the Ecosexual Position,* for the University of Minnesota Press. I watched their film last night. It's fabulous. It made me laugh. It made me cry.

ECOSEXUALITY: IMAGINING EARTH AS A LOVER

RLM: I know that everybody wants to talk about Annie, how she went from being a porn star to getting a Ph.D. We may get to that later. But first, we're going to talk about your new project, which is ecosexuality. I'm going to read from your book:

Ecosexuality is a new sexual identity, an environmental activist strategy, and an expanded concept of what sex is and can be in our culture. Ecosexuals imagine the earth as a lover, a romantic partner, and they experience nature as sensual, erotic, or sexy. Ecosexuality is a way of being in the world, wherein giving and receiving love with the earth increases pleasure. Sex with humans is also a part of ecosexuality, as humans are part of—not separate from—nature.

That's from chapter 21 of your book.
How did this come about? Let's take it from the top.

Beth Stephens (BS): This is back ten years ago, almost to the day. Our anniversary passed recently; we had a performance-art wedding

---

*Editor's note: The fourteenth edition of the documenta art exhibition that took place in 2017 in Kassel, Germany, and Athens, Greece.

as part of a series. But in this particular one, we married the earth. When we did, we started thinking, *What does it mean to* marry *the earth?* We realized that it meant that we needed to love, honor, cherish the earth, and take care of it—to really try and pleasure it as we would with any lover or partner. We started thinking deeply about our relationship with the earth. Our approach aims to go beyond using the earth's resources without thinking or feeling guilty. Because we're hurting the earth, which I don't think is a useful position.

Annie Sprinkle (AS): I had ecosexual feelings going way back to the first time I went to your Health Sanctuary at Wilbur Hot Springs with Juliet Anderson, a porn star aka Aunt Peg or Juliet Car. So when we married the Earth, we looked back at the times when we had essential, erotic, connected times with the earth, the sky, and the sea. We just dove deep into that idea. We've been doing art about that for ten years. We say that we do art theory, practice, and activism. So ecosex for us is an art project. We've developed the theories and environmental-activism aspect around it. The practice is enjoying the sensuality of nature, although non-human nature is the wrong word because we *are* nature.

RLM: When you're talking about the Earth as a lover, do you mean that as a metaphor or literally? For example, years ago, many of us were called tree huggers. I'm sure you remember that.

BS: Oh yes, we're tree huggers, too.

RLM: Tree huggers isn't a metaphor. We literally hug trees, put our arms and legs around them, close our eyes, and hold on to them. Is this similar to your ecosexuality—and, if so, how?

BS: It's both metaphorical and an embodied practice of being in the world. When we walk outside on the streets or out in the field, we're giving the earth a massage with our feet. It's shiatsu. When we're breathing the air, we're having intercourse with the air. So we're physically intermingling with everything on the third biome clouds of the soil, trees, and plants. The Earth is keeping us alive, both through the beauty it exhibits and the nourishing qualities of all the elements we engage with lovingly. Definitely, the metaphorical part of ecosexuality helps us be conscious of how we are with the Earth. But physically, we're also always hugging the air that we breathe. There's nothing more intimate than drinking a glass of water.

RLM: That is absolutely brilliant.

AS: Going back to the trees, a lot of people like to critique ecosex. They generally do it by saying, "Oh, they're tree huggers." They think we're actually having some kind of intercourse with trees, and that's the big joke. They don't see the *forest* for the trees. They just imagine that we're putting branches inside us. We aren't unless they're nicely carved. People automatically think about trees when we say ecosex, but it's a lot bigger than that. We're not having sex with animals and trees—but what is sex? Where does our body start and end? We ask these questions. We try to communicate with trees. People also say, "What about trees not consenting?" We have to try to ask for consent, and some trees don't want to be had; they have poison ivy around them. So we use a lot of humor, fun, and play. And we also critique ecosex, because it can be laughable and silly—like getting "pounded" by the ocean waves. Once we did a workshop and we had a whole line of people naked. The ocean waves were in just the right position where we all got spanked, and we're rolling around. It was so joyous, and we were all laughing. It was so real because we had our ecosexual gaze on; we were all thinking about the Earth as a lover. These were seasoned, sex-positive, advanced people and they were having innocent fun getting slapped in the butt by the waves. We're having pleasure with water, with wind, with sun rays penetrating our skin.

BS: There's a little interview in our film, *Water Makes Us Wet,* that alludes to the metaphorical play we engage in when we drink a glass of water. The water does literally make us wet, and it's the wetness that keeps us alive. Cells can't divide in the absence of water. If they do; they just die. So we're positing that ecosexuality is part of a powerful life force, and that playfulness, joy, sexuality, and titillation can reunite us with the Earth. When we're all so connected to our computers and kids aren't getting outside as much as they did, it's important to get people outside and connected to the earth so that they care about it. Otherwise, corporations are going to gobble the earth up for resources, and then we're in a lot of trouble. I think ecosexuality helps us face that trouble. All of the talks about climate change and global warming can be incredibly overwhelming. It makes people feel powerless that there seems to be nothing we can do when, in fact, we can do a lot. We believe that, as an activist strategy, love is the most important motivating force to counter the greed of large corporations. We're getting an amazing show from our federal government right now. They're taking protections away from national parks, drilling, fracking, and exploding things in ways I never thought I would see again. So in fact, ecosexuality—as playful and joyous as parts of it are—also gives us the strength to face environmental devastation.

AS: We *are* anthropomorphizing Earth; it's beyond human qualities, but we can still imagine Earth as a mother. So if we're drinking a glass of water, it's as if the mother is keeping us alive. But the mother has also been a lover. So we can morph and change. The Earth can be a friend, a sister—it can be whatever helps us access a closer, more intimate, loving connection with the nonhuman and the human. Really, when you're making love with a human what you're making love with is 70 percent water with some stardust sprinkled in and some other minerals. So we like being experimental in our thinking about sex. Also, as a sex educator myself, I'm interested in exploring new forms of pleasure—or, rather, calling attention to various forms of pleasure that are easily accessible to people who don't have partners. When I heard the earth could be a lover, I was able to access nature more easily than I was able to access humans because my mother was, frankly, a bitch at times. I was much more interested in sex and sexuality. So that opened the door for me, but it's not for everyone. And we're not saying Earth is not a mother as well.

ART REIMAGINING OUR CULTURAL
ATTITUDES TOWARD SEX

RLM: But you are using the art form to create cultural change. You are all about changing our attitudes towards this planet that we're part of—and how we relate to it. You're using your art and sexuality as an entry point to having deeper dignity and respect for our totality, people, earth, rocks, other animals, everything.

BS: You got it, Richard. Maybe you want to come out as an ecosexual?

RLM: I think my wife Jolee and I would like to join you, and consider ourselves ecosexuals.

BS: The nice thing is, you don't have to give up anything else that you are. You just add it to the rest.

RLM: But even before we became familiar with your work, my wife Jolee would talk about making love to the air and the ocean in front of our home here in Mendocino. So we applaud you. You're educating us about the intersection of ecofeminism, sustainability, and queer theory in relation to ecosexuality. So with that introduction, please talk about those.

BS: I'm at the university a lot, so I go to a lot of talks and lectures. In the last twenty or twenty-five years, a lot of feminists have been talking about how we can break down certain hierarchies—especially binary hierarchies—that have privileged culture over nature, male over female, or even corporations over individuals. We see ecosexuality as a way of contesting that through pleasure, because honestly, hierarchies are not pleasurable. Maybe some people get pleasure out of power, but more people than not, don't. It's making life horizontal so that we're all just creatures of the Earth, including animals and plants. But it creates a more loving environment. Again, love is the most important thing in this moment when we're seeing so many things blowing up and falling apart. It's almost a natural cycle of life that things fall apart, but the question is, "How do you feel okay about that, instead of getting scared and then retaliating?"

RLM: It seems that there's a global political movement that seems regressive for some of us. There's a move towards "strongmen," such as Trump in this country, Theresa May in England, and dictators, such as Putin around the world. With the Supreme Court's Citizens United decision, we created a situation where corporations almost *are* people. You're pointing out that most people enjoy sensuality and sexuality over power. Yet we have to be cognizant of that small, powerful group. Maybe less than 5 percent of all of us enjoy inordinate power, over everything else. And, so often, they're leading the way. Can we get to them? Do you two have a sense of hope that we can reach those people who are willing to stand up in front of the world and, for example, swear to us that nicotine isn't addictive?

BS: I think so, because sexuality provides the possibility for power from *below*. In ecosexuality, we firmly acknowledge ecosystems. So I believe that each different strategy for reaching those people is important, and we need to work as a system to reach them rather than any individual movement or person. I don't know if we can change those people because they're addicted to profit over everything else. That is the truth. That's what capitalism is—the production of profit. I think something needs to change to allow us to continue to live on a thriving earth that can provide the things we want without profit. The Earth doesn't work on a capitalistic profit basis; it works on a reciprocal basis where the sun gives back to the earth. You can't just take and take forever. That's why, seeing the earth as a lover, we feel that's a more reciprocal relationship than the power from above where the patriarchal or matriarchal power issues orders and everyone follows along. That's not reciprocity, and reciprocity is important.

AS: On our new business card we put that we do *social sculpture,* which is a term that German artist Beuys created. I don't think the word *ecosex* is going to reach people because they like to pooh-pooh the idea. But we're creating culture. For example, there's a whole sex toy industry that's now more green and eco conscious. There are porn stars making ecosexual porn. Now, they don't *call* it ecosexual, but you can be sure that some people are connecting and making love with the natural world around them. It's going to reach them. Sex is a common denominator. Not everyone likes sex. But a lot of those people who are after the almighty dollar like that kind of porn. We're also pushing against sex-negative culture. It's taboo to enjoy the sensuality of nature, to masturbate with a hose, to take pleasure with water. Sex is a taboo outside of monogamy and marriage. So any kind of pleasure that's not about monogamy is going to be pooh-poohed. We've been on Breitbart, Fox News, and all those, and to read the comments is amazing. Largely, people are freaked out by sex. So we're pushing against that taboo-ness.

BS: People are also freaked out by thinking of the Earth as a source of pleasure rather than a resource they can use for profit. We're seeing this pushback in the federal government now. Scott Pruitt, the EPA administrator, is undoing every rule that was put in place since the seventies to protect water and forests.* I'm from West Virginia originally and what's going on in that state is Armageddon. It's horrific with this mountaintop removal, coal mining with fracking, and the way the people of West Virginia have been manipulated to buy into this. They told them, "You have to have jobs, no matter how crappy they are, no matter what they're doing to the environment." It's a deal with the devil, and the devil is Trump right now. It's heartbreaking to see that. I know where society can go unless we fight those powers trying to take everything they can from the earth. We're seeing it at Standing Rock and with plastic in the ocean. It's overwhelming. So we're trying to galvanize people around what they love. The earth is life; water is life. The indigenous people at Standing Rock are absolutely right about that. Our culture is going to have to choose: Do we want life or do we want a death culture, which capitalism is handing us on a platter?

---

*Editor's note: Pruitt's controversial span as head of the EPA ended with his resignation on July 6, 2018, amid a cloud of federal investigations.

AS: By the way, if people are interested in learning more about what we're doing, *Goodbye Gauley Mountain: An Ecosexual Love Story* is on iTunes. You can buy or rent it on YouTube. It's about West Virginia and mountaintop-removal coal mining. In fact, Don Blankenship, who just lost an election there, is in our film. They can also get our book *The Explorer's Guide to Planet Orgasm.*

CHANGING HYPOCRISY TOWARD SEXUALITY

RLM: I want to come back to something you said about the stigma of sex. From your perspectives as activists as social activists, how are we coming along in changing the culture's attitudes, particularly the negative or hypocritical attitudes, towards sexuality? Are we still in the era of shaming women who enjoy sex and championing men who do as studs? Have we moved beyond such derision of women? How are we doing with regard to the "sexual glass ceiling"?

AS: There are different ways to look at that. Obviously, the #MeToo movement is having a huge effect on sexuality, all the proliferation of pornography and feminist porn. That's like saying, "How are we doing with life and culture today?" Sexuality is ginormous, and there are so many ways to look at it. I think that we are moving along. There are a lot of "erotically gifted young people." But there are also some really fearful young people. We were around young people a lot, students and interns, and some of them are interested in sex but don't know how to go about it. Some are getting misinformation. Obviously, taking away abortion rights is going to affect a lot of people. So I don't think there's a simple answer to that question.

RLM: I know, it's a tough question. Asking how we're doing in life is a tough question but an important one. There's a major struggle going on between power and capitalism on the one hand, and what you might call humanism—sexuality, respect for the Earth, and for all living people. It sounds like you are saying that there's still uncertainty as to how much we've made progress with regard to our attitudes towards sexuality. I've wondered whether the proliferation of pornography has made it easier for people to express their sexuality. After all, you can now see more things by pushing a button than most people ever saw in their entire lifetime.

AS: Yes, that's true. It seems we've made two steps forward and one step back. We were very promiscuous in the seventies and early eighties. I'm grateful I lived at that time, and we're far from that. We were having a lot of sexual adventures and freedom until AIDS and herpes came along and sex became dangerous. So these young people have grown up in an era where sex kills. That's put a damper on things. On the other hand, we do have more education available online. People can learn about any topic on Wikipedia.

BS: I teach a general education course about erotic art at UC Santa Cruz called Ars Erotica. It's interesting because I show a lot of alternative art that's sexually explicit—films about people who are otherly abled having sexual relationships, sex around queer, trans sex, people of color, and Cyborg sex. You notice that, of course, the queer students love the queer films, and students of color love the characters of color. But it gets complicated, because most of these kids have watched mainstream pornography, and they have set ideas about what porn and pleasure are. So, while there's this proliferation of pornography, I'm not sure that mainstream pornography is putting out a message different from the hot female who's submissive to the dominating stud.

RLM: Exactly.

BS: There has been freedom for people who are in other groups than that to make pornography and to get it out on the internet, which is empowering. But I think, now, our federal government is pushing back against that with their stance on trans people in the military or homosexuality. They're horrible, racist policies. Those things do affect how we're doing with sex and sexuality. But it's quite a remarkable moment.

TINDER'S EFFECT ON
OUR CULTURAL SEXUALITY

RLM: Do you think websites like Tinder are having an effect on cultural sexuality?

AS: I think everything is having an effect on sexuality. Pornography is a mirror of society.

RLM: I didn't know that, Annie—I thought it was a mirror of a bunch of guys down in a big warehouse in Los Angeles.

AS: If you look throughout history, you'll see different sexual styles between men and women, trans people, and our erotic heritage through pornography. So it's both. These days, we often observe people showing signs of a misogynist society. But you also have many alternatives now—what we call post-porn, feminist porn, queer porn, and alternative heterosexual erotica. It's so huge. If you've seen one porn movie, you haven't seen them all.

BS: My great-nephew told me about Grindr, which is an app for gay men. It was like, "Oh, Auntie Beth doesn't know about Grindr!" At first, I thought, *This is a great idea.* You can walk down the street, and your Grindr can locate someone else's, and you can go grind somewhere. But I was talking to students at Santa Cruz about online dating apps, and they're not feeling safe because you meet someone you haven't been around for long. You don't know their body language. You don't even know who they are. On one hand, it's liberating to have anonymous sex. Someone may have signed up and given you certain information about themselves. But I know when I broke up with my last girlfriend years ago—Annie and I have been together almost eighteen years now.

RLM: I've got to interrupt you there. The reason for the interruption is to applaud you for your eighteen-year relationship. One of the most wonderful parts of your movie is your relationship—the way you touch, hug, and kiss each other. As you're walking, you're arm in arm. In and of itself, that says so much and makes your movie more enjoyable. It's a great film. Those of you reading this, contact Juno Films, contact Beth and Annie, or look for it online. If *Goodbye Gauley Mountain* is anywhere near *Water Makes Us Wet*, you want to see them both. The film I've seen is spectacular. I was so touched by it. I don't want to give away too much by talking about it.

BS: Thank you for that, Richard. The best way for people to see *Water Makes Us Wet* is to contact us. We can put the film in film festivals.

RLM: Okay, what's the best way to reach you two?

AS: Just go to *sprinklestephens.org*. There's a contact email, and Beth and I will get it. Also earthlab.ucsc.edu, where you can sign up for our occasional newsletter.

BS: We won't fill your inboxes—but I want to go back to online dating: I went onto an online dating site and I saw my former partner's profile. It was nothing like the person I had experienced. So I was glad that I met Annie in the flesh.

RLM: Maybe my wife and I were too idealistic because we were thinking that possibly these hookup sites were leading to a more matter-of-fact relationship with sexuality, where sexuality became more accepted as just part of us, the way you two accept it. You accept sex like drinking water, eating food, and voiding. They're all just part of the human condition. But as you two know, sex, especially premarital sex, is demonized, because of religion. Sex is in its own category, by itself, in part because of the stigma and the pleasure. When is the demonizing of sex? When will it just be something pleasurable, like it was in the seventies, as you pointed out, Annie?

AS: Grindr is not that different than going to a bar and cruising people* and a lot of people are enjoying Grindr and other dating apps. My brother came to San Francisco and he got on one of those apps. He met three different women he rather liked. So you're right,

---

Cruising is gay slang for going out in public looking for a sex partner.

Richard—although one thing to think about is how sex has become corporatized and people are making billions of dollars. "You have to have the right garter belt, the right sex toys; you have to be on the right websites." Sex is very commercial now, whereas ecosex is going back to basics.

DECOMMERCIALIZING SEXUALITY

BS: You don't need to buy anything to be an ecosexual.

AS: If you think about all the pornography on servers, the electricity, resources, and the plastic waste, there's all kinds of crap going on. In terms of the commodification of sex, even strip clubs have become corporatized.

RLM: Is that right?

AS: It's so huge, and it's a lot about money. Sex is political. People want to control other people's bodies and sexuality. We love the topic of ecosex because it at least raises questions about some of those practices.

RLM: Ecosexuality also gives people a way to have sensuality and sexuality without it costing money. Reading from your book:

> Rubbing a velvety sage leaf and inhaling its scent; enjoying the feel and taste of a sweet, juicy strawberry. Some practices are more intense, extreme, and even kinky, such as running naked through a field of stinging nettles or getting pounded and submerged by ocean waves. These are things that don't cost money. You're talking about making love with air and having squishy wet clay between your toes.

I'm purposely doing this, Beth and Annie, because I want people to get what you're talking about with examples of things they can do after they listen to this program. "Feeling the grain of a wooden conference table during a faculty meeting." It's so beautiful. I've done that myself, and it's a wonderful feeling.

BS: It can really calm you down during a meeting to face it.

AS: How many people straddle the hot-tub jets? I'm sure your particular audience is a hot-tub-jet-straddling crowd. People use the water and take advantage of the water, but how many actually pleasure the water back and thank the water, tell the water, *I love you?*

RLM: It's hard to damage an environment that you're making love to on a regular basis.

AS: Yes, we have to love the damaged environments, too.

RLM: In order to heal them, exactly.

AS: It's wonderful to think about the Earth as a lover.

RLM: So many things that we do in our daily existence become sensual and sexual when one takes on what you're talking about because sensuality and sexuality can literally take place walking down the street, anywhere, any time, without it costing money.

AS: Why fantasize just about people? Why not fantasize about the little creatures in the soil, walking barefoot, and massaging them? It's expanding your fantasies. People are taught that fantasies can be good, but they should only be about people. Why not fantasize about the wind when you're riding a motorcycle? Or the colors on earth? I can get off just looking at the flowers onscreen or the colors of green and a redwood forest. There's so much pleasure to be had. It's expanding your fantasy and imagination; a lot of it is very conceptual. We take it pretty seriously, and at the same time, we can laugh about it.

RLM: Before we come to a close, what's your next project?

BS: Writing our book *Assuming the Ecosexual Position.* And then we're going to take off on a cross-country summer trip to document other artists doing environmental artwork. I'm also going to offer an online class on environmental art, and believe me, my idea of environmental art is an expanded one. What's so exciting is that they're allowing me to experiment with how I do the class. I feel I can reach a large audience in ways that maybe even our art doesn't reach through the teaching online. I was actually against online classes because I felt that it was important for people to be together in a classroom—I still feel that's important, but I see how many of my students are married to their computers. So I'm thinking: if you can't beat them, at least try to join them.

RLM: Can our readers get involved and check in on this online class?

BS: If they contact me at the university and they look for Beth Stephens, the former chair of the Art Department at UC Santa Cruz, they'll get my email address. I could find ways for them to engage in this project. Some of them could be testers to see if what we're doing is actually interesting. I'm thinking about framing it as a sort of TV show. So it's going to be fun.

RLM: That sounds cool. When you take this summer trip, are you going to be taking your pollination pod with you?*

BS: No, we're just going to take the big E.A.R.T.H. Lab van. We got a new one exactly like the old one. So we're going to take the Evan and build a platform on the roof for our cameraman who's going to be living up on the roof at night. It's going to be an adventure.

RLM: Jolee kept asking me during the film last night, "Where's this cameraman? Where do they have him stashed? He's always around. He seemed to be everywhere."

BS: We have cameramen stashed at every port, Richard.

AS: Richard, I'd like to see you, in our future, slowing down and having more ecosensual pleasure. I'd also like to see the future at Wilbur Hot Springs your amazing, beautiful place.

RLM: I would love you both to come.

---

*A stylized trailer that Annie Sprinkle and Beth Stephens used when they toured the U.S. giving talks on ecosexualism. An image of the activists and their vehicle is featured on the cover of *Water Makes Us Wet*.

AS: Richard, I want to thank you for creating a place filled with eco-sensual delights and pleasure. Your Health Sanctuary at Wilbur has brought many people so much joy and knowledge. I've been to the Women Vision Conference there. You've done an amazing amount of pleasure activism. So thank you.

RLM: You're very welcome. It's my privilege to be involved. Next time when you two come to Wilbur, maybe we'll get you to give a talk on ecosexuality.

AS: Happy trails!

The Sex Industry

Have you ever wondered why people who sell pleasure in our culture are held in such low regard? We ostracize sex workers along with the chemically dependent and mentally ill people who we disparage as *psychos* or *crazies*. Please consider the genesis of this international conspiracy to condemn females who sell sexual delights for their living.*

Prostitution is not the oldest profession, as is often quoted, but it may be the fourth oldest after hunting, fishing, and gathering. As far back as 1700 BCE, under the *Code of Hammurabi,* the property of a prostitute was protected. However, for most of history, sex workers have been exploited dramatically, and almost always by males.

The ancient Greeks established government-supported brothels. However, once Christianity came upon the scene, the lives of sex workers have almost always been in extreme jeopardy. There have been

---

*Editor's note: It's interesting that Jesus was notable for not dehumanizing this category of people. In the famous story where King Solomon said he would cut a baby in half in order to discern which alleged mother would concede to spare the baby's life, those mothers were both prostitutes. In today's courts, the judge would have taken the baby from both women into the "care" of the state.

exceptions, such as when the Greek Council of Venice in 1358 declared prostitution to be "absolutely indispensable to the world." And, when, in 1547, King Henry II of France regulated prostitution. But, when Pope Sixtus V came into power in 1586, he mandated the death penalty for prostitution, and it has been downhill for these downtrodden laborers of physical love ever since.

In a world where sex work is demonized and illegal, those who have no choice but to do this work face the brunt of our cultural shame. In many countries, sex workers have been, and are still, institutionally whipped, beaten, raped, and murdered. Here in the United States, the chances of a sex worker being murdered are between 80 and 120 times as great as a non–sex working female. Can any of you name another occupation in which your chances of getting killed on the job are that much higher than average?*

In addition, the social stigma that our culture has placed on sex workers is one of intense ostracism, which is what some sociologists and psychologists consider to be the most severe form of human punishment. Sex workers' children are thrown out of schools. Retired sex workers are fired when employers find out about their former occupation. Google *children of sex workers* and see what you find. One might rightly say that sex workers and their families are treated as lepers. I ask you, why are sex workers so thoroughly debased in our culture? We don't do this to any other workers. Why do we pay women for sexual favors and then turn around and cruelly demean and attack them for what they provide? Why do we not *thank* sex workers and glorify them for the sensual delights that they afford us? Why should sex workers be any less celebrated than chefs? Why do we use religion and misguided morality to undermine the self-esteem of these hard-working folks who place their lives on the line while merely attempting to make a living in the world?

When will we take into consideration what the stigma we attach to sex workers does to their children and their families? When will

---

*See "Is sex work still the most dangerous profession?" by Lucy Platt, published in London School of Hygiene & Tropical Medicine.

we be willing to stand up and say out loud, as one people, that there is nothing dirty or inherently bad about sex? When are we, as a people, going to look ourselves deeply in the eye and come to grips with the fact that we ourselves are not dirty when we, *as sober consenting adults,* engage in sexual activity? Is it not true that when we say a sex worker is bad, that we're saying that sex *itself* is bad? And, perhaps most important of all, when will we realize that by criminalizing the vocation of sex workers, we are putting their daily lives at grave risk?

I ask each of you, have you ever frequented the services of a sex worker? Have you ever enjoyed pornography? If so, do you think that for engaging in these behaviors you deserve to be whipped, raped, beaten, thrown in jail, or murdered? Would any of you marry a sex worker who made $300,000 a year? $500,000? $1,000,000? How would you feel if your child married a sex worker who was a prostitute and sold sex products for over a million dollars a year? Does the amount of money a sex worker earns affect your attitude about their goodness or badness as a member of our community? What word can you think of that we launch toward males that comes close to calling a woman a whore or a cunt? Might you be willing to help a sex worker if they were in need? Would you hide them in your home?

The late Margo St. James and I became instant friends upon meeting. At the time, she was already famous as an outspoken, hard-working prostitute. I was working as a clinical psychologist at a clinic I co-founded named The Gestalt Institute for Multiple Psychotherapy in San Francisco. Because she had been arrested for prostitution, Margo had a difficult time getting legitimate work and when a position opened in my clinic, I hired her.

Margo did excellent work and all the clinic patients adored her. Then one evening, on group-therapy night, when there were over sixty patients in the clinic, Margo sat at her desk, totally naked, mindfully typing the whole time. Even in San Francisco in the 1960s, that was enough to freak out many of the group therapy participants. It was Margo's way of giving notice. Apparently it had been enough of the straight job for her.

My time with Margo was a crash course in the life of the working girl. All my misguided myths about women who sold themselves were destroyed. Yes, some were abused as children, but some, like Margo, came from normal loving homes. Yes, some sex workers took drugs, but others neither drank nor drugged. Yes, some sex workers were quite uneducated, yet others had Ph.D.s and even law degrees. Yes, some sex workers were trafficked, owned, and enslaved, but others worked entirely of their own volition.* Yes, some sex workers did it only for the money, but others loved sex and were thrilled to get paid for engaging in it. And some sex workers, such as Norma Jean Almodovar, whom you will meet later, are in forty-year marriages.

Margo went on to create the first prostitutes' union, COYOTE, which stands for *Call Off Your Old Tired Ethics.* To fund COYOTE, Margo founded San Francisco's famous Hookers Ball, which, at its height, had 20,000 attendees.

In 1980, Margo sought the Republican Party nomination for president of the United States. Margo cofounded the International Committee for Prostitutes' Rights and organized the first and second World Whores' Congresses, held in Amsterdam in 1985 and at the European Parliament in Brussels in 1986, which led to the World Charter for Prostitutes' Rights. After her return from Europe in the 1990s, she was appointed to the San Francisco Task Force on Prostitution.

In 1996, she narrowly failed to win election to the San Francisco Board of Supervisors, and in 1999 was one of three founders of the St. James Infirmary Clinic in San Francisco's Tenderloin, which provides health care to the sex worker community.

As an international political activist for the rights of sex workers, Margo was a force majeure.

Margo left her body on January 11, 2021, but her legacy lives on. To learn more about her legacy of protecting and destigmatizing

---

*Editor's note: Sex trafficking is a form of slavery. It should always be categorized as such, distinct from voluntary sex work. A sex-trafficked child should never be called a prostitute. Rape should never be called sex.

sex workers, visit *margostjames.com*. Donations will be gladly accepted to help the movement carry on.

I hope that, through this section, you will deeply consider the existential questions being raised about the human rights of sex workers, how our treatment of them is a mirror for our own shame, not theirs, and how they deserve to be treated as people, and as workers.

11

Maggie McNeill

The Honest Courtesan

Though she isn't a professional therapist, Maggie McNeill's decades of studying human sexuality from very close up have given her a remarkable degree of insight into sexuality, relationships, and many other related topics; people have therefore long sought out her advice on such topics.

Maggie McNeill was a librarian in suburban New Orleans, but after divorce, economic necessity spurred her to take up sex work; from 1997 to 2006 she worked first as a stripper, then as a call girl and madam. She eventually married her favorite client, retired, and moved to a ranch in the rural South. There she writes a daily blog called *The Honest Courtesan,* which examines the realities, myths, history, lore, science, philosophy, art, and every other aspect of prostitution. She also reports sex-work news, critiques the way her profession is portrayed in media and treated by governments, and is frequently consulted by academics and journalists as an expert on the subject. *The Honest Courtesan* is quite possibly the largest single-author blog on the internet, containing over 3,500 essays written over the past decade. You can find her book *Ask Maggie* and its subsequent volumes on Amazon.

Dr. Richard L. Miller (RLM): Our guest today is Maggie McNeill, who, having earned a BA in English from the University of New Orleans and a master's degree in library science from Louisiana State

University, identifies herself as a retired, or perhaps *semi*retired, sex worker—is it retired or semiretired, Maggie?

Maggie McNeill (MM): It's semiretired, Dr. Miller. I don't take new clients anymore, so I only see my existing clients.

RLM: Is the term *sex worker* appropriate or comfortable for you?

MM: Sex worker is fine. It is a broad term, but most of the specific terms for my type of sex work are either a little rude or too legalistic. *Escort* works.

RLM: Let's hear what the rude ones are.

MM: Whore, harlot, hooker—lots of those.

BECOMING COMFORTABLE
WITH THE SEX WORKER'S LIFE

RLM: Please tell us about the incident where you were at a dinner party with highly educated people and someone said, "Well, Maggie, why don't you tell us what you do?"

MM: The hostess had always been friendly to me, but I'd started escorting recently. She didn't seem to mind when I was a stripper but escorting seemed to bug her. So the conversation around dinner was that we all had advanced degrees, and none of us worked in our subject. Then, the hostess said to one lady, "Maggie has an interesting job—don't you, Maggie?"

The lady innocently turned to me and said, "What do you do?" I said, "I'm a whore." She said, "Excuse me?" I responded, "A harlot, a hooker, a lady of the evening, a *fille de joie*," and probably six other expressions. She was surprised but polite about it. But it clearly took her off guard. I think the hostess was trying to embarrass me, and she ended up embarrassing herself instead.

RLM: Because you were matter-of-fact about what you did. You're comfortable with your occupation. Is that correct?

MM: Very comfortable. Yes.

RLM: How did you become comfortable being who you are in a country that is so hypocritical and nasty about people in your line of work?

MM: My mother inadvertently did me a favor. She was reticent to discuss anything related to sex. Even growing up, if I asked her questions about anything remotely sexual, she would say, "I thought you would know that already," or, "Go look that up," instead of answering me.

I never got any kind of programming regarding sex from my mother—neither good nor bad. She didn't tell me sex was dirty. I didn't get anything at all. So, I formed my own opinions, and those weren't negative. By the time I hit high school and got exposed to a wider culture—TV and movies—my brain had already solidified how I would see sex.

RLM: Where did you go to high school, Maggie?

MM: I went to a small-town parochial school through eighth grade. Then as I got to high-school age, there were only public schools in our county—or parish, as we say in Louisiana. My parents had that old-fashioned Catholic approach of cherishing education. So they didn't want to send me to public school. They wanted to send me to a Catholic school.

The nearest one was in New Orleans, thirty miles away. For four years, I rode a bus every day with all the other kids for over an hour in the morning and over an hour in the evening.

CATHOLIC CHURCH VERSUS SEX EDUCATION?

RLM: The Catholic religion has some strong and strict teachings concerning sex. How did that affect you during high school?

MM: It's funny. It seems like the Catholic schools—at least in New Orleans, were making a big effort to be reasonable in the seventies. So I got sex education as part of my ninth-grade religion class because the diocese's philosophy was that if they had to do sex education, they would do it within the context of the Catholic faith. So, we got quite a good sex education.

I've seen some of the materials used now in the abstinence-only programs, and we had nothing like that. It was much better than that. The main problems with the sex education I got were that they exaggerated the failure rate of birth control methods. They spent a lot of time on awful pictures of diseased penises from gonorrhea, and on abortion. After all, they were Catholics. But as far as the mechanics of sex education, I can't fault them. It was not as bad as what's being taught now.

RLM: After high school, did you continue your education?

MM: Yes. I went to the University of New Orleans. My undergraduate degree was in English. I originally wanted to do physics, but I could not handle the math, which was humbling. Integral calculus was the first class I ever failed. Later on, I spent a few years out and then went back to get my master's degree in library science from LSU.

RLM: When was your first sexual experience? Was it with a boy or a girl?

MM: It was with a boy. My first one was on my fifteenth birthday. The reason was that my older cousin, unlike my mother, could see where I was going. When I was fourteen, he felt as though I was heading for early promiscuity. So he made me promise I wouldn't have sex until I was at least fifteen. People have asked me, "Why not sixteen?" I think he realized I was never going to wait that long. So he figured fifteen was a good compromise. I waited until my fifteenth birthday.

RLM: While you were in parochial school?

MM: Yes.

RLM: How did that sit with you? Were you comfortable with it, or were you guilt-ridden?

MM: No guilt. It didn't go how I expected because, being a fifteen-year-old, I had no idea. I knew the mechanics, but I didn't understand how easy it is to have bad sex. He didn't know what he was doing. He was an eighteen-year-old LSU freshman who lost his virginity with me, and neither one of us knew what we were doing. It was terrible. Some people romanticize their first time, but I think most people's first time is probably terrible. It didn't take me long to figure it out, but I didn't feel any guilt.

RLM: It didn't take you long to figure *what* out?

MM: To figure out how to make it better. One of the things I hit upon was that this guy was too young to know what he was doing.

After I got into college, it got easier because the guys I was seeing were much older. I don't believe I've ever been with a guy under eighteen. I didn't like young guys; I liked mature guys.

RLM: When you're saying "make it better," am I correct in thinking you mean "to feel better"? More pleasure?

MM: Yes.

RLM: You said your cousin sniffed you out as a girl who was headed for *promiscuity*. That word is used most typically by men to be negative about a woman who enjoys sex the way a man supposedly enjoys it. It's a put-down word.

MM: I agree with you on that.

RLM: In this case, your cousin was saying he sniffed a familiar person, also interested in sex. You were like him.

MM: Yes, exactly.

HOW DOES ONE BECOME A SEX WORKER?

RLM: At some point in your life, you decided to transition from having social sexual relations—evidently primarily with males—to selling sex as a product, so to speak. How did that come about?

MM: Only the first time was with a guy. I switched back and forth frequently. That caused me some guilt at first because it was hard to understand for myself. Even the books I had encountered that discussed homosexual activity didn't even recognize bisexuality. It was weird because I kept seeing treatments describing the attraction to women as an aversion to men. That wasn't my experience.

So I got even more confused, and it took me until I was in college to realize that there are a lot of ignorant people writing about this subject—it's not that I'm a freak. My first encounter with a girl was probably no more than six months after my first one with a boy. Then it went back and forth through high school and college.

RLM: How did a sexual experience with a girl six months after starting your sexual life come about?

MM: It was a good friend of mine at high school. After school, I went to her place, and we were sitting on the couch. It's funny how you remember these things. We were discussing Mae West movies. Somehow, we had gotten to the topic of gangsters like John Dillinger and his legendary giant penis.

At some point, we stopped talking, looked at each other, and started kissing. It just happened. It wasn't planned. In those days, nobody cared. Nobody saw anything weird if I stayed at her house and slept in the same bed. She and I had a relationship for a while.

RLM: In my day, they called them girls' pajama parties. The girls got together, in pajamas, and had parties. But at fifteen, how did you move from kissing to licking her vagina or sucking on her nipple? How did you know to do that? Or did it just come naturally?

MM: I think it came naturally. It seemed like the thing to do.

RLM: I certainly wouldn't expect that, in those days, two fifteen-year-olds would know about dildos.

MM: No. Nothing like that was involved. When I got to college and started hanging around with people who identified as lesbian, I was informed that dildos were verboten. In those days, a lot of women in New Orleans were very controlling about what other women should be doing in their lesbian activities. I remember a woman much older than me telling me, "There is no space for a dick between two women." That's how she put it. I never forgot that. So dildos didn't take part in any of my lesbian activities for a long time because I internalized that prejudice. Also, as a bisexual woman, I figured, "If I want dick, I'll go with a guy. Why would I want that from another woman?"

RLM: Somewhere along the line, you decided to bring money—sales—into your sex life. Let us in on how that occurred.

MM: It's a funny story. I even told it once at a stand-up open-mic night. I was a broke college student. I had just turned eighteen. I had moved into an apartment of my own. My parents told me they were willing to pay for my tuition, a good education, and food, but not for an apartment rather than the dorm. So I had to scramble.

RLM: I'm laughing because I've heard that many times from countless parents. "We'll pay for your food, tuition, and clothes, but we're not going to pay for an apartment. You're going to stay at a dormitory." That's a way of saying, "No sex."

MM: Yes. I remember when my mom found out I was having sex. When she found out that it had not only been recently, she acted as if I had shot her. She was utterly distressed. And my dad got angry at me.

RLM: It's hard to imagine that it was easy for you at the time, even though it's easy to talk about it now.

MM: No, I've never taken well to being yelled at by people I care about. Being yelled at by strangers doesn't bother me. Being yelled at by people I care about does. So I'm looking for extra opportunities for money, and I get into a friend-of-a-friend situation. There was an engineering professor at Tulane whose wife was also an engineer. At that point, three things happened simultaneously. The husband had to go to an academic conference; the wife had a business trip; and a roofer they knew had promised to give them a cut rate, as long as they waited for a week in which he didn't have any other jobs.

So these folks wanted a reliable college student to whom they could give a key and who would go to their house and let the builders go up on the roof. They didn't want a bunch of strangers, and I came recommended. This was in 1985, and they were willing to pay me $5 an hour, ten hours a day for seven days—three hundred fifty bucks, which was my rent. I was to get the key and act as a chaperone so that the builders could go to the bathroom. But the job was quicker than they had expected. So they got done on Friday instead of Sunday. The husband also came home on Friday. So I'm showing him the extra shingles and stuff the builders asked me to show.

As we're walking around, I'm thinking about the money I would be missing. This was a hundred dollars less than they had promised me since I would not be there over the weekend. Therefore, I wouldn't have my rent. I realized that the professor, who was in his fifties, was subtly coming on to me. He put his arm around my shoulder. Finally, because I didn't appear to be picking up on his cues, he came right out and said something. I don't recall what words he used, but I do recall my response because it just popped out of my mouth.

I said, "Can I stay on the clock?" He responded, "What?" So I said, "I was expecting 350 for this gig. Now, it's only going to be 250. Will it still be 350?" So he said, "Sure." Half an hour later, I left. I realized that was the easiest hundred dollars I'd made in my life. After that, I started playing a game. When guys asked me out, I would say, "I'm in a terrible mood because my phone bill is due, and I don't know how to pay it." Then the guy would say, "How much is your phone bill?" "Seventy-five dollars." "What if I gave you the money?" This little charade would go on. So I got a reputation. I didn't advertise anywhere. It was the same group of guys that knew me.

WHAT DOES THE TRAINING OF
A SEX WORKER LOOK LIKE?

RLM: In most endeavors—whether it's carpentry, surgery, psychology, or library science—there are ways to learn the skills of the occupation. You went to library science school for an advanced degree. I went to graduate school to get my doctorate. Plumbers work with older plumbers. How does a young girl learn how to perform as a sex worker?

MM: That's a good question.

RLM: A guy says to you, "A hundred bucks for sex is no issue." But you've never done this before. How do you know what to do? Do you suddenly have the courage to start zipping down his fly and sucking on his penis? Nobody had yet taught you anything.

MM: I did exactly the same I did with guys that weren't paying me, and he was happy. So I kept doing it.

RLM: I'm a little confused. I would assume with guys that you weren't charging, you would start by kissing and fondling, then petting and taking the clothes off. You did the exact same thing?

MM: Yes, only a little faster because I wanted to move it along. Fewer preliminaries but the same thing. That served me well my whole career.

RLM: So then you went on to charge other people fees for sex during your college career. And word got around that you would perform sexually for a certain amount of money.

MM: Yes.

RLM: You started, like any other business, to build up a clientele. And you had repeat customers.

MM: Yes. It was all repeaters from a small group. One of my friends once asked me, "How many guys were in that group?" I honestly can't tell you, but I would think no more than a dozen. It was a fairly small number. I also had a friend who was ten years older than me. She was divorced. She had a child, and her ex-husband was kind of a ne'er-do-well. He was often late on child support.

If she needed money and it wasn't forthcoming from the ex, she would tell me, "I guess it's time to turn a couple of tricks." She would call up a small group of men. I think I borrowed that pattern from her. You can call them up when you need it. Sometimes they call you. In those days, everything was by regular phone. There was no texting or caller ID.

RLM: Am I correct in assuming that, since you were a college girl, your customers in this group of twelve were connected to the school?

MM: All of them—mostly graduate students, a couple of professors.

RLM: I'm correct in assuming that you were physically safe with these men?

MM: I felt completely safe.

RLM: You didn't have to deal with the concern that somebody's going to beat you up and push you out of the car.

MM: No, nothing like that.

RLM: You had a safe entrance into the business of sex work.

MM: Very safe. In fact, they were invested in making it look normal because a lot of guys don't like thinking they're paying for sex. So we did it like a date. There was no specific time. It was very casual. So one guy might give me 75 bucks, and we might go on a three-hour date. Another guy might give me 100 bucks, and we would go on a two-hour date and see a movie. We would eat, go back to my place, we would screw, and then he would leave. But to exterior people looking at it, it looked like a college girl dating—except when it was the older guys. I noticed most of them didn't want to do too much in public. New Orleans is a small town. I suppose they didn't want it getting back to the wrong people.

RLM: They didn't want the faculty to know about their sexual exploits. Then you took a two-year break before you went to graduate school.

MM: Three maybe.

RLM: Did you continue the sex work during that period? Or did you take a break?

MM: I stupidly accepted a proposal at the ripe old age of twenty and stopped working because I was young, dumb, and had illusions. That relationship was on-again-off-again. It was a stormy relationship. We would argue, break up, and get back together. This went on for seven and a half years. We got married like we shouldn't have. Then, in January of 1995, he took off—just got up and left. So I tried to hang on for a while. I did not take the breakup well. I've never been a person who gets romantically attracted to people easily.

So it's difficult for me when I do invest that effort and do get involved. Breakups are hard on me because I've got a lot invested. Within a few months, I couldn't manage to go to work anymore. I was not in a psychological state to do it. This dragged on for a couple of years, and I got a sugar mama who cared for me. One of the peculiarities of my sexual development is that, in that early period, I had two sugar mamas. I never had a sugar daddy, which is odd, but that's the case.

RLM: Did you have a sugar mama while you were with this man for seven and a half years?

MM: No, I did not. I had her at the beginning, right when he and I started to date, but we weren't exclusive yet. The second sugar mama was after he left me.

RLM: I see. So during the seven years of your first marriage, you were on a break from the sex business?

MM: Yes, and he's gone.

DAILY LIFE AS A STRIPPER

RLM: Take us into the next phase of your work life in the sex industry.

MM: He left me in January of 1995. I managed to hold on by working with the sugar mama and through help from friends. I sold the house, and I used that to pay rent in advance. But by September of 1997, I realized there was no way I could continue not to work. Something had to give. For some reason, I didn't think about escorting. So I worked as a stripper for two years. By October of 1999, I was sick of stripping. I didn't like it. My best friend told me, "Why don't you do escorting?" So I said, "You think?" She said, "You would be good at it." I thought back to college and thought, *I sort of did it before.*

RLM: Let me interrupt for a moment because a lot of young women consider going into stripping at some point in their lives to make some money. Before we go into your escorting phase, give us some flavor of the life during your two years as a stripper. What do you want to share with the public about what being a stripper was like?

MM: Stripping was harder for me because I was almost thirty-one when I started. Most of the girls I was competing with were eighteen to twenty-one, very young. So I got tired more easily than they did. I still had an outstanding figure, but I was aware that I was competing with girls ten years younger. So I was always very open. I was the extras girl. Some strip clubs don't like extras girls, and some realize it'll happen anyway. If you go into the VIP room, the guy can slide the extras girls extra cash, and they'll do something in the VIP room, which you're not supposed to do.

RLM: How far do you go? A hand job or a blow job?

MM: Hand jobs, blow jobs—that sort of thing. You can't risk doing anything where you could potentially get caught. Some strippers believe that, "When you do that, all the guys expect all the girls will do that." My response to them was, "You're twenty-two years old.

We'll talk if you're thirty-one and still a stripper." I needed the extra money.

RLM: Tell us something about the flavor of daily life when you're not at the club.

MM: I'm a very OCD person, and my ex had left me with a big debt load. I wanted to get that debt off my neck. So I worked at the club every single day. I took no breaks at all. Even some managers said, "Don't you think you ought to take a few days off?" I only responded, "Nope." I was there, whether rain or shine, slow or fast. I was there all the time, which is part of why I burned out.

I was living with a good friend. We still live together. But she had another job at that time. Nowadays, she's older and not in good health, so I support her now. In those days, she had her own job. So we palled around, and my life outside of the club was the same as before. Hanging around with friends, watching movies. Nothing out of the ordinary.

RLM: It is important for the public to know that your job, though it happened to be in the sex industry, was first and foremost, a job.

MM: Absolutely.

RLM: So your days were regular working days. People might have some fantasy that sex workers' daily lives are somehow different than the lives of the rest of us.

MM: No. It's true—people think that, and I always leaned in on it because it became more pronounced when I became an escort. I started agency escorting in January of 2000. We already had the internet, and independent girls were using it, but I wasn't one of those clever people who had it figured out early. So I was working for an agency, which meant carrying a cell phone all the time. If the agency gets something, they call you.

When I got the call, I might be in a grocery store or at a friend's house, and I would be honest with the guys. The guy would say, "You sound great. How soon can you be here?" I would say, "I'm in the grocery store right now, so I'm about to check out. My apartment is five minutes from here. I'll put my stuff away, and then I can be on the way so that I can see you in maybe forty-five minutes?" So I would lean in on it and reinforce, "This is normal."

I remember one night, it was pouring. This guy called, and I was baking cookies. He said, "How soon can you be here?" So I said, "Well, I've got one last tray of cookies to put in the oven, and they'll be in there for ten minutes. As soon as they're out, I'll be on my way." He goes, "You're baking cookies from scratch?" I said, "Is there any other way? Would you like me to bring some?" So he said, "What are they?"—"Chocolate chip."—"Yes, please." So when I got to the hotel, I knocked on the door, he opened it, and I handed him a bag of cookies.

Even though I wasn't doing it on purpose that way, I think that helped protect me during that time because it was hard. It's hard for guys to dehumanize you when you act so human.

RLM: Point well taken. Underlined in red. You gave yourself a certain amount of extra safety.

MM: I think you're right.

RLM: You're reminding me of something that Veronica Monet, who wrote *Sex Secrets Of Courtesans,* told me. Quite often men hired her, and there was no sex involved whatsoever. During her many years as a courtesan, escort, and call girl it was common for her to get fully paid without any sexual activity. The public doesn't know that, Maggie. The public has fantasies of what goes on between customers and sex workers.

MM: Oh, sure.

RLM: What does "Oh, sure," mean?

MM: "Oh, sure," means the public doesn't know, as you say, but every sex worker knows. As you become more experienced and older—as you charge more—you have less sex. It really is true.

RLM: The more you charge, the less sex you have. That's an interesting phenomenon—please elaborate.

MM: The more you can create the feeling of a regular date, the more money you can command because that's what most guys want. This is one of the infuriating things about prohibitionists. Prohibitionists want to pretend that sex workers' clients are monstrous people, that they're dehumanizing girls. None of this is true. I hear from lots of girls that if they do both dating and working, clients treat them better than their social dates.

Once I started escorting, I didn't date socially anymore, so I didn't notice that dichotomy. But I did notice from the past. The guys I dated for free, way back in college, didn't bring me flowers every time. They didn't take me to nice restaurants.

MOVING ON TO AN ESCORT AGENCY

RLM: In the year 2000, a few years after you finished working as a stripper, you moved into working as an escort with an agency.

MM: Yes.

RLM: You felt safe; you weren't getting harmed.

MM: No.

RLM: You didn't live in terror of what the next experience will be.

MM: No.

RLM: I love your story about the cookies.

MM: The funny thing is, I remember telling one guy I was at the grocery store. He said, "Out of curiosity, at what grocery store are you?" I said, "It's right down the street from you." So he said, "If you want, you can put your groceries in my fridge." So I showed up and knocked on the door holding two bags of groceries.

I said, "This one's not cold. This one's cold. Let's put this one in the fridge." I hung the other one on the doorknob, saying,

"Because I don't want to forget my cold groceries when I leave."

RLM: I love that story. Let's continue with your life story now. What happened next in your career?

MM: I didn't like the agencies I was dealing with and, later on, I did find one whose owner seemed ethical. I liked and trusted him, and he became a good friend. But before I met him, I realized a lot of these agency owners are terrible people. There's nothing like a Better Business Bureau. So you can be a terrible person and still be in this business. It's okay, and people won't stop you.

So I started my own agency because I wanted young girls to have a place where the owner was looking out for them. It didn't take too long for the word to get around. Some girls in New Orleans would only work for me. The other owners didn't want to deal with newbies when a girl called to apply. They would just send them my way because I would give them the whole talk. That went on for a few years.

RLM: Given that sex for money is an illegal activity, how does a newbie who's never done sex work before find sex for hire?

MM: It was in the phone book in those days, and they just called. I got calls from girls who wanted to work twice a week.

RLM: What would you put in the phone book? Would you tell them this was a sex-work agency?

MM: It was under escort services.

RLM: Nowadays, it would be on the internet in the same way.

MM: Yes. But the internet has almost killed escort services. They still exist, but they're much more specialized. It's not like it was back in the early 2000s. In fact, by 2006, the market consisted mostly of independents. I wasn't getting many phone calls from new girls anymore because they were all going independent. So I decided to close my doors and shift to the internet for my own work. But then, in 2006, I was retiring again because I had gotten married to my favorite client.

RLM: That's great.

MM: We stayed married for a few years, and then we did eventually get divorced, but it didn't have anything to do with my work. If it did, it was the opposite in the sense that his view of me was romanticized because he met me as an escort. Once the daily grind had gone on for years, and he had seen me sick, with my hair pulled back, putting on a little weight, throwing up, and yelling at him, the bloom was off the rose.

RLM: He had married a fantasy.

MM: Sure. We had an amicable divorce.

RLM: So the divorce didn't wrench you.

MM: No. The first part was hard. But even though nowadays you don't require the other person's approval to file divorce papers, he played it the old-fashioned way. He waited until I was ready to divorce, and then he said, "Let's go ahead and do it." I'm very grateful to him for making that much easier than it would have been. We still talk. He still texts me often. He remarried, and we chitchat. He's a huge *Star Wars* fan, so I'll text it to him if I see some *Star Wars* thing. If he sees a *Doctor Who* thing, he'll text it to me. So we're still friendly.

ARE SEX WORKERS USED TO FEARING THE LAW?

RLM: Coming back to what you did after leaving the sex-for-hire agency, where does the fear of the law fit into sex work for you?

MM: I've always been kind of an anarchist. I've never had a comfortable relationship with authority. When my mom would tell me to do something, my immediate response was, *"Why?"* I didn't take well to arbitrary declarations, to people saying, "You must do this because we are over you." My mom was always frustrated because, all through school, she was wondering, "How can you possibly make

A's in subjects and C's in conduct?" The answer is that I would not listen. I would *not* mind the teachers. I would most of the time, but as soon as I viewed something as arbitrary, I couldn't do that. When it was something like, "Let's be quiet now because we're going to have class," that made sense to me, so I would be quiet.

So I've always had problems with the idea of criminalizing a thought. If I did the same thing for free because I like a guy, it would be completely legal. Because I'm doing it with a profit motive, that thought in my brain makes it illegal. This is thought crime. This is Orwellian. This should not *be* in a free country. It had always seemed like an illegitimate law to me, so I've ignored it. Now, the fact that cops are out there trying to trick sex workers put a condition into the work that I had to deal with. So one of the main things we were looking for when we screened guys on the phone was whether they're a cop. In the almost seven years I owned an agency, most of our problems were not bad clients but cops having a sting or trying to trick girls. In the whole time, I only had two girls get arrested, one of them was me, and both times we had a lawyer on retainer. So as soon as we realized what was going on, we called the lawyer. He went down, got her out, and helped her navigate the system. "Do you want to plead guilty? Do you want to pay the fine?"

RLM: What did you do in your case?

MM: I just paid the fine. Nowadays, I would do something different, but in those days, I was married. I didn't want to make waves. I just wanted it to go away.

RLM: Of course. Do you recall how much the fine was?

MM: Three hundred bucks, which was what I was charging in those days.

RLM: Some people might consider it a cost of doing business.

MM: Yes, but I don't like that I still have that criminal record.

RLM: Was it a misdemeanor or a felony?

MM: It was a misdemeanor. Originally, they also threatened me with a felony. This is complicated, but I'm trying to give a short version: under Code Napoleon, which is the form of law in Louisiana, you're required to spell out every crime. That's why the Louisiana law code is way bigger than that of most states. Somebody realized they technically couldn't charge sex workers with what they called "crime against nature"—i.e., oral or anal sex, which was a felony. They realized it hadn't taken place. So sometime, probably in the eighties, they passed a new law called "crime against nature by solicitation," or CANS, and that made it a felony even if you only talked about it.

After *Lawrence v. Texas* struck down sodomy laws in 2003, the Supreme Court said sodomy laws were no longer allowed, but CANS wasn't technically a sodomy law. It referred to talking about it, not doing it, and that stood. The Supreme Court didn't make any effort to do anything about it. They used to charge a lot of street girls because it let them throw in a felony in addition to plain old misdemeanor prostitution. Originally they threatened to hit me with that in October of 2005, shortly after Hurricane Katrina.

But when my lawyer pulled up the charges, it wasn't there. His theory was that the DA realized I was connected when I had a federal judge call the jail to let me out as a favor to my lawyer. So they must have said, "Let's just hit her with the misdemeanor. If we hit her with the felony, she's going to fight, and we'd rather get the money and be done."

RLM: A critical aspect of the story, to everyone reading this, is that *talking about something* was made into criminal activity. Talking was criminalized.

MM: Yes.

RLM: It's like throwing gasoline on the fire of making sex work illegal, which in itself, in my opinion, is heinous.

MM: Yes.

LEGALIZATION VERSUS DECRIMINALIZATION

RLM: Keeping sex work illegal is an act against women, perpetrated by men. It's a horrendous thing that sex workers are considered criminals and are arrested for their work. I hope we're making progress, and that your coming out in this interview will contribute to the cause of legalization.

MM: I hope so—or that decriminalization is what we prefer.

RLM: Yes. Let's talk about that for a moment.

MM: Sure. A lot of people get confused because the terms are used the opposite way in sex work as they are in drug legalization. In drug legalization, decriminalization is closer to criminalization than full legalization is. In sex work, it's the opposite.

RLM: Why?

MM: My friend Mistress Matisse believes the reason is that substances are not people or acts. In other words, if you have marijuana, you can make a law saying that any possession of marijuana at any time is illegal. It doesn't matter what your reason is. With prostitution law, you can't do that because all the acts are legal. It's only the profit motive that makes it illegal. Legalization is what they have in Nevada. That's what Americans would be most familiar with.

RLM: Speaking as a semiretired sex worker, why is legalization not preferable? That's "Get out of jail," end of the discussion. Why would you not prefer that?

MM: In sex work, it doesn't mean that. Here, legalization means certain narrow conditions under which prostitution is *allowed*. If you step outside those bounds, you're still committing a crime. Many people are shocked to hear Nevada has the highest rates of arrested sex workers of any state in the country because they aggressively pursue anybody outside of the brothel system. In the UK, prostitution itself is legal, but so-called brothel-keeping, meaning to keep a place where you see clients, is illegal. If I have an apartment where I see clients, which I do, that will change the act to an illegal one in the British system.

RLM: You're telling me that if you bring a client to your apartment in England, it's called a brothel, but if you have sex with him in an automobile or on a bicycle, that's okay.

MM: Or his hotel room or his house, yes. It's bizarre.

RLM: I'm getting educated, and I appreciate it. Now, let's say that Nevada changed their laws to decriminalization. Then the working girls, no matter where they worked, would not be prosecuted. Is that correct?

MM: Correct. Under decriminalization, sex work is treated like any other work. Prohibitionists will sometimes say, "You don't want any regulation. All businesses have regulation." We're not saying that. We're saying that this is not a *criminal* matter.

I like to use a restaurant as an example. There are health codes that govern restaurants. If an inspector finds violations—a dirty floor, or whatever it may be—he writes a report. He gives it to the manager or owner. He says, "I'll be back next Monday, and you'd better have this cleaned up. If you don't, I'm going to fine you."

He doesn't come in with a squad of cops, beat everybody up, arrest the owner, the cook, the wait staff, the customers, put their pictures in the paper, and call them names. That's all we're asking for with decriminalization. If you want to come up with rules that say, "No brothels within a thousand feet of a school," this is part of modern living, unfortunately. That's the way it is. In New Zealand, they have decriminalization. They say up to four women can work from the same premises before it becomes a brothel. If you and your three friends are renting an apartment, that's okay. If you add one more, it's a brothel, and you have to get a license. It's all zoning stuff.

WORKING AS A SEX WORKER
IN YOUR SEVENTIES

RLM: You've taught me about aspects of legalization that I hadn't understood. I work sitting in a chair, and as long as my heart and head are okay, I can continue to work. I'm eighty-three years old, and I'm still in practice seeing patients. But in many fields of endeavor—baseball, athleticism, carpentry—as one ages, it becomes more difficult to maintain their occupation. How does that work in the sex industry?

MM: It all depends on the person. Most women who do sex work may go in and out of it. You might have a lady who does it for a while when she's in college; then, she quits and goes on to have a regular career. Then she gets divorced and needs the extra money, so she goes back in for a while. Then she gets remarried and quits. This is exactly what I did. I bounced in and out for a long time. A lot of women treat it that way. Only a small number make it a lifelong career.

RLM: Is there sex work for women in their sixties and seventies?

MM: I don't want to still be doing it in my seventies, but there are many people. These two sisters were in the Red-light district in Amsterdam, the Fokkens sisters. They both worked until their late sixties. One of them retired at sixty-seven because she had a bad hip. The other one worked until sixty-nine. It happens.

For the most part, I'd say it's less physical, and more a case of you getting tired of changing conditions. It becomes so much to keep up with. One of the reasons I semiretired is because the ad sites keep changing. When the pandemic started, everybody shifted to online work. I feel like I'm too old to learn. I don't want to learn all those new tricks. I want to keep doing things the way I've been doing them.

For me, it was good to semiretire because I've got established relationships with my clients. I don't have to worry about new ads, changing my model, or learning new skills that I'm disinclined to learn. I can keep going the same way I have been. Now, I say that, but

I have friends who aren't much younger than me, yet they're right on it. They're aces. I've got other friends who are of similar age to me who semiretired long ago. They've got all the regulars they needed, so why bother?

RLM: I get it.

MM: I think what keeps you from burning out in any profession—not just sex work—is finding the aspects of the job you hate, eliminating them, and only keeping the parts you like. I like seeing guys; I like talking, stroking, touching, sex, and going out to dinner. I want to keep seeing my guys. What I don't like is having to write new ad copy. What I don't like is, "That website's rules changed." I don't want to say, "Now we don't see people in person anymore. It's all Only Fans." I can't handle all that. It's too much.

RLM: I'm laughing with you, Maggie, because I love clinical work. I love radio work and book writing, but I hate administration and paperwork.

MM: Exactly.

RLM: We're coming to the end of our time, and I have one last question for you. You can take all the time you want to think about this. What did we not cover that you'd like the public to know?

MM: So much, but I think the most important thing that I want to emphasize is what you said at the beginning, which is that sex workers are not any different than the rest of the people. The major difference between sex workers and most other women is that we're more comfortable with sex. I say women because most sex workers are women, although men and nonbinary people make for a certain percentage. The law certainly tends to focus on women.

Other than being more comfortable, we're just like any other woman. On my Twitter account and blog, I've been putting a lot more emphasis on my stuff that isn't sex work over the past couple of years. I bought a farm on the Washington coast, and I've been adding an extension in the back with a bathhouse and guest cottages. I published pictures of my work. I learned to weld, and I showed pictures of myself welding. I was writing about *Dr. Who* episodes that I watched. I'm doing this to show people I'm a nerd. I have a regular nerdy, older-woman life. It's not that different.

RLM: I can see the headline of one of your blogs being *Sex Work and Chocolate Chip Cookies*.

MM: Exactly.

12

Norma Jean Almodovar, Carol Leigh, and Veronica Vera

Three Perspectives from Sex Workers

Norma Jean Almodovar is an American author, sex workers' advocate, and activist. Norma Jean worked for ten years as a traffic officer in the Los Angeles Police Department. In 1982, she quit her job with the LAPD to work as a call girl. In 1984, she was arrested, convicted, and thrown in jail. Two years later, Norma Jean ran for lieutenant governor in the California gubernatorial election as a libertarian. In 1993, Simon & Schuster published her autobiography, *Cop to Call Girl*. Norma Jean is the founder of the International Sex Worker Foundation for Art, Culture, and Education. Since 2012, she has served as executive director of the Los Angeles branch of the sex workers' rights organization COYOTE (Call Off Your Old Tired Ethics), founded by Margo St. James.

Veronica Vera is a human sexuality writer and performer. She's best known for her films, *Times Square Comes Alive*, Gerard Damiano's *Consenting Adults*, *Mondo New York*, and *Rites of Passion*, as well as her work with the world-famous photographer Robert Mapplethorpe. Veronica is a former Wall Street trader known for founding the world's first cross-gender academy, Miss Vera's Finishing School For Boys Who Want To Be Girls. She is the author of three books based on her academy. The first bears the same name as the school and was published in 1997 by Doubleday. Veronica is currently working on a memoir of her life in the 1980s. She is a doctor of human sexuality.

Carol Leigh, also known as the Scarlot Harlot, is universally credited with being the first to coin the term *sex worker*. After obtaining a BA in creative writing in 1977 and continuing to study creative writing in a master's program at Boston University, she worked as a prostitute. Having been a red-diaper baby, an anti-war activist during the Vietnam War, and a feminist, she naturally embraced issues of prostitutes' rights when she started working as a prostitute herself. Leigh was raped early in her career, which solidified her dedication to protecting sex workers from the violence, which accompanied the stigma and criminalization.

In the late seventies and early eighties, Leigh began writing poetry from the perspective of Scarlot Harlot, which developed into a play, *The Adventures of Scarlot Harlot,* performed at the National Festival of Women's Theater. Leigh joined the AIDS activist organization Citizens for Medical Justice, a precursor to ACT UP, and organized many demonstrations and press conferences while collaborating with the Sisters of Perpetual Indulgence. Leigh has received awards from the American Film Institute for *Yes Means Yes, No Means No, Outlaw Poverty, Not Prostitutes,* and *Mother's Mink.*

In 1999, she founded the Sex Worker Film and Arts Festival. In 1993, she was one of the chief contributors and lead writer for the Board of Supervisors' San Francisco Task Force on Prostitution. In 2006, she received a grant from the Creative Work Fund to establish, in collaboration with the Center for Sex and Culture, the Sex Work and Media Library.

Dr. Richard Louis Miller (RLM): Today, it is my privilege to bring you three distinguished women, Norma Jean Almodovar, Carol Leigh, and Veronica Vera, who have courageously dedicated their lives to advancing the lives of others—namely, sex workers. A hearty welcome to you all. Let's we start with each of you to making an introductory statement.

Veronica Vera (VV): I feel that my work, in terms of standing up for women's rights and our rights to do what we want with our bodies, arose from early repression from religion. Repression inspired me— knowing from the beginning that I wanted to experience the pleasure in my body, being told that was wrong, not understanding why, and completely disagreeing with it. That's how I started: associating with the idea of women who were called "whores." It seems these women had answers I wanted to hear. For me, religion was the big abuser and, unfortunately, this is often still true—not just for women, but for many especially in the LGBT community.

RLM: Thank you. Carol, would you like to go next?

Carol Leigh (CL): Sure. My life has been focused on sex-worker rights, activism, and arts, since I started doing sex work in the late seventies and coined the term *sex work*. I'm seventy now, and also a cancer patient. I'm thinking and writing about the sex workers' movement from a global and historical perspective. I've been especially interested in the development of the sex-worker rights movement. There are so many ideas and there's so much diversity amongst sex workers that it's even hard to talk about them. I do glorify sex workers. I think that's needed, maybe in the model of Grisélidis Réal in Switzerland, a great artist who was a sex worker. So, I'm focused on sex with artists. I've run a film festival, *Sex Worker Film and Arts Festival,* for about twenty years. I teach, and I'm involved in various sex-worker rights organizations.

ACTIVISM FOR A REALISTIC VIEW ON PROSTITUTION

RLM: Thank you. Hi, Norma Jean.

Norma Jean Almodovar (NJA): Hi. The last thing I did was travel to China as an NGO delegate to the women's conference in Beijing.

At that conference, we encountered well-known anti-prostitution activists like Melissa Farley and Donna Hughes. There were five sex-worker activists. During our time there, we worked hard on inserting a paragraph into the Platform for Action. The original paragraphs said, "All pornography and prostitution are incompatible with the dignity and worth of the human person and must be eliminated."

So, the five of us worked for two weeks lobbying and we changed the paragraph by one word. At the end of the conference, they voted on it and changed it to, "All *forced* pornography and prostitution." We got that in the Platform for Action. That was an amazing accomplishment. The problem was that the abolitionists back home were saying, "It doesn't matter; it's all forced—all prostitution, all pornography. Women cannot *choose* to be sexual. Anyone who says they are doesn't know what they're talking about." All of these lies came out and changed people's opinions about prostitution. So, I started doing research—basically, because I take care of my disabled husband and I don't go anywhere, except to my computer. All the facts and statistics are out there—from the FBI and government sources, not from radical feminists. I found that all of these things were not true. They were just pulling numbers out of their posteriors.

So, I put together what I call *Operation Do the Math*. It's on my website, Police Prostitution and Politics. The work that I put together takes all government statistics every year. I put them in a format where people can not only click on the link to the FBI website where I got the information, but I add all numbers up so that people can see the actual numbers, which vastly deviate from the reports. Let me read one of them. If we take the claim of 100,000 to 300,000 children trafficked into prostitution, we can put that next to 102 confirmed cases from 2014 to 2019.

So, how one can extrapolate from those numbers and come up with 100,000 to 300,000 children, doesn't make any sense. 1.81 percent of all arrests for prostitution are children. That means the majority of people arrested for prostitution are adults. One of the other abolitionists' arguments is that child prostitutes are forced to see between ten and twenty-five men a day. When I was working, I would be lucky if I saw two or three men a day. I'm sure most sex workers would love it if they would get ten on a consistent basis.

So, when you do the math, you say, "Wait for a second, if there are 100,000 children, and they see ten to twenty-five men a day, how many men do we need to accommodate them? If they're only 1.81 percent of all prostitutes, how many men do we need to accommodate the adults?" You realize you would need *billions* of men. So, my question is always, where are we going to get them? We have to import them from Mars.

SEX WORKERS' BACKGROUNDS

RLM: To segue from that, there's a belief in our culture that women who go into sex work come from parents who are drug addicts and mentally ill. People assume their childhood has been terrible. You three are experts on this—what can you tell us about the variation of the backgrounds of people who go into sex work?

NJA: I can say I was born and raised in a fundamental Baptist family. I have thirteen brothers and sisters. I was enrolled in Philadelphia College of the Bible; I was going to be a missionary. I was a straight-A student. I was in the accelerated classes. I've never done drugs; I don't drink; I don't smoke. The only thing I ever did was spread my legs for money. That's the most hideous thing I could possibly do, according to society. So, all of those theories about how we're all from horrible backgrounds, it doesn't ring true to most of us.

CL: Sex workers are so diverse. Most people see us monolithically, as stereotypes—as wealthy call girls or abject victims. You always have to look at these statistics, as Norma Jean teaches, just to understand that we're real people—mostly working-class and mostly mothers, by the way—who support our families. But sometimes the statistics are skewed. There are a lot of political goals for statisticians—usually anti–sex work goals.

So I do think it's important to know real sex workers and understand the day-to-day realities of our lives. Each locale may have different populations of sex workers. I know, as an early sex worker, I'm ashamed to admit, I was busy saying, "I'm not a drug addict. I'm not poor." I wanted to prove that I was not a certain stereotype, but that's wrong. It's easy to use the details of our survival strategies against us. There's so much stigma placed on individuals and people of backgrounds that are more marginalized. Sex workers suffer most from the stigma.

As we're moving ahead, our movement and the general public always need to be conscious of not portraying that dire condition as something that would make people afraid of us. We need to be proud of our strength and the wisdom that adversity brought us.

VV: Now, you're seeing more activists among Black and Brown sex workers. People used to think of the sex workers' rights movement as a movement of white women. Now that's changed, because Black and Brown sex workers—especially trans sex workers—are speaking out.

You have to look at how economies change, too. Part of what lifts people and gives them the ability to speak up for themselves and their rights as sex workers is that, economically, things are getting better. Another part is improved education. So the diversity of the movement's spokespeople is changing. Sex workers have always been a diversified group. We're now seeing more and more diversity in the movement leadership, which is great.

RLM: When you three refer to sex workers as a diversified group, do you mean some of them do come from terrible childhoods, some from wonderful childhoods, and everything in between?

All: Absolutely.

RLM: What about the public perception that sex workers, in order to do this "dirty business," are always under the influence of drugs? They have to be—otherwise, they wouldn't be doing this. Please comment on that.

NJA: When I was working for the LAPD, an awful lot of my colleagues drank a lot, smoked a lot, and did drugs. In fact, when you went to a cop party, the cops were doing all the drugs that they had confiscated. Some of the cops came to work drugged out. Look at Wall Street—how many of those guys are doing cocaine?

RLM: So, Norma Jean, we're dealing with abject hypocrisy amongst leadership in our country with regard to sex workers. Namely, the very politicians and cops who are anti-prostitution and anti–sex worker are doing the very activities that they're arresting and prosecuting the sex worker of doing? Having worked for the LA police department for ten years, you speak with authority.

NJA: That's what I'm saying. I worked for them for ten years. Now I collect stories of cops who hired or raped prostitutes. People don't get it. Prostitution is not going to go away. The more you repress it, the more corruption you have. I would think that people would want a police department and a justice system that actually contributes to justice, not police engaging in as many crimes as the people they arrest.

CL: I tried to figure out which population of prostitutes uses which drugs and why, and whether governments have brought the drugs into the community. I don't really know. Now, some of my friends were middle-class, maybe more adventurous women. I smoke pot; I'm not saying I'm not a drug user. When I was young, I didn't want to use drugs, but I used all kinds. I would try LSD.

We're missing important information as we stigmatize, reject, and disrespect sex workers. We need to respect survival strategies—getting by when you come from a family that struggles. The general public and media have a middle-class notion of success and ignore the strength and accomplishments of those who surmount so many challenges. We need to understand various relationships between sex work and poverty.

People who take an anti-prostitution stance often blame poverty alone and believe there wouldn't be prostitution without it. Even our movement hasn't looked into what the link is. Society needs to understand this better. How does it manifest? What are its variations?

There's needing money and then there's *poverty*. So, what about that continuum? Our movement hasn't quite been able to delve into it. I haven't seen it in the academy, either. So, I think that's an important subject.

VV: It's a big picture, too, because you hear people say, "I'm a sex worker, and I'm making more money than I would as a secretary or stocking shelves in Target." So, there is the economic element, and it's important to look at that. But, there's also the idea of, "Oh, you chose sex work, but that's still so terrible." Then, it intersects with how people feel about sex in general, about keeping sex for marriage and for making babies. In the movement, we believe in the three Rs of women's rights: sex for reproduction, sex for recreation, and sex for remuneration. True women's liberation rests on that three-legged stool.

DO PEOPLE GO INTO SEX WORK SIMPLY BECAUSE THEY LOVE SEX?

RLM: We hear so often from professional athletes how much they love what they do. They're so happy to play baseball and get paid for it. So, comment on how many people are motivated to go into sex work simply because they love sex; people who enjoy it and think, *What the heck? I like to do this and if I can get paid for it, that's a great thing.*

NJA: I think it varies by every individual. In my case, I needed to earn a living. I was already giving away sex to a lot of cops, really bad lovers. The interesting thing was when a couple of the cops offered me $200 if I would have sex with a retiring captain. I said, "If I'm going to be a prostitute, I'm going to do it for myself, not for you guys." But it depends on the individual and what motivates them. I enjoyed being a sex worker. Did I like every client I had? Not really. But I liked the work overall, because if murder is the worst thing you can do to your fellow human being, giving them an orgasm has got to be one of the best.

RLM: I remember, Norma Jean, in our first interview some years ago, you told me how the cops in the locker room were forcing you to give them blowjobs. So you said, "What the hell, if they're going to force me to do that for free, I might as well start charging them."

NJA: I don't know that it was so much forced as it was expected.

RLM: Okay, fair enough.

VV: When I got involved in the sex business, I had a nest egg. I had worked on Wall Street and I had some money. But, I got involved as a writer and I met other people who were writing for a sex magazine. Through that, I met other people exploring human sexuality, especially other women. So, for me, part of it was getting allies, the camaraderie of the other people who wanted to get rid of sexual ignorance. Some idealism was involved, and it was fun. It was an adventure to go from being a repressed Catholic girl to being a bachelorette around town, "giving it away," making a few hardcore films, mainly writing about sex and the commercial sex life of New York, especially Times Square. Annie Sprinkle and I became best friends right away. Other porn stars and I became friends.

So, men didn't get me into the porn business—women did. It was the camaraderie of the women. You build your own support system, your own families, and that encourages people to explore sex with like-minded people.

CL: I was sexually adventurous, but I was always working out my sexuality. So, I was fascinated with prostitution. But, I dare say now, I am a privileged prostitute. There's even an additional privilege to speaking out from the activist's perspective the way all of us do. I do have a lot of sex-positive friends. Sometimes, I've seen with other people, that being sex-positive is inversely proportional to how you're forced to feel economically. But also sometimes it's the opposite! Embracing sexual pleasure is also a kind of survival strategy for some. Anyway, I am always interested in why and who is sex-positive.

I was also fascinated with sexual politics, and I see that in my friends. But, I certainly see a lot of women—my group—who were just fascinated with sex, too.

NJA: When it comes to the topic of people in prostitution being sex-positive or not, I like to bring up how many people who have to clean up the urine, feces, and vomit of complete strangers earning minimum wages are cleanup positive. How many of them love scrubbing toilets? Yet, we don't try to outlaw or ban people from engaging in that activity if that's the only work they can find.

RLM: That's true.

THE DANGERS OF BEING A SEX WORKER, IMAGINED AND REAL

RLM: So I'd like the three of you to talk from your personal experiences about the dangers of being a sex worker. Please comment about what you know, personally, and what you've heard from your work about the dangers of sex work.

NJA: First of all, let's do some statistics: Again, the FBI posts this information on its website. Let me give you these statistics on murders by circumstances from 1991 to 2019: there were 326 prostitute homicides. By comparison, law-enforcement homicides totaled 1,637; there were 891 children were killed by babysitters; 1,371 people murdered during rapes; and 4,254 were murdered during a romantic triangle. So a lot of prostitutes have been murdered, and that *is* a horrible thing, but the overwhelming statistics that people cite just don't show up in the numbers reported by law enforcement.* And, again, these are the actual numbers from the government.

RLM: So, you're making the assertion that the number of on-the-job deaths of prostitutes is much lower than what we're told.

---

*Editor's note: Almodovar's assertions are difficult to verify as the FBI website has changed.

NJA: I believe so. It's not that those deaths aren't important. They're very important. The problem is how the cops follow up on these— they don't. In fact, the police have a term for a murdered prostitute; they call them *NHIs,* which stands for "no humans involved." It's abominable that they would even consider that a prostitute's murder wasn't important at all. "It's not a human being, so what do we care?" We have to look at the reality and not look at all the people murdered in prostitution. Instead, let's look at the ones murdered who are not getting justice. Why do cops feel they can call a murdered prostitute "not human"?

RLM: But, is it not the case that, compared to an office worker, prostitutes get hit more often by clients?

NJA: Possibly. But, compared to cops and women involved in romantic triangles, we're not even up in the top numbers. So, there are a lot more dangerous activities for women than prostitution. All three of us have been trying to make sex work safer by making it possible for us to have someone on the outside know where we are at all times, maybe even a driver. Unfortunately, if you're a sex worker and a driver takes you to work and has phone contact with you from outside, that person can be charged with sex trafficking, which is a felony. That can send them to prison for a long time. We've got to change these laws so that if you're going to have someone on the outside who's making sure that you're safe, they're not penalized. We have to work on making sex work safer by decriminalizing all consenting adult commercial sex.

VV: Right. The *laws* are the biggest danger to sex workers. Another thing that contributes to sex workers being thought of as throwaway people is how TV and movie stories kill off prostitutes. It's part of the drama. There's a new documentary, *Disclosure,* about transgender portrayal in the media. In it, the transgender people say, "As a performer in the movies, I was always either dying in bed as a transgender person or already murdered." That's how it is with prostitutes. It's enough. Producers are getting rich on dead prostitutes.

CL: Wow. I think about that every night, too. I think there's a lot of good work in academia and research that examines prostitution and oppressive systems. You might compare the United States to New Zealand where sex work is decriminalized. The research shows that systems targeting the client are so much more dangerous for sex workers. There's an enormous amount of good research validating that. But you don't see it in the media. I don't think it's gotten around, although they're clear about that in academia.

When I think about the dangers for other types of sex workers, I'm also concerned. I have an informal helpline that people call, and I'm always hearing about abusive husbands who might get child custody because the wife is a stripper. I hear that so often. Then I hear about people whose families evict them because they're sex workers, trans people who can't find other options because they're stigmatized. Then, because they're more stigmatized, they're more likely to be arrested. I do hear a lot about the struggles in this criminalized situation.

RLM: Did you want to say something, Veronica?

VV: I wanted to say something on the idea of sex positivism and pleasure. There's this idea of pleasure activism, and how we learn about ourselves by exploring our sexuality. To me, that's what sex-positivism is about—exploring our sexualities as a guide to learning and accepting who we are as human beings. For instance, a lot of the people who come to my academy are adults from the world of straight men. Their feelings are confusing to them because when they cross-dress, they feel that they want to be attractive to other men, but only in their feminine modes.

But exploring that part of their sexuality is frightening to them because it might mean giving up the male privilege they've had. So when we get into this idea of exploring pleasure and sexuality, we have to look at shaking up society, people losing privileges. This is why people want to hide their sexuality. Who can reveal *everyone's* sexuality? The prostitute, the sex worker. So, we have to keep her down because they could spill the beans on everybody. That's another reason why sex workers get repressed.

RLM: You mentioned your school, and I'd like you to give it a plug. Tell us how readers can find out more information about your school, Miss Vera's Finishing School For Boys Who Want To Be Girls.

VV: Just go to the web, *missvera.com*. We haven't been doing in-person classes during COVID. I've written three books about my school, so you can find plenty of information.

RLM: Give us the name of one of the books.

VV: The most recent one is *Miss Vera's Cross Gender Fun for All*, which encourages everyone to find a cross-gender self. The motto is, "Bye-bye, binary." We're at the end of the gender binary.

RLM: Can someone attend your school on Zoom the way universities and colleges are doing now?

VV: We've started to do it on Zoom.

RLM: Say the name of the school again.

VV: Miss Vera's Finishing School For Boys Who Want To Be Girls.

RLM: Oh, it sounds delightful.

VV: I'm thinking of making it Miss Vera's Cross-Gender Academy now, because it's not just boys who want to be girls. There's more flexibility—there are girls who want to be boys and people who want to explore all avenues. I don't believe we have to stay in one gender. Women had a lot of freedom because we were put down for so long. We got to explore ourselves more than men. Men have had power but they've had to stay in emotional straightjackets. Women have been able to explore and rise economically, but they're still fighting for more.

RLM: You're doing great. You mentioned that you got a doctorate in human sexuality—you got it from the Institute for the Advanced Study of Human Sexuality in San Francisco, correct?

VV: I did.

RLM: Under Wardell Pomeroy?

VV: No, under Ted McIlvenna.

RLM: I took their Sexual Attitude Restructuring (SARS) course many years ago. It was a wonderful ten-day course on sexual attitude restructuring, which opened up my consciousness a great deal. Let's move on to the topic of pornography. I'd like to hear from the three of you: What can you share about the nature of the work for women who go into pornography? Is this a decent job? Is it a decent way to make a living? Is it dangerous? Are there problems? Can you support it?

VV: I have one funny thing to say about that. Annie Sprinkle and I went to the Second World Whores Congress in Brussels in 1986, right after I met Margo. So, all kinds of sex workers were there. We thought, being porn stars, we were at the top of the pecking order until we heard from call girls who were doing it more privately. They thought we were at the bottom of the barrel because we were so open about it. It really gave us a lesson not being on our high horses.

RLM: They looked down on you because you were exposing yourself publicly and doing what they were doing in private.

VV: Exactly.

WORK CONDITIONS AND PECKING ORDER IN THE PORN INDUSTRY

RLM: So, there's a pecking order and there's diversity of experience in porn work. What about the modern woman who's considering going into pornography as an occupation? What can you offer us about that?

NJA: Fortunately, porn is now legal to do. Back when I was on the police force, it was illegal. The cops used to go out and confiscate porn movies, which by the way, they used to show at the parties where they were using confiscated drugs. When I was arrested, my husband and I wanted to make videos on how to have good sex. But, under the law, that would have been prostitution. So, before Hal Freeman filed his lawsuit,* which ultimately overturned the prostitution laws, my husband and I filed a lawsuit with First Amendment attorney Stanley Fleischman. Unfortunately for me, by the time the California Court got around to responding, I was already back in prison. I was hoping to save myself from prison and that pandering would be overturned. But, our lawsuit was declared moot. Fortunately, Hal Freeman's lawsuit won the day and pornography was then decriminalized.

It's just a job, like prostitution. I didn't want to do it because I'm a private person. I'm not interested. I didn't want to become an actress either, even though I met a lot of movie stars and producers when I was with the LAPD. I don't want to do sexual things publicly. I like to do them with a person in private. But other people find being in pornography not any different than working on a regular movie set.

RLM: I'm trying to get a sense of the working conditions in the porn industry, because we've been led to believe that, while some working conditions were okay, some were brutal and women were coming away bleeding, particularly from anal sex. Pornographers aren't always pillars of the community or scrupulous about what they do, who they hire, and how they treat people. That's true of many occupations. So, I would say it stands to reason that that would be similar to other jobs, that some people in pornography would find conditions to be untenable.

CL: I think the legal situation makes it more likely for exploitative people to be there, putting the worker in a more vulnerable situation. Of course, there's a range. I'm not an expert, but I would like to promote my paid job. I make the best pornography. I'm a fabulous pornographer for money. Visit *pornyoga.com, orgasmicyoga.com,* and

---

*Editor's note: In 1987 the State of California prosecuted porn producer Hal Freeman, charging him with pandering and prostitution, in an attempt to shut down the porn industry. Although initially found guilty, the case made its way to the Supreme Court, which overturned the ruling, eventually resulting in the legalization of hardcore pornography in California.

eroticmassage.com. I've been working for the company that produces those sex-ed websites as an editor. It's sexual health, but the best. I'm so proud. We even have *Rights of Passion*, starring Veronica Vera, on the Web.

I see a lot of women-owned erotic media companies. It's very exciting, but not an easy way to make a living. It's very hard. My boss, Joseph Kramer, is an excellent businessman and a legend in the community. He knows so much about sex and sexual health, freedom, and expression. He's been a leader in many communities, originally focusing on gay sex and now expanding across genders and orientations. I'm fortunate to work for him. So, I want to encourage everyone to check out the brilliant, instructive material produced by contemporary pornographers.

RLM: What is the website for people to go to?

CL: We have several. This is my job for over twenty-five years. It's fabulous. Our sites include the ones I mentioned: *pornyoga.com, eroticmassage.com, orgasmicyoga.com,* and *yogaofsex.com.* I've edited most of the movies there. I also do the graphics and general IT.

RLM: Those are the ones you work for. You mentioned you have some personal websites?

CL: Oh, please, yes. I made a porn art movie starring myself with House O' Chicks. I directed *Annie Sprinkle's Herstory of Porn.* I was featured in *Sluts and Goddesses Fabulous.* I would have liked to do more. I have a lot of websites featuring my movies, especially *scarlotharlot.com.* I'd like to direct people to *sexworkermedialibrary.org,* which includes my library of sex-worker movies in conjunction with the Sex Worker Film and Arts Festival.

VV: Fabulous library.

CL: Some of my sites are there. But, you can also find *Collateral Damage* and the trafficking material that I've been working on for ten years. I'm most proud of that project.

NJA: If people want to know where I get the statistics, they can go to my website, *policeprostitutionandpolitics.com*. Everything has a link to the original source—unlike the abolitionist websites, which completely ignore where they got it. They just make statements without a basis for what they say.

ONLYFANS, GERIATRIC SEX WORK, AND SPECIALIZING AS A DOMINATRIX

RLM: I was reading last night about one woman who made three million dollars her first year on OnlyFans. On OnlyFans people sell pictures of themselves, not doing sex acts necessarily, but sex talk while wearing lingerie. They're communicating directly with men who sign up by the month. It's a combination of chat and Instagram. The actresses get subscribers, and while never leaving their homes, they make big money just by showing themselves. Carol, have you heard about OnlyFans?

CL: Sure. I'm just a spectator in that phenomenon. I know that's how people are making money. But, I don't have the details. I want to know, so go have somebody on your show for that!*

RLM: All of us here, to put it diplomatically, are getting on in years. What can you tell us about geriatric sex work? Is there work for older women in the sex trade? I see you shaking your head, Norma Jean.

NJA: I'll be seventy this year. If I wanted to, I could probably do sex work again. But, I don't have the energy or time because I take care of my husband. But there *are* women out there. I had a friend up in Canada who was seventy-five and still seeing clients. So it's possible, because men aren't necessarily seeking a young beautiful, svelte body but someone who's mature and has knowledge of human sexuality and knows how to give pleasure. Yes, it's absolutely possible for women in their seventies to continue to do sex work. And why not?

---

*Editor's note: At the time of this writing, OnlyFans is an $18 billion company used by porn stars, celebrities, and everyday people alike to share private content for subscribers.

RLM: One could call sex workers "sexual athletes," and athletic careers most often end in one's twenties or thirties. But you're saying sex work doesn't necessarily end in your twenties and thirties.

NJA: I didn't start sex work *until* I was in my thirties. I can't say how long, but I worked until my forties. So you don't have to give up your career in sex work because you get older.

VV: Especially if you're a dominatrix. An older dominatrix? No problem.

RLM: Tell us about the specialty of being a dominatrix, Veronica.

VV: In domination, it's sex as theater. Another powerful element is giving people permission to have the kind of sex they want. Those are the two things that make domination attractive. When I started to explore sex, I wanted to explore BDSM, because to me, it was the perfect segue from Catholicism and all of that religious repression. I think that's part of its power; it fits in with everything that we learned earlier.

So BDSM goes back to childhood. It's very powerful, and you can be creative with it. There are some creative, dominant people. There are also people who will just take a script from someone and follow along with whatever the person paying wants. So, like everything else, it can run the gamut.

RLM: Remind us what BDSM stands for?

VV: *BDSM* is "bondage, discipline, and sadomasochism." Usually, we think of sadomasochism as corporal punishment or some kind of deprivation.

RLM: If somebody is reading this and they say, "Well, that sounds interesting. I'd like to give it a try," are they going to get hurt?

VV: There are safe rules. There's a whole etiquette involved. You can google etiquette for S&M play. The Center for Sex and Culture runs great events on this. Carol was talking about how there are different sex shops run by women—not so much during COVID—where they'll have an expert in who gives her expertise on how to be dominant. Usually, one of the big things before you start S&M play is to define a safe word. So, if it goes too far, you know it's time to stop when the partner says, "yellow" for example. But, there's an etiquette, with rules to follow to maintain safety, just like with other aspects of life.*

RLM: So, tell us about sex work in the COVID era. What are sex workers doing? What's happening to business?

NJA: A lot of sex workers are doing e-sex where they do it, just like we're talking on Zoom—only they perform sexual activity on themselves and have sex talk. A lot have found that this is an easier way to work than having to get dressed and go somewhere.

RLM: So, they're doing virtual sex?

NJA: Virtual sex, electronic sex, whatever you want to call it. All sex takes place in the mind. The rest of your body follows along, but if your mind isn't there, it's not going to happen. So, if you can get to somebody's mind—visually, on camera, or by words, by typing—that's going to get somebody aroused. That's just as good—sometimes better—than physical, in-person sex because you don't have to travel anywhere and the client doesn't have to get dressed and be on time. For a lot of sex workers, doing e-sex is the way to go.

RLM: I'm trying to picture sex workers doing it *in vivo*†—with masks versus without masks—because all the other occupational groups where I worked and lived, during the pandemic, were trying to figure out some way to operate. The restaurants were trying to do outdoor offerings, the beauty parlors moved outdoors. I don't think many of the sex workers were doing outdoor sex work but I would guess that it's been damaging to the occupation just as it has been to many other enterprises.

---

*Editor's note: The subject of consent (part three of this book) is historically most consciously addressed by practitioners of BDSM (bondage and sadomasochism) where the participants enjoy the illusion of danger and power play, while creating strict protective boundaries and measures.

†In the body.

NJA: Oh, sure, for a lot of the sex workers that don't have access to the internet and computers. It's decimated their businesses.

CL: Actually, one of the exciting things that I've seen is how sex workers have risen to address community needs and formed mutual-aid organizations and projects. I've never seen this energy from the sex-work community, and it feels like a model for other communities. It's developed into a new movement. I'm also witnessing people who are more vulnerable as BIPOC or people of color, trans people. We're a role model for solutions.

MALE SEX WORKERS

RLM: We've talked almost exclusively about female sex workers. What can the three of you share with us about male sex workers? Very little is known by the public about male sex workers. Can you shed some light on that particular group?

NJA: I can't speak for male sex workers, but I certainly know enough of them. I know that the pandemic decimated their work, too. But, there's as much interest in male and trans sex workers as in females. They just don't get the same attention. In fact, the abolitionists don't care about male sex workers.

All they care about is us poor exploited women. But, I have a lot of male friends who were sex workers, and their businesses were just fine. We have some long-term activists, in Canada, the United States, and around the world. These guys have been doing sex work as long as I've been around.

RLM: Men who sell themselves to give pleasure to women for a living?

NJA: To men, usually.

RLM: Men who sell themselves to give pleasure to other men are more common?

NJA: Yes. Women are just not likely to want to have to pay for sex. Yes, there are women who do, but let's face it: a woman can go out, find any guy, and get laid. She doesn't have to pay. Whereas, guys have a harder time because of the whole male-female interaction. They don't want to be deemed as a sexual predator. If these producers in Hollywood would just pay for sex, they wouldn't all be in trouble.

VV: That's right.

RLM: That's absolutely right. You're correct that any woman can go out anytime and—if she wants to—pick somebody up and get laid. But that's not the same as hiring a professional for sex. When you hire a professional, you're going to get a professional who's going to do you in an extra pleasurable way in order to ask for a fee.

VV: Also, it's easier to find a man to pay, because it's easier for a man to find a woman sex worker. It's not so easy for a woman to find a male sex worker. Women have been brought up to get the money from men, not to give them money.

RLM: Yes, that is what's taught in the culture.

CL: I remember, when I was in Taiwan, I was surprised that people were explaining how they had a whole scene of male sex workers for women. Everybody knew about it and I thought it was interesting. We don't know about it around the world. I think this is another place where academia is failing us. Why don't we know about the cultures where that happens, and the differences? It's crazy. I think we need so much work. We need the Institute of Sex Work studies; we need graduate programs focused on sex, because with our questions here, we can only offer conjecture based on stereotypes. We need more serious research. It's crazy the world has not brought this forth.

VV: About such an important subject.

NJA: Very true.

RLM: I was teaching at the University of Michigan in the late 1960s when I moved to California. I took a sabbatical to test out the coastal environment and opened a clinic on Sacramento Street near the Children's Hospital. I went to a social event, met a woman named

Margo St. James, and we became close friends. For a short period of time, she worked for my clinic. She said it was the first straight job she'd ever had. It was fun having her there because you know what Margo was like. She usually got to the office a bit before me in the morning. One day, I walked into the office and Margo was sitting at her desk typing, totally naked. She spent the entire day sitting there totally naked. Patients came and went, talking to her. It was fascinating, because nobody ever mentioned a thing. Nobody ever said, "Doctor, do you know your secretary is sitting there totally naked?" It was like the emperor's clothes.

I'd like each of you, as a tribute to her, to tell a Margo story of appreciation for who she was, because we know that she has left us.

CL: My Margo story is so long because I'd heard about her before I knew her. It was in the mid-seventies, and my mom was a member of the National Organization for Women. She invited Margo St. James to speak to all the housewives on Long Island. Rather than one story, I can just say: Margo spoke in political haikus. I joined COYOTE when I moved to San Francisco. At the beginning of COYOTE, of course, Margo was the leader. She was a fascinating presence, and she always got to the point of things. I found her completely intriguing. She understood that, when it comes to movements, we need to prioritize those who are most impacted. She taught that, along with Priscilla Alexander and many others.

NJA: I met Margo when I'd been arrested and my lawyer, who knew her well, contacted her for me. We got on the phone, and I said, "Oh my god, there's a prostitutes' rights movement?!" It was amazing. When I got arrested, we had a fundraiser. I went twice, as a matter of fact. She and another sex worker came down, and we had a fundraiser at the Masters Club in Los Angeles, which is for actors. Margo was just phenomenal. But, when I first got involved with COYOTE in San Francisco, my main concern was that they were going to think I was working undercover, that I was still working for the police. I was terrified of what they were going to think. Actually, it turned out that they didn't think that at all, and I'm so glad.

VV: I'm a New Yorker, so I didn't spend much time with Margo, but I met her. I had heard about COYOTE and the Hookers Balls that 20,000 people attended at the high points because I was writing for sex magazines and interviewing people in Times Square. One day, I heard that Margo was going to give a talk at Judson Memorial Church. So I wanted to meet this person. It was Margo and Gayle Pheterson from Europe, addressing about 150 to 200 women activists. There were groups. Wages for Housework was one group that I remember. So Margo, Gayle, Dolores French, and Gloria Lockett were all there to talk about the Second World Whores Congress* and to encourage people to visit. I was all fired up. I was doing some work for *Penthouse Forum,* so I pitched my editor to send me and Annie Sprinkle to the conference. This was an amazing experience. We could go there as delegates as well as journalists. We were the only people who could do both. There were 150, maybe 160 different women from different countries, and also some male prostitutes. In the European Parliament, we were all wearing headphones. We had translators explaining what the word *blowjob* meant in different languages. This was mind boggling to me.

When I came back, we had PONY in New York, but it inspired me to help reorganize PONY with other people.† So Margo had a huge influence on my life, even though I didn't get to see her that much because she was on the West Coast. Actually, I've gone back and I'm now a member of Judson, a social justice place. They're into the arts. It's not a big God trip. I've organized the December 17th vigils, which honor sex workers who've died from violence, at Judson. The Judson community is very supportive of sex workers' rights.

RLM: You also mentioned another dear friend of mine who I've interviewed, Annie Sprinkle. So I want to give a shout-out to her. She didn't make it today, but she'll be with us again. She's been promoting her new interest in ecosexuality.

---

*Editor's note: The Second World Whores' Congress was organized by the International Committee for Prostitutes Rights (ICPR), a global network of sex workers headed by Margo St. James and Gail Pheterson.
†Prostitutes of New York.

VV: Exactly. *Assuming the Ecosexual Position: The Earth as Lover,* Annie and Beth Stephen's new book.

RLM: We're coming to the end of our interview. This is the time, if you have any final words—or a final plug—that you want to get in.

NJA: I just want to say I'm so glad you invited us old whores on your show. Because, I've met some amazing people—men and women—and, as we get older, people forget about us. But there's nothing like a group of old whores. We have so much history and camaraderie, so many interesting stories to tell about our lives. It has been amazing to be part of it.

RLM: One of the most important things for me about this interview, that's going to come across clearly is the abundance warmth, and humor, that the three of you have brought to our readers. You have a profession—sex work—that the public is uncertain about, doesn't know about, and is afraid of, among many other views. Some people may be sex work abolitionists, some sex positive, but nobody with an open consciousness can miss the warmth that you three have brought to the discussion. You've represented your occupation beautifully, with human feelings, and that is so important to all of us. I wish the readers could see the beautiful expressions on your faces. You're three beautiful women.

NJA: You know what the word *whore* originally meant?—*Beloved one.* I have to say, I love my fellow beloved ones.

VV: Yes.

RLM: Beautiful place to end. Thank you.

NJA: Thank you, Richard.

VV: This has been a pleasure, and we like pleasure.

13

Veronica Monet

Confessions of an American Escort

Veronica Monet is an American author and activist for sex-worker rights. Her early activism focused on debunking stereotypes about sex workers and advocating for the decriminalization of all sex work. Today we are discussing Veronica's book, *Sex Secrets of Escorts,* talks about sexuality in America and the world.

Dr. Richard L. Miller (RLM): Our guest today is Veronica Monet. Veronica graduated with honors from Oregon State University, and she has training in Tantra, human sexuality, and ancient sacred prostitution. She's accumulated more than a decade's experience with the practical and political aspects of sex work, having worked as an erotic model, a porn actress, a prostitute, an escort, and a courtesan.

Her political activism has included memberships with Bay Area Bisexual Network, COYOTE (Call Off Your Old Tired Ethics), and the San Francisco and Sex Worker Outreach Project. Welcome, Veronica.

Veronica Monet (VM): It's wonderful to be here, Richard. Thank you.

PROSTITUTE, ESCORT, COURTESAN— WHAT'S THE DIFFERENCE?

RLM: In the introduction, I said you've worked as a prostitute, an escort, and a courtesan. What is the difference amongst those three?

VM: Mostly, we say *sex worker*. Some people do have an issue with that. I wanted to call out the different ways there are to work in the sex industry, because some of them are extolled in certain circles and some vilified. As a political movement, it's all of one fabric.

When I first started working, I was a college graduate. I'd been clean and sober for many years, but I was working by the hour. I had transferred from a secretarial job into prostitution. I called my level of work *escorting,* if you want to call it a "level." This is the problem with anything in a capitalist society—not that I'm against capitalism, but everything is hierarchical. And the sex industry is especially so, because there's so much shame and fear around law enforcement, people's taboos, and stigmas.

So, when I say *prostitute,* I want to identify with those people. If you look up the word *escort* in the dictionary, it means "to go somewhere with someone." So, if you're doing what they call in-calls, where somebody comes to your place, you're not *escorting* them anywhere. I started with in-calls. Then I started doing out-calls, or going to somebody's home, but still not going anywhere with them. Eventually, I started escorting people to dinner, theater, the symphony, and museums.

Working as a courtesan is a different level. That's where my career in the sex industry took me. As a courtesan, you're more of a muse or confidante. It's borderline *mistress,* but not quite. I had a very select group of clients. As a courtesan, I would go on a three-day trip with one gentleman. I might fly out to New York, Los Angeles, or Seattle and spend a week with said gentlemen as his guest. That's different than when sex workers are touring. They go into a city and let everybody on their social media know they're in that city so they can make an appointment and come to their hotel.

Here, you're the guest of one gentleman who prizes you as his closest confidante, and he tells you things he doesn't tell anybody else. You develop a very personal relationship where you sometimes help him make some of his life and professional decisions.

RLM: So an escort, a prostitute, and a courtesan spend different amounts of time with their clients. Is that correct?

VM: If we think about it in terms of time, we're dumbing down this whole process. I want you to think about it more on the level of interaction: When I started working as what I would term a *prostitute,* I was thinking about the hours. I'd spend an hour with this person, and I'd charge by the hour. When you get to being a courtesan, you're charging by the day and not clocking in as in a factory. It's about spending *time* with this person. They give me money, we go to these places, and it's not focused on the hours.

It's even a matter of what sex acts occur. I can think of one instance in particular, where I traveled up to Seattle to spend a week with someone and there was no sex, but it was still sexual. There's flirtation, warmth—a sexual vibe—but it doesn't always lead to sex. If you're working at the level of a prostitute, it could happen that there wouldn't be any sex, but it's rare. The focus is on sex acts and time.

Here's an example I've often used: the difference between a barber and a hairstylist. Maybe you go in and you tell the barber, "This is what I want, and please take a little off the edges." But then, when you go see one of these fancy hair stylists that charge hundreds and hundreds of dollars like I used to, they don't want you to tell them what to do. They tell you what kind of a hairstyle you're going to get.

RLM: I can relate to what you're saying in my profession, because when I see a patient for an hour, I charge by the hour. And, even if I see a patient for three or four hours, I'm still charging by the hour. But if I take a couple for a residential weekend, there's a fee by the day or weekend, and it's a different kind of arrangement.

VM: Exactly.

RLM: It sounds similar. When people come for treatment with me in groups, for a whole week, they're getting charged for the week, not by the hour. That I understand.

THE PATH FROM GRADUATION
TO SEX WORK

RLM: Evidently, there was a transition in your life. You graduated with honors from Oregon State and then went on to do other work. Sometime after that, you went into sex work. What led to that transition?

Here's what I mean by "what led to it?" When I interviewed Norma Jean Almodovar, the current president of COYOTE, she told me that she had been working as a policewoman in Los Angeles. When she was in the locker room, the other cops were aggressively demanding blowjobs from her regularly. So she said to herself, "If they're pressuring me to do this, I'm going to start charging for it." That was her entrance into the world of sex work. What was your entrance? How did that transition come about?

VM: My experience was similar. I worked in corporate America for seven years. I graduated from college and went straight into an office-manager position. Then I made a lateral move to another company, where I became a department manager. After that, I worked as a marketing representative for a radio station in Santa Cruz.

In every one of those jobs, I experienced two forms of gender bias that I found intolerable. One of them was that my positions were denigrated. In the first job, they fired my boss, and for an entire month, they routed all his phone calls and put all his paperwork on my desk. They could have put me in his office, but God forbid I sit in the royal chair.

They had all of his technicians come to my desk to be dispatched. The only thing they wouldn't let me do was to sign their paychecks. Everything else fell on my shoulders for a month. I brought department revenue up that month, and as a reward, I got to train my next boss.

Granted, this was a few years back, so I'm hoping things have changed, but when I talk to young women today, many things are still the same. When I went to work for that radio station, my sales manager said to me, "Veronica, you take this account. He likes a good-looking pair of legs." Mind you, I was getting a 10 percent commission on radio sales. I thought he was literally pimping me out. At that time, way before the #MeToo movement and before HR got savvy to sexual harassment on the job, I had to take it. If you want to work, pay your rent, and eat, you deal with what's happening in the workplace.

I went out to see that client. I didn't flirt with him; I didn't go out to dinner with him; I just went and tried to sell him spots on our radio station. Sure enough, he propositioned me. After making repeated attempts to get him to sign with us, he told me, "The only reason I've been seeing you is that I wanted to date you." At that point, I thought, "If this is how I'm seen, then I'm going to make money doing it, and I'm going to cut out the middle man."

It was sexual harassment. I had briefly entertained the idea of possibly going into acting. I thought I would get out of the office and do something in movies. But acting didn't appeal to me as much as producing and writing films. So, I'm down in Hollywood, out on a date with this big-time producer that a friend of mine had arranged. No names here. I'm not even going to tell you which production house it was—that's one thing I do; I know how to keep people's secrets. I thought we were going to talk shop, but at the end of the evening, the guy tried to kiss me. I pulled away. He looked at me and said, "I thought you wanted to be an actress."

I said, "Actually, I don't. I want to be a writer." And I walked out.

People often assume that sex workers have no boundaries. In my case, it was the exact opposite. I had better boundaries than most and decided to make an expeditious decision about my income and working conditions.

THE PRACTICAL SIDE OF LEARNING TO BE A PROSTITUTE

RLM: Tell us about the first time you charged money for a sexual act.

VM: I started working with my girlfriend. I'm bisexual, and I was dating a woman who was working as an escort. She was married and she had three kids. She was beautiful. She had been the centerfold in men's magazines, and I had no idea I would decide to go into her profession.

Initially, with my feminist ideology, I felt sorry for her. I thought it was sad that this woman was allowing all these men to denigrate her. I'd been hanging out in feminist circles for so long. I considered myself a feminist throughout my entire sex-work career, but it changed. My brand of feminism changed, and one of the reasons was that this woman was so damn happy. She didn't do any drugs. I've never even seen her finish one glass of wine. She's a little health nut. She worked out every day and took care of herself. So I thought, *Isn't happiness one of the things we want out of life? She's obviously found something that works for her.*

Initially, I asked her, "Could you teach me how to do what you're doing?" I want to highlight that, at this point, I'm a college graduate. I have seven years in corporate America—training as a manager, training in sales—and I'm asking this prostitute to teach me what she does. Most people would say, "What's to learn?" As it turns out, there was a lot to learn.

This woman was a successful entrepreneur. First, she said, "No, I won't teach you because I don't want the responsibility."

Then I said, "I'll go do it on my own."

She knew that would have been a disaster, so she changed her mind.

The first thing she did was trot me down to City Hall to get my tax ID so that I would start paying quarterly taxes. Most people think sex workers are outlaws. She wanted to adhere to the law as much as possible while disobeying this one misdemeanor.

We started doing doubles. That's two girls and a guy, in our case. I suppose it could be two male sex workers and a girl, but that's rare. In all honesty, male clients drive the sex industry. I've had female clients; I've had trans clients; but, by and large, male-identified people drive the industry.

Sometimes, they're looking for two girls, and that's what we did at first. We would put on girl-girl shows and make love with each other in front of the client. It was a lot of fun. Understand: I was already making love with her. To do it in front of somebody and get paid for it wasn't a big stretch.

RLM: When this was going on, was she at times literally giving you directions? I don't mean in terms of you two making love with each other, but directions as to when to bring the man into sexual play or how to act towards the man?

VM: I followed her lead. It's not an overt thing. Here's the thing about sex work: I want to say that it's quite a performance, but people will use that to say, "Somehow or another, it's fake." That's not true. Think about it—when you go to see a play, do you call that fake? No. You say, "Wow, what a grand performance. I felt transfixed or transported. All these emotions came up. It was an amazing experience. I can't wait for you to go see it so you can understand what I mean." That's what I mean when I say "performance."

It's a beautiful flow. You're bringing an energetic gift to the client. When you're doing that, you certainly don't want to be stilted, artificial, cold, or detached. You want to be fully present and engaged in order to bring in sensuality, beautiful emotions, and content. It's still a performance because your eye is on the audience, and the audience is the client. You want to make sure that they have a peak sexual experience.

RLM: Yes. At the same time, if you're working by the hour, you still have a little bit of your consciousness on the clock, which also has an effect.

VM: How is that different than a stage performance? They know exactly where they're going to step on stage because somebody has marked it off with tape. They know exactly when the act ends, and the play has to end on time.

THE FIRST TIME SOLO WITH A CLIENT

RLM: Take us to the time when you were alone with your first client. That must have been a big experience. You no longer have your friend with you for safety, and you're now going into the hotel room or the house of a complete stranger, or you invite the stranger to your place for an in-call.

VM: That's how most people would envision it, but that's not how it was. My girlfriend loved me and cared about me. So the first time I saw a client by myself, she had already screened this person. She knew them, and she could tell me what they liked, their history, personality, and what they did for a living. So I didn't see a stranger; I went to see a friend of my girlfriend.

The experience was still shocking though. I was taking my assumptions from my white-collar jobs, where somebody handed me a job description and told me my duties. So I assumed male clients would be telling me what to do, and that's not what happened. Now, I'm not saying the experience will be the same for every sex worker, or that all clients are the same. But with the kind of clients my girlfriend saw, they were expecting me to be the professional, tell them what was going to happen, and create the experience. That was unnerving for me because I didn't know what I was doing, and I didn't have the background that I currently have in sex. I'd *had* sex, but the professional sex worker has got so much expertise, knowledge, and experience. I lacked those aspects initially and was dumbfounded about making a session go.

I quickly educated myself. I took classes in Tantra and sacred prostitution because I needed to figure out what defines my profession. I had no idea the men were going to basically lay there and expect me to do whatever it was and tell them what to do. That was a shock, but a welcome shock. I thought, *Oh my God, somebody wants me to be in charge.*

RLM: So you did what almost all of us do when going into a new job. You got mentoring and you took classes. Is that correct?

VM: Absolutely. For the first nine months in the sex industry, I technically worked for my girlfriend. It's a warm, loving relationship, and I was rather content working with her. Basically, this woman taught me how to screen a call to tell if this was a desirable or undesirable client, and also how to tell if law enforcement was calling you. She taught me the difference between an actual client and somebody pretending to be one. She taught me to pay your taxes, and how to apply a condom in an unobtrusive and sensual way.

MISREPRESENTED STATS ABOUT VIOLENCE IN SEX WORK

RLM: It seems to me that a person going into this business for the first time, even after having a mentor as you did, must encounter a certain fear when entering that hotel room and taking off your clothing. Am I incorrect? You're an educated woman, and you know as well as I that between 30 to 75 percent of sex workers have been raped at some point. We do know that a certain percentage of sex workers—much more than the average woman, except for policemen's wives—have been hit by people that they didn't vet well enough. How did you deal with that? Or are you fearless?

VM: Let's talk about those statistics for a minute. As you know, I'm a sex-worker rights activist. So I'm familiar with those statistics, and I know where the data comes from. A lot of that data is mined from street prostitutes. If you're working on the streets, it doesn't matter if you're selling drugs, sex, or stolen radios, your risk of violence is increased dramatically.

The parts of cities where they allow street prostitution and occasionally come through to take people to jail are the most dangerous. The type of people who go to see prostitutes in those parts of most cities is more likely to be dangerous. Somebody who works in the streets is exposed to those elements.

But an independent escort—who is screening her calls, has the freedom to say yes or no, works for herself, isn't living hand to mouth, *and* isn't doing survival sex—is not going to conform to those statistics. Her rate of violence or her exposure to violence is far reduced. I have a background in domestic violence. I was trained as a domestic violence counselor when I was going to college, and I work with clients who suffer from domestic violence today.

The incidence of violence is higher in intimate relationships. What fires me up more than anything is the way we demonize people who are marginalized in society as being vectors of disease, being the place where violence occurs because we don't want to look at the violence in our own homes. College was far more dangerous to me, and nobody has ever asked me, "Weren't you scared to go to college?" They have a mythology about being frightened of sex work. I found sex work to be far safer.

RLM: Safer than going to college?

VM: I did. The numbers bore that out. During my college days, I was raped twice. As an escort, I worked for seventeen years, and I had the misfortune towards the end of my career of booking a serial rapist as a client. That was the least traumatic rape I ever experienced. College was far more traumatic. I was raped by a coworker when I was working in telecommunications. That was probably the scariest encounter I ever had. So I'm a rape survivor, and any rape in any venue is a serious matter. I don't want to downplay the serial rapist who preys on sex workers because I encountered it towards the end of my career. But we know we've got a high incidence of rape on college campuses, and yet people would rather look at sex trafficking.

They've inflated statistics about the violence because they look at street prostitution and not independent escorts. A lot of them are going to work for years and never encounter a rapist. As far as being hit by a client, you're far more likely to be hit by your boyfriend or husband. Still, I was afraid at first, thinking, *What am I getting into here?* I'm part of the culture, and I believed those statistics. These people are probably right in saying it's a dangerous profession. But I felt safer and more in control of my life in the sex industry than as a young girl in college or working in corporate environments where I was sexualized and sexually harassed and felt powerless. As a sex worker, if I didn't like somebody, I walked away or hung up on them.

WHY CONDOMS ARE STILL THE BEST DEFENSE AGAINST DISEASE

RLM: Is the sex worker's first line of defense against disease condoms?

VM: Absolutely, and any professional worth their salt knows how to use a condom like nobody's business. If you look at the box of condoms, it'll tell you there's a failure rate of about 5 percent. So it's not considered the most effective form of birth control, but it is considered your best defense against disease. If it's got that failure rate for birth control, you have to think it's probably the same for protection from disease. But the people who put that statistic on their box are measuring use with amateurs. Now imagine that you use a condom multiple times a day; you have got to get pretty good at it. That means you're going to have a far-reduced failure rate. So yes, you use latex barriers of all sorts, including finger cots, condoms, latex gloves, and something called a dental dam, which is used during cunnilingus.

RLM: You seemed to have a certain advantage in that you went into sex work when you were about thirty years old. That's different than a girl going into sex work at twenty because she's a lot less mature. What recommendations do you have today for a woman who wants to go into sex work?

VM: If I were to give advice to anybody that wants to go into sex work, then the government could, unfortunately, consider conspiracy charges, saying that I'm engaging in sex trafficking. So I don't advise anybody at all ever. But I believe nobody should go into the sex industry until they are college-educated and capable of making money some other way. That's not always possible. Some people go into it because they feel they have to. In all the child sex-trafficking statistics, they particularly mention underage runaways, who probably ran away from an abusive parent who might have been sexually abusing them. They wind up on the streets and can't get a job because they don't have a job record, a résumé, any education, or experience. Some don't even have IDs—perhaps because they're immigrants.

Those people have to engage in survival sex to survive. We must find ways to give them alternatives so that nobody ever *has* to do sex work. And if somebody *chooses* to do it, please take self-defense. You'll never need it probably, but you'll carry yourself with confidence, and that's important. One of the statistics that I like to point people towards is that somebody who lacks confidence is more likely to be a rape victim. They did a study where they asked convicted rapists, "Which of these women would you most likely pick on?" Surprisingly, it wasn't the girl dressed in scanty clothes who's walking down the street like, "Don't you dare mess with me." It was the girl that had her shoulders humped over and was shuffling her feet down the street. You want to have lots of confidence, resources, and options. I walked into this with tremendous privilege. I was college-educated, clean and sober, and knew I could get another job in any field I wanted, any day I wanted to.

MALE CULTURE'S INFLUENCE ON SEXUAL RELATIONSHIPS

RLM: That jibes with other information on pickpockets; they pick people who look like victims. Let's talk about your book *Sex Secrets of Escorts*. I appreciate your listing ten different things people can do to enhance their sexual activity; but let's begin with some of your thoughts on male culture and what it brings to the sex-work relationship.

VM: Of course. I wrote my book about seventeen years ago, and I want to say the culture continues to evolve. We have increasingly fluid definitions of gender. But let's talk about dominant paradigms around cis-gender males. In general, there's a lot of focus on performance in males that always astounded me. Somebody paid *me* for sex and still worried about *their* performance, whatever that means to that particular human being. Oftentimes it means they've got to maintain an erection and make sure they don't come too quickly.

It's okay to have those benchmarks in one's sexuality, I suppose.

But unfortunately, sex is not a cerebral event. It's an energetic flow, and people are oftentimes focused on doing this or that particular sex act, as opposed to, "What kind of energy am I bringing to this? How am I showing up for this *energetically?*" As an escort and courtesan, my focus was on getting men energetically embodied, helping them to connect with their breath, bringing their chakras alive, and helping them relate to their chakras and pressure points.

Unfortunately, male sexuality is very penile-centric, and people will complain that the man is selfish. I would counter that and say that men don't enjoy sex as much as they could because they're so focused on their performance and their penis.

RLM: When you read the literature on male sexual activity, one issue constantly discussed over decades is that the average man orgasms and ejaculates in a few minutes. Relatively rapid male orgasming has led to problems because men become aware of orgasming quickly and stop while leaving the women feeling incomplete or hanging. We know that after males have their ejaculation, like all the other animals, they are much less interested in the female. What have you found in your personal discovery concerning that event?

VM: It takes some reeducating because the dominant culture has made penis-vagina sex the main event. You said he ejaculates, and the woman is left hanging. Why is she left hanging? You still have a tongue. You still have fingers. You maybe have some sex toys. She shouldn't be left hanging. If you think that without an erect penis, there can be no sex, then I have no idea what the lesbians are doing. Because it's sex. Sex happens without a penis. So if you think that the penis is the center of sex, then, of course, you're going to think everything is over once it's not erect. That lacks imagination.

RLM: If you look at the other animals in the barn, when the male orgasms and ejaculates, he immediately pulls away and disappears. If we apply that model to male behavior, the male withdrawing is more than a matter of the male maintaining an erection, as you're pointing out. Yes, the male is able to show affection, perform cunnilingus and pleasure the female. However, if he is finished psychologically after the orgasm, there's no motivation to continue. I'm wondering if a man hires a woman for an hour and he comes after two and a half minutes, what do you do with the other fifty-five minutes?

VM: Lots—believe me, Richard.

RLM: Well, I do believe you. I believe you're the expert.

VM: But it's not only a matter of what I do but of what *he* does. I can remember one guy ejaculating when I opened the door. He didn't say, "Thank you, ma'am, here's your money," and walk away. Of course, he was embarrassed but still interested. This idea that a man loses interest after ejaculating is not my experience.

RLM: It's important to know that stopping after orgasm is not universal.

VM: Furthermore, since you brought-in animals, our closest genetic cousin is the bonobo. It looks like a chimpanzee, but it's vastly different. They're incredibly sexy. They're having all kinds of sex all the time, and they don't rely on an erect penis for their sexual gratification. Bonobos engage in cunnilingus. They engage in fellatio and do something we refer to as *frottage,* where the females rub their clitorises together. The animal kingdom knows all kinds of sex— particularly this primate, our closest cousin. I feel sorry for men who lose interest in sex because they ejaculated, but it's not biologically mandated. It's not even my experience, having seen hundreds of men. So I don't know about that particular story as a sex expert; I'm going to say I don't believe it.

MEN SHOULDN'T HIDE THEIR VULNERABILITY

RLM: Talk to us about the issue of vulnerability in a sexual relationship.

VM: You have to understand I was dating a woman. I'm a feminist, and I was identified with what we would call the feminists who aren't sex-positive. It's, "Down on men!" That's how I came into the sex industry. And that quickly changed, because of how vulnerable, sweet, and emotional I experienced my clients being. Am I saying all sex worker clients are that way? No, I'm just telling you all of mine were. Sometimes they would cry in my arms after they had an orgasm. I was touched and moved by this, and I was thinking, *Wow, men are far more vulnerable and sensitive than I ever thought.*

I had had sex with men before I went into the sex industry. You'd think I would've been exposed to this, but I discovered as a sex worker that the men who paid me for sex were far more honest and vulnerable. They dropped the facade. In college, the guys I dated were always trying to be macho and prove whatever they were trying to prove. As a sex worker, I got to see this human, vulnerable side of men. As a sex worker, I *fell in love* with men.

RLM: You're saying there's more room for men to be vulnerable in all relationships.

VM: I can't say every woman will respond the way I did, but when men are vulnerable, I just melt. I've been a relationship coach for seventeen years, and I encounter two things with the married couples I work with—I'm talking about people that have been together for ten or twenty years: Often, the cisgender women are focused on how they look and don't seem to know much about initiating sex through foreplay. I teach that in my book because I wanted women to start initiating and expressing their desire overtly. I can't tell you how many men tell me their wife or girlfriend kind of hints that they're interested. Maybe they put on a sexy outfit. What's wrong with them saying, "I would love to make love with you"? Seduce the man with your words and actions. Don't just try to be the flower attracting the honeybee.

I also see that men are often so focused on maintaining the power dynamic in the relationship. Maybe they consider themselves the provider, the breadwinner, and the protector—even if both partners have jobs. They like to think of themselves as egalitarian; they share all decisions and power. I still see this power dynamic come into play where masculinity becomes a performance. If you're performing masculinity in your relationship—and a lot of men do—then you're going to be less vulnerable. That creates a distance, especially during the sex act.

People often revert to their prescribed gender roles, which is sad. Mix it up. There's a term in the BDSM community—we call it *switching,* which means you could take either a submissive *or* a dominant role. If you switch, you know how to inhabit both places. I think it would do a lot of heterosexual, cisgender couples good if they could learn how to switch back and forth between leading and following. The sex becomes a beautiful dance. When you mix it up, everybody gets to express their masculine and feminine side—to be vulnerable and receptive, hungry, and have that animalistic passion rise to the surface.

GET CLEAN, BE ATTENTIVE, BE INTERESTING

RLM: You give ten tips in your book, and I'd like to discuss as many of them as possible, starting with your number one tip, which I think is spectacular: *get clean.*

VM: That came out of working with men who sometimes didn't seem to know how to clean themselves down there.

RLM: I've interviewed many people in your business, and one of the biggest complaints I've heard is, "Oh my God, this guy smelled like a garbage can; his breath was like old tomatoes. He doesn't seem like he's washed his penis in ten years. I couldn't stand it." So I loved it when I read that you start with "Get clean."

VM: Let me say this. If you have skid marks in your underwear, stop it. Learn how to clean yourself back there because if you want her to go down on you, she doesn't want it to smell like she's kissing the toilet.

RLM: You're not allowed to give advice to sex workers because of a concern over being indicted for conspiracy to illegal acts. But I can advise because I'm a doctor of clinical psychology, and I'm saying if you're a sex worker reading this, you have a right to demand that a client take a shower before engaging physically.

VM: I'm hoping wives and girlfriends also have the right to say that to their husband or boyfriend, "You have a stinky butt—do something about it."

RLM: Exactly, let's move on to number two, "Be attentive." You start by saying that everyone wants to feel special.

VM: I was married most of the time I was working as an escort.

RLM: Did you have children with him?

VM: He came with children. I had a parenting journey with them, from toddler to teen. It was beautiful, and I loved them. One time, I wanted to hire a prostitute for us because we were swingers. So we went to see this prostitute, and she just laid there. I thought, *What are you doing? I just paid you. You're lying there like you're God's gift to the world.* This is the script for a lot of women. They're given this gender script. I don't fault them, but they're trying to play the good girl—or maybe the diva, I don't know. But women must break free of just lying there and *allowing* access to their bodies.

Get up and do something; be engaged; initiate; be creative. You've got to have some techniques. And if you don't, study and learn. Most men are attentive and eager to please, even when they're paying for sex. They want to know what the woman wants and how to make her feel better. I'm sure there are selfish guys out there, but I wasn't working with them.

RLM: Number three, "Be interesting." Talk to us about a woman or a man being interesting.

VM: Okay. Women listen to men, but they don't know how to tell their own stories or be dynamic players in their own movies. To break free of that and have something intelligent to share, that's sexual foreplay. As a courtesan, I would go out to dinner with a gentleman, and we would talk for five hours before we went back to his hotel room. An intellectual conversation is a fabulous form of foreplay.

INFORM YOUR CHARACTER
AND YOUR SEXUALITY

RLM: "Be informed," is your next tip. How does that relate to sexuality?

VM: If you have something interesting to say, you're a more intriguing person. I have a theory about infidelity, and it does not conform to Esther Perel's idea that "We all want variety." I think people start to take each other for granted, and they think they know everything there is to know about their partners, so they stop asking questions. So the first thing you should be informed about is this year's version of your partner. Ask them—don't assume you know what foods or music they like. Somebody at the office will probably be interested and ask them a bunch of questions. That's where the flirtation happens. You start feeling like the other human being is interested in you, cares about you, and sees you as the person you are *this* year, not the person you were twenty years ago.

That's often where an office romance will start. Being informed about each other is important. You have to be ongoingly curious. You also need to exercise curiosity about yourself and the world. If you get into a relationship rut where you take everything for granted because it's comfortable, your relationship can only take two directions: it's either growing and evolving, or it's dying. If you want your relationship and sex life to be vibrant, get informed by being a curious person. Ask lots of questions; don't take things for granted.

RLM: Your next tip is to become experienced. Do you mean experience at sex, or a broader experience?

VM: When I wrote that, I was specifically talking about the female reader's experience around sex. At that time, a lot of women lacked sexual experiences. They wanted me to target housewives in Ohio. That's who I wrote it for. But I think this pertains to all of us. Having sexual experience doesn't necessarily mean that you have to be promiscuous and have sex with as many people as I did. It doesn't *hurt*—and I'm not going to say you shouldn't if you feel called to do that. But if you don't, you can get sexual experience by learning about your *own* body. That would be a great place to start. Don't expect your partner to figure it out.

You should be spending a certain amount of time self-pleasuring to get to know yourself and what it is that you like. It's not a matter of telling your partner, "I like it this way or that way." It's about developing *your* connection to all of those neurons. That takes time to develop. If you learn how to move into a sensation with yourself, that will translate into a better partnered sex life. Your first place of experience is as close as your hand—and any kind of sex toys that you gift yourself. Take some Tantra; you don't have to go to a class. You can find it online. Learn how to pair your breath with sensation. That would be the most fruitful line of experience you can have.

RLM: That's excellent advice. The advice you're giving about your hand matches that of my dear friend Dr. Stella Resnick, of LA, who has written books on human sexuality. Stella said, "If you don't learn how to pleasure yourself and figure out what you like, how can you possibly expect your partner to figure it out?" It's like offering them a multiple-choice game endlessly. Now you recommend being adventurous. What does it mean to be adventurous sexually?

VM: It's going to mean different things to different people. But try to open your mind; try something new. You have *got* to break free of sexual shame. You asked me about the fear factor of becoming a sex worker. By definition, sex workers are adventurous people. For a layperson to imagine doing sex work is scary, but sex workers are risk-takers and have a certain level of confidence. With that confidence, you develop competence. But more and more, monogamous couples are opening up their relationships.

You can be sexually adventurous in a lot of ways. You can try new things if you want, but you could also be adventurous by taking risks in the relationship. What causes the sex life to become stale is that people stop taking risks in their interpersonal connection. You think, *It's not worth talking about that because it's just going to lead to a fight, so never mind.* You do that repeatedly for ten or twenty years and your sex life is guaranteed to die because there's no risk in the relationship. You're playing it safe. You're being disingenuous and not showing up to be your authentic self.

So I would say, take the risk, enroll in the adventure, in your truth, and in finding out what your partner's truth is. Learn creative ways of conflict management; take on the things you don't want to argue about anymore. See a counselor or a therapist. Become the person who can take risks in conversation and emotional intimacy. It's going to be easier when you have sex to be vulnerable and authentic *around* your desires and emotions.

OVERCOMING THE FEAR OF ORAL SEX

RLM: What do you say to couples who seem to have a fear or aversion to oral sex?

VM: We have a lot of shaming around female genitalia. "It's dark; it's dirty; it's ugly; it's smelly." It's important to reframe that and realize that the vulva is the first religion; it's *sacred*. It's a place from which life can emanate. It's a portal to the other side. It's an amazing creation, evolution, or however you want to look at that. But it has so many moving parts and so much beauty. You can become inspired by the vulva, see it, and learn about all of its intricacies and its responses. I'm going to give a shout-out to a fabulous book by a colleague of mine, *Women's Anatomy of Arousal* by Sheri Winston. If you get a chance to read that book, it will blow your mind about the vulva and its sexual response. The book is all about arousing the female body.

Whether the man is reticent or the woman is shy, finding out and understanding the vulva is the first step because it has, unfortunately, been kept mysterious. I love referring to nature for examples of healthy sexuality, such as oral sex—particularly cunnilingus. Fellatio is rare in the animal kingdom. The Bonobos do it, but most animals don't orally copulate with the male member, whereas almost all animals perform cunnilingus. That's always a prelude to sexual intercourse. If you're looking for examples, thousands of mammals perform cunnilingus. I had a mated pair of dogs, and that was my female dog's favorite sex act.

RLM: Talk to us about being assertive in your sexual behavior.

VM: It's probably true that most cisgender males don't need lessons in assertion. They need to learn to be more receptive—not so that they can please her, but to please themselves. But a lot of cisgender women shy away from being assertive because they've been taught to hold back and be the gatekeeper. If you're in that position, think about it: a gate only allows or denies entrance; it doesn't do anything else.

If you think of yourself as the person who says "yes" or "no," then you're a gatekeeper. That's a dull way to approach sex. You want to think assertively. Take an active role and assert that you would *love* to have sex—or say that you're not in the mood for sex now, but that you might be later. If you're in the mood for sex, communicate what kind of sex you would like.

It always comes with a responsibility to be curious about how your assertion is impacting the other person. Are they enjoying it? Are they frightened? You have to become adept at reading body language. Throughout the sex act, always be tuned in to your partner, paying attention to their breathing, what's happening with their eyes, their facial expressions. Is their body tensing up? Is it relaxing? It's a full-body experience. Showing up to notice what's happening for your partner is also a way of being present and assertive.

THE TRANSITION FROM SEX WORKER TO POLITICAL ACTIVIST

RLM: You have a beautiful way of describing the sexual act as both a skill and an art form. I bow to you for that. I'm guessing you made a substantial amount of money as a sex worker, and I imagine that you make less as a relationship coach and anger-management coach. You must make considerably less as a political activist for the good cause of advancing sex work. How did you deal with that differential in pay? Aren't you ever tempted to go back and pick up some easy money?

VM: Yes. You're being the psychologist now. I feel read like a book. People often ask me, "Why did you transition?" I'm a spiritually based person, keep in mind. I was clean and sober for several years before I got into the sex industry. I brought prayer to my work with my clients. I woke up one morning and told my husband, "I'm going to stop escorting, sell the house, and move us to the mountains. Then I'm going to write a book, because it's time. And the book deal is coming." He said, "You're crazy. You can't know there's a book deal coming. That's ridiculous." I said, "I do, and I'm going to act upon that."

Part of it was a career transition. It was time to move into the next thing. Part of it was that, as an activist, I had been on every major network and international television for years. They say you get fifteen minutes of fame. I had seventeen years of major media exposure, and I was recognized in the streets. Sometimes, it was upsetting. I can remember when I was in a restaurant with my family and children. The staff all gathered at the door. They're pointing and looking at me because I'm the lady from TV. That day, I even tried to wear a baseball cap to hide. There was no hope. I also was getting interference from law enforcement. I got arrested and audited. I was getting sick of that. The public exposure made me want to go to the mountains and live in a cabin for a while.

RLM: I can relate to that. You tweaked my memory with what you said about being in the restaurant with your family and kids. I've come across quite a few sex workers who had a difficult time because their kids were made fun of at school or were pointed to in restaurants while they were working. There's been a tremendous amount of shaming in their post-sex-work life, and it's challenging for former sex workers to adjust. Some of the stories are heart-wrenching. People have had to take their kids out of school because other kids shame them about what their mothers did for a living. Do you have any comments about that, Veronica?

VM: My children were stepchildren, and I think they were more identified with their birth mother than me. It seems they were fortunately spared that suffering. My husband, however, would get mercilessly teased at the office. He worked as a sales manager, and they would say, "Saw your wife on Geraldo." They *had* to invite us to the company Christmas party, but we didn't get invited to other parties. It was weird how people cut you out of their lives.

RLM: Not getting invited to a party should be the worst thing that happens to someone.

VM: It hurt my feelings.

RLM: Of course. Do you want to say anything about the effect of your sex work on your relationship with your husband? What was it like for him? I'll tell you a cute story about that. When I interviewed Norma Jean, she said, "Being a sex worker was just my going to work, and my husband also went to work, and it was very normal."

I said to her, "Are you telling me that you're sitting at the dinner table with your husband, and your husband says to you, 'How was work today, darling?' and you say to him, 'Oh, that last guy was hung like a horse and pass the salt, please?'" She replied, "Yes, it was exactly like that."

VM: I know her husband, Victor, and I've had dinner with them. It's the truth.

RLM: They were just two people going to work—that's how she makes it sound. After work, they might talk about work, and then they go on to other things.

VM: I told my husband everything. I would come home and tell him, "Oh my God, this client is amazing. I couldn't believe I had such a good time. We talked about this, we went here, and we went there." He would go, "That's great, honey. I'm glad you had a great time." Other times, I would come home and say, "I don't think I'm going to see this guy anymore. He's a jerk," and I'd tell my husband why, and he'd go, "It sounds like you shouldn't see him anymore." There were times that I'd say, "I'm not sure I should go see this person because I've never seen him before. Would you listen to his voice and tell me, do you get a good or a bad feeling when you hear his voice?"

RLM: Very smart. But my gosh, Veronica, after doing what you did, to come home to your husband and then make love, you've got to have an Olympian appetite.

VM: No. . . well, okay: guilty as charged. I do have an Olympian appetite. But my husband asked one thing of me, and that was not to have orgasms with my clients, and I agreed to his terms. So, when I came home after work, I was incredibly aroused. What that meant for my husband was that I was ready to go. He loved it. He had a horny wife.

14

Maeve Moon

Profiting from Trauma

Maeve Moon is a former sex worker turned trauma recovery coach. As she shares with us her story of recovery and victory, Maeve goes through her harrowing, heartbreaking journey as a young woman in the sex industry, and what it took for her to escape and find her true sense of self. She is now using her story to provide hope and enlighten other women in the industry. You can find out more about her on her Instagram and podcast, Profit from Trauma.

Dr. Richard L. Miller (RLM): Our guest today is Maeve Moon. She's going to be talking to us about healing from severe trauma. Welcome, Maeve.

Maeve Moon (MM): Thank you.

EARLY TRAUMAS

RLM: Maeve, you've had a life of trauma, and now you're working with trauma victims. Let's begin with your life experience. I believe you had your first experience with trauma when you were as young as four years old.

MM: When I was four, my mother chose to foster children—a selfless act in and of itself, but it resulted in older children staying with us. And they reflected onto me what was going on in their life and what happened to them. That resulted in sexual assault that went under the radar and wasn't dealt with at that time. My mother was also physically and emotionally abusive. She did all the things a mother should do except the things you need from a mother, the care and nurturing. I became homeless at sixteen; I had a hard couple of years. Honestly, that was a traumatic time in my life. At eighteen, I went into the sex industry and started speaking to sugar daddies. And, at twenty, I fully went into escorting.

RLM: You became homeless at sixteen?

MM: Yes.

RLM: How did that come about?

MM: It wasn't a snap decision. My mom and I cannot coexist. It's a hatred that can't be resolved, and it resulted in a lot of physical violence when I was a child. As I grew older, it didn't stop. I'm a big woman. So when my mom decided to start tackling me as a teenager, it backfired on her. I was no longer squishable. I couldn't be pressed under her thumb. So I moved out when I was about fifteen and moved in with a friend. But at sixteen, I was old enough to go into a homeless hostel for vulnerable adults, aged sixteen to twenty-five.

RLM: So you voluntarily went to this homeless hostel where they had other teenage children who did not have homes?

MM: Yes. In part voluntarily and partly because my mother was constantly kicking me out. So I made the decision that I had a right to leave right then.

RLM: Tell us what it was like living in that homeless shelter.

MM: It was better than my home, if I'm honest. But it was difficult. I lived in emergency accommodations initially. All those rooms were on the hostel's ground floor for short-term residents. So it was only a room with a bed, toilet, desk, and a bolted window. Adjacent to the window was a ten-foot wall. It was depressing and dark, but better than being in a constant state of danger. At least I felt safe there.

I lived in the shelter for about six months before moving into supported housing with another homeless girl. That escalated into various other living situations.

RLM: Did the people at the homeless shelter help you find the supported housing situation?

MM: No, that was an agreement between the other girl and myself. We decided we would apply for housing and government-funding benefits, and she happened to know a family friend who was a landlord. So we moved into a house together.

SEEKING ARRANGEMENTS IN SURREY

RLM: How did you eat and support yourself at sixteen, seventeen years old?

MM: I worked underhand. At that time, the law in the UK, which has recently been changed, stated that you were not entitled to housing benefits if you earned over five pounds a week. That kept people in a loop of never finding work because you would lose your housing benefits. I worked as a freelance session musician. That was my passion when I was growing up. I was trained classically, so I worked at the studio and sang.

RLM: What instrument did you play?

MM: I sang. I was also playing guitar at the time, but I was not recording.

RLM: At some point in this difficult home situation, you were also taking singing lessons; you got classically trained.

MM: Yes. I joined a choir when I was six, and then the choir tutor, who was a professional opera singer, took me on as a private client. I was lucky to be trained that way. My mother did provide. She was quite wealthy and gave me many opportunities to learn and develop skills as a child.

RLM: Did you say your mother was wealthy?

MM: Yes, she was a police officer.

RLM: I see. So now, you're living in supported housing. What happens next in your life?

MM: I had a huge fight with the girl I was living with. She really hurt me, and I ran away. So I lived in a caravan for a while in somebody's garden. Then I moved back into the hostel where I knew I was safe, and I lived there for another few months until I finished my diploma at college and went to university. I moved down to Guildford, Surrey. Later, I got into the Academy of Contemporary Music in Guildford.

RLM: Did you go to college at the academy?

MM: Yes.

RLM: Did they also give you a place to live?

MM: I found student housing.

RLM: What happened next? Did you complete school?

MM: No, I didn't.

RLM: Something happened?

MM: Yes. I did go to university. For the first year, I was extremely committed, I got a boyfriend, and I thought, *I'm starting this new life.* I believed this would be a new chapter. I changed my name to Maeve—my birth name is Rhiannon—and I thought, *I'll move to the bottom of the country, as far away as I can. I'll leave Rhiannon behind. Her life was so difficult, so I'll start fresh in this wealthy part of the country.*

I had a fantasy that relocating would fix me inside; it didn't— I just went somewhere else. But all of me was there while I was in Surrey. I did a year and a half of the degree and finished it with a higher diploma. But about halfway through, as I turned twenty, I broke up with my boyfriend, signed up to *SeekingArrangement.com* properly—a sugar daddy website—and started meeting men.

RLM: You signed up? What does that mean?

MM: I made an account. Another girl from university and I had these delusions of signing up there and making loads of money to travel and go shopping.

RLM: How old were you?

MM: I had just turned twenty.

RLM: Okay, so you go on the website. Have you ever done anything like this before in your life?

MM: I had been speaking to men from the age of twelve.

RLM: Had you been engaging in sexual relations with them or just talking?

MM: Just talking. My first intimate relationship with an older man was shortly after my sixteenth birthday. A teacher had groomed me because I got validation from speaking with men online, which backfired. Have you heard of Omegle?

RLM: No, what is it?

MM: It's an online chat room where you get paired with somebody random from across the world. They never pair you with people nearby because it's quite dangerous. So if you and I went on Omegle, there's a chance we would match in this chat room, and we would be able to see each other and connect. Still, you're so far away from me that nothing would happen if you or I were a dangerous person. I ended up meeting a twenty-six-year-old man who lived at the bottom of the country in Devon. He was a teacher, we connected, and he spoke to me for a year until I was sixteen and happened to be in Devon for one night. It went south. I met him for a drink; he spiked me, drove me out of the town, and assaulted me.

RLM: He spiked you with a drug in your drink?

MM: Yes. We were drinking wine at a club.

RLM: Then he assaulted you out in the country?

MM: Yes.

RLM: Then what happened?

MM: I was staying with my father in Devon. When I came around from this horrendous situation, I had twenty missed calls from him. I didn't know my dad. This is why I think I went on that date: My dad couldn't stop me because he had never been in my life, and this was the second time I had ever met him. We had gone to Devon to collect my brother. Then, this guy drove me back to his grandparents' house. They knew what was going on. It was bizarre. The police were called, I was put under the Child Sexual Exploitation Act, and I was under 24/7 supervision for a while.

RLM: Would you say that was your entrance into sex work?

MM: Yes. In my mind, it set the precedent that sex isn't anything that should be valued, that I can use it as a commodity. I had gone through sexual abuse as a child, and then again in my teenage years. So I didn't have the mindset that sex is precious. Once I was twenty, I thought, *I already don't enjoy sex due to my past experiences, so I might as well make some money out of it.* I enjoy money—I knew that. So it made financial sense to turn my body into a commodity.

RLM: Was that the time when you got together with your friend and enrolled on this sugar daddy site?

MM: Yes.

THE FIRST CONNECTION GOES SOUR

RLM: What was it like the first time you connected with an older man via the internet and got together? Can you remember what it was like to meet a complete stranger for the purpose of selling your body as a commodity?

MM: Clear as day: it felt exhilarating at the time. I felt like I'd taken back my power. I felt powerful, and so did the other girl. We signed up as a duo. We looked similar, so we thought we would be like a fantasy: *We're living in a fantasy, and we can become a fantasy for other people.* So we met this man, and we agreed to 1,000 pounds for the night, split between us. That would include going to a hotel, going out for a meal, and then having sex with him. He said, "How about 800 pounds, and the champagne's on me?"

He drove up from Southampton to Guildford—about three hours. I think it went exactly as everybody expects a fantasy to go. Guildford's a wealthy area. We went to a lovely hotel; we had champagne; we went out for Thai food; we went back to the penthouse suite he'd booked. Then we had a threesome. He paid us each 400 pounds, and I remember both of us walking out the next morning in our heels, feeling gross and naughty—I liked that feeling, actually. I had just made 400 pounds from having sex. I just looked at the money and said, "That was the easiest money I've ever made in life." When I was on benefits, I received fifty-seven pounds a week.

RLM: Here, you made 400 pounds for hanging out in a hotel, eating Thai food, and having sex.

MM: Right. It makes it logical in that sense.

RLM: Yes. Given that it went well, that you weren't beaten, hurt, kidnapped, or one of the terrible things that could happen with a stranger off the internet, it was quite something. Also, you were with a friend. So you took precautions regarding your safety. I would think it's more difficult to do something terrible to two people than one person.

MM: That was also our reasoning. We were both nervous. We had never done this, and we both had the fantasy of doing it. But we had never done it alone. This time, it was real. When I had spoken to men on SeekingArrangements at sixteen, the interest was there, but not the intention. I wasn't going to meet these men. I had enough on my plate—I was trying to pay bills, work, and go to college. I didn't have time for sugar daddies, but I was interested. Now, we'd done it, and we did feel safer doing it together.

RLM: So that was your first experience. You walk out of there with your friend; you're both smiling and happy with 400 pounds each. What was next on your agenda?

MM: That man invited us to America on that night. We both agreed and didn't think it would go ahead, but it did. I had a connection with him on that first night; she didn't. She started meeting men on her own. So I developed a relationship with him for the next three months. He chauffeured me down to his place from Guilford once a week to date and sleep together, and he paid me a weekly allowance. Then, all three of us booked tickets and went to America.

RLM: In which city did you land?

MM: We landed at JFK. He had a lake house in Connecticut.

RLM: So now, the three of you are living in Connecticut.

MM: I'd say we were there only for a week and a half, but it was interesting.

RLM: You were in Connecticut for a week?

MM: Yes, and we moved to New York. We left him in his house and went off together.

RLM: Why did you leave him? It sounds like a wonderful arrangement.

MM: It does. What drives me to share information online about this world is that, of course, it's nice when it's nice. But I met a man on the internet, got on a plane with him, went to another country where it was illegal to do what I was doing, and I was twenty-years-old, so I wasn't even legally allowed to drink in America. Finally, he ended up being aggressive. He transformed into this person I had not met. I trusted him for some reason. On Thanksgiving eve, he took us to a bar full of motorbike guys. I started speaking to somebody, and it deeply upset him.

But the night before we were going, he had engaged with the other girl without me. That wasn't okay because I was in a relationship with him, but he was not in one with her. So the idea was: we either all have sex together, or he only has sex with me. That's how normal threesomes work. Then, I started speaking to somebody; he didn't like that and left the bar. She got spiked at the bar, collapsed outside, and people gathered around us. We looked completely out of place. She was Finnish; I'm English. We looked bizarre. We stood out like sore thumbs. Then, the bouncer called the police and ambulance.

I was not interrogated, but I felt like I was. Three cops stood around me, going, "What are you doing, ma'am?" I said, "I'm an escort. I don't know. I'm staying here, and the man has left us. I don't know what to do, and I'm unsafe." I spent the next eight hours in hospital with her. We went back to the house, collected our things, and her sugar daddy booked us a cab from his house to New York and a hotel room to get us away from him. It was bad.

RLM: That was your first experience, and it went badly when you got to the States.

MM: It was so dangerous.

RLM: But by then you had embarked on that life.

MM: There's something tasty about that danger when you don't feel fulfilled with your life. I completely turned my back on who I was, and I became "Jasmine." She was fun and crazy, just a dangerous woman. I loved being her. She allowed me to live in my ego all the time, without a care in the world.

FROM ESCORT TO PROSTITUTE

RLM: What happened in the next chapter? We're moving towards you becoming a coach to help others.

MM: I realized it was too much emotional investment and that I actually wanted money. So I decided to become a prostitute rather than wasting time with sugar daddies. That would cut out all the dining and other escort services. I did that for about a year and a half as a freelancer.

RLM: Did you do that in the United States, or did you go back to England?

MM: I came back to England. I worked for my student accommodation. I then moved to London and worked in a few brothels. I trained as a dominatrix; I started working in dungeons and from my apartment in London.

RLM: Tell us about what it was like working in a brothel.

MM: I worked in two, which were vastly different. The first one was in the center of London, and the men I was getting were very poor. They would take everything that they could get in that situation. We had cameras, and the pimps were adjacent to our apartment. So they were right outside, and they were nice. Again, I'm lucky that he happened to be this six-foot-seven gay Polish guy. He was lovely. He said, "I'm here to protect you if you need me." He paid me fairly. The second brothel was in Bradford, in the northwest of England—again, in a very poor area, but this one was different.

I was working with a Romanian girl who I could tell didn't want to be there. I don't think she had a choice to be there. I ended up being kicked out of the brothel without my passport, without any of my luggage or money. I was left with a client who kindly let me stay in a warehouse with him overnight because he was married. He had kids and couldn't take me anywhere else, but he felt obliged to look after me. It was a mess because I was badly ill at the second brothel. I had tonsillitis, I was on my period, I had copper poisoning from the coil,* and the pimp still expected me to work.

RLM: Typically, how many men would you have sex with at the brothel per day?

---

*Editor's note: Referring to the coil from an intrauterine device.

MM: They would book an hour, which cost 200 pounds—including anal—and 140 pounds without anal. The goal was to get them in and out within fifteen minutes so that you could sleep with at least four men in an hour. Then, you could make upwards of a thousand pounds in one day's work. You want to keep 500 pounds because the other 500 pounds go towards the pimps. It's fifty-fifty.

RLM: For how long did you work in the brothel?

MM: About a week and a half.

RLM: Oh, not for months or years?

MM: No.

RLM: During that week and a half, you were making about 500 pounds a day.

MM: Yes, thereabouts.

RLM: So you saved up some money. But at four men an hour, you were having sex with maybe twenty to thirty men a day.

MM: Yes, depending on how long I worked. You can work for five hours and then be satisfied with what you've made. The body does have limitations. At client three, my body is at capacity already because that's a lot on the body. Also, at that time, I was not having sex because I wanted to have sex, so my body was not self-lubricating. I'm forcing my body to do something that it doesn't want to do.

RLM: Yes. So then you left there, and you went out for a while freelancing before you had the Ayahuasca experience.

MM: Yes. I worked at two brothels, saying, "I'm not doing that again."

RLM: Wasn't freelancing frightening in terms of, who's going to protect you if the man is aggressive?

MM: Yes. But honestly, the money was more important to me. I didn't have any protection, and that did result in rapes and assault. But as I said, it made financial sense. If you work three hours a week, you can make enough money to survive that week. If you work eight hours a week, you can make the money to survive the month. But that's not taking into consideration that out of those three clients you take in the day, the second one rapes you. Then what do you do for the rest of the week? Do you force yourself to continue working? Are you so shook up, in fight-or-flight mode, or so shut down that you physically can't work? Or do you force yourself? At that point, it stops making financial sense. When that's your only source of income, you have to force yourself to continue having sex. If you've just been assaulted, you don't want to have sex. What do you do? Do you go broke, or do you force yourself?

RLM: I understand. These things are always important for the public to hear, because there are very few rights for sex workers. And very few people or organizations are looking out for them in any way, as you well know.

THE AYAHUASCA REVELATION

MM: Eventually, I went on an amazing Ayahuasca retreat, and I had the revelation that I had soul ties to all these men. I had an addiction, and I hated my life. So I just told myself, "I'm never doing this." I gave up my apartment. I took myself off the AdultWork site. I took myself off SeekingArrangements. I closed down my dominatrix account and moved back in with my mother. I said, "I'm starting again," and I started Profit From Trauma. I simply started blogging about my life experience and gave advice on Instagram. It has grown into an amazing community—a movement and platform I'm honored to be a part of now.

RLM: Something then occurred that made you take this Ayahuasca and have this revelation.

MM: Yes.

RLM: Tell us how that came about. How does a sex worker suddenly take Ayahuasca and open up the door to a complete change of life?

MM: Although I was making unconscious and unintelligent decisions, I was aware that I was an intelligent woman. And I did have prospects—I did have a potential future if I wanted to make one. Throughout my final year of escorting, I started to research, "What's going to fix me? What could get me off weed and cocaine? What could stop me from doing this?"

I came across Ayahuasca retreats in Peru, and I thought, *That's it then. I need to go to Peru. I'll take Ayahuasca, my addictions will be cured, and I'll be back to normal. No more eating disorders, no more weed addiction. Everybody's happy.* Unfortunately, that's not how it works. Again, another delusion, but a more promising one. In the brothel in London, I'd met a client who had Mother Ayahuasca tattooed all over him. It was divine timing. This man walked into my life, and I asked, "What are those tattoos?" So he told me. He put me in touch with shamans, and I was able to go to a retreat in the UK. I was so ill when I went to the retreat, just completely depleted. I felt like I was at the end of life at twenty-one. That feeling of not seeing a point anymore was simply unbelievable.

I sat with the medicines—San Pedro, mescaline, Ayahuasca, DMT, and Kambo. It made me see the reality of my life. I found reverence for my life—that my life is important. I saw hundreds of men on a wall, hundreds of faces. I looked at all these faces, and I could see that I've got soul ties to each one of those men. They're in me, and I'm carrying all of their energies every day. So I said, "I can't do that to myself anymore." I made the decision then: "That's it. I end it now. I stop smoking, and I quit. I don't know what I'll do, but I've got to make that decision."

RLM: How old were you when you made that decision?

MM: Maybe twenty-two. I was only in the industry for two and a half years.

RLM: You got out early while there was still a way. You're very fortunate.

MM: Yes. It's like a whirlwind. When people hear me talk, they may think I was a prostitute for thirty years. I have to remind them, "I'm only twenty-three years old. I can't have been doing it for *that* long. Think about it."

PROFIT FROM TRAUMA

RLM: Now, tell us about how you came to the title, Profit From Trauma. That's totally new. We want to hear you talk about profiting from sexual trauma because that's part of your expertise personally.

MM: Your reaction is exactly what I'm looking for from people. I want you to look at that title and go, "What on earth does that mean? That's so heartless. This woman is financially profiting from other people's trauma." But that's not what I mean. I want you to think that, so that you click on my name, come to my account, and see what I'm talking about, which is: You can profit from your own experiences in life.

You can take the trauma and experiences you've gone through, hold them on a pedestal as absolutely invaluable, and you can profit emotionally and spiritually. While *you* can profit financially, I'm not trying to profit, financially, from your trauma. I see "profit" as post-traumatic growth—not discarding the trauma you've gone through, but instead acknowledging that it happened. You can use that to advance your own life and those of the people around you, if you want to.

RLM: That is what you teach in your classes?

MM: Yes. I want you to acknowledge your trauma, to ask yourself what you've learned from it. Be introspective about what you truly learned. When I have a one-on-one client, we look at a day-to-day action that isn't supporting them, their well-being, or their lives. Then, we ask about the root. We go further and further backwards, asking, "What started that core belief?"

Then, we ask, "How can you change that core belief? How can

you understand it and have that compassion for yourself?" The next question is, "How can we transform that into something that's going to advance your life rather than harm it?" Simply having compassion for yourself at that moment can be the advancement you need. It doesn't have to be some great action where you start a charity, jump out of an airplane, and raise money. Compassion can be the pinnacle of that introspective moment we share.

RLM: Where did you learn all this? You talk just like a psychologist.

MM: I read, I listen, and I care. I've had such a drive to become a psychotherapist for years. I kept applying. I got accepted into university to do an MA. Then I got offered the opportunity to do a master's degree in contemporary arts psychotherapy. But they rejected me because they would only offer it on the condition that I give up my social media activism. That doesn't look good for the university or the ethics board. So I said, "Actually, I'd rather keep my dignity and my platform than work with an institution that tries to shut down my human experience." Victor Frankl wanted to publish his book anonymously but then decided not to because people could recognize him as a person, and his human experience helped them.

RLM: Are you referring to his book *From Death-Camp to Existentialism*?

MM: No, *Man's Search for Meaning*.

RLM: It was the same book. It was published separately as *Man's Search for Meaning*.

MM: Okay. Then yes, that's the book I'm referring to.

RLM: I had the pleasure of knowing him while he was alive.

MM: That's incredible.

RLM: Yes.

MM: I felt this overwhelming "No" come through me when they asked if I'd accept the ultimatum. I felt the *No* of people who have changed their lives and the world against the odds. I said, "I'm not doing that," and I applied for Gabor Maté's Compassionate Inquiry course. Again, I was rejected.

RLM: Why did Gabor turn you down?

MM: Because I'm not a professional.

RLM: I know Gabor, and I think he opens up some of his classes to nonprofessional people. Have you looked into Bessel van der Kolk?

MM: I have read the start of *The Body Keeps The Score*, but I have not looked into any courses.

HELPING SEX WORKERS THROUGH TRAUMA

RLM: Tell us about your social media platform. Do sex workers come to you now for coaching on changing their lives?

MM: They do. I also have mothers of sex workers coming to me who need support because they don't know what to do. They feel powerless at that moment. I think sex workers come to me because they can relate, and that's key for them. Sex work is grossly misunderstood. If you don't understand the mental processes that go on when you decide to sell your genitals to all and sundry, it can be hard for you to relate to a client as a therapist. Clients may also feel they can't relate to you or don't trust sharing their information with you.

That's what I've learned from the women that come to me. That might not be the case across the board—I can't know that—but they're able to be honest, share their entire human experience with me, and feel that I'm not judging them. They can feel that I get it, and that I'm not trying to change them. I'm not seeing these people as broken. We're not doing goal-oriented therapy—I'm not a therapist; I'm a coach. So we just work the process, and currently, their life experience is being a sex worker. Let's work with your current situation and not try to change it. But let's *go in*. If you're not happy with it, ask yourself why. The change will come about on its own when we address the *why*.

RLM: It must be gratifying for you to help sex workers after the experiences of that time in your life and the horrors you faced.

MM: It is, and I feel different things arise within me. Sometimes, I feel triggered, and the money switch in my brain might switch on when I see these girls making so much money. Part of me remembers making that amount of money and sitting around all day, but I also remember the hard side. I wrote a course called 15 Days of Introspection, and I've run it twice with women worldwide. After a class where we've done two hours of introspection—which is a lot for girls who have never looked inside themselves—I go to bed feeling complete. I've never felt so full in my heart.

RLM: That's marvelous. Does that contribute to your healing from the trauma you've gone through? What else are you doing to address the trauma?

MM: Good question. I've started the Moving into Wholeness course by Process Work.* That's a nine-month course, which will lead me into the diploma at the end of this year, and that is world work, somatic experiencing, and getting into your body, which is challenging for me but so valuable. We finished the first module yesterday, and I've never been so aware of what my body is saying. That's the most beautiful thing. Once I finish this course, I hope to pass this back out into the world, teach and guide from a healing perspective rather than my ideologies. Also, I work in a spiritual retreat center, so I'm in the community. I'm living the prayer—with the medicines, the plants, Ayahuasca, and San Pedro. I'm helping people as they come through the center.

DOES SEX WORK NATURALLY LEAD TO TRAUMA?

RLM: What else would we like our readers to know? Would you recommend a sex worker's job to a young person under certain conditions?

---

*Editor's note: Also called Process-oriented psychology, Process Work, is a depth psychology theory and set of techniques developed by Arnold Mindell.

Could this be a business without the trauma, or is psychological trauma inherent in selling one's self for sex making it not worth the amount of money that one earns?

MM: That's a difficult question, and I hear it a lot. I always want to put myself on the knife's edge because I don't know what's right for everybody else. I can only speak from my subjective experience, and I can't be so objective as to say, "It's right for this group of people and not right for that one."

I don't know what's going to be right. It was a huge learning experience and valuable—I wouldn't take it back. But did I need to go through all of that? I don't know, and I wouldn't recommend it to anybody since you might end up going through the same experience or even a similar one, and that's highly likely, given the nature of humans.

When we talk about sex work, people forget that we're putting this blanket cover on all the people paying for sex. But all those people have different intentions. Out of ten people, how many do you think have malicious intentions towards you? How can you possibly know? You take that risk every time you meet a client. You don't know, and you're probably not protected, so I would never recommend it.

RLM: That's one of the most critical points which any person thinking of this work needs to consider. You said it beautifully: Of every ten people who are hiring you for sex, what percentage of them are going to be abhorrent enough to do you damage? Those percentages accumulate the longer you stay in business, so the likelihood of some horrendous event will increase over time.

MM: Precisely, and it only takes one abhorrent person deciding to harm you to affect the rest of your life.

Consent

What does it say about a culture when its most esteemed institutions normalize and ignore sexual abuse? Many believers still turn to faith for moral support, while church leaders systematically silence the suffering their institutions cause.

Whether or not we are believers, the actions of religious leaders determine the course of public discussions in our everyday lives, especially if we live in red states where the religious right has a stronghold on laws and policy.

If we accept those influences in our lives (not that we have a choice), what weight does it carry when Pope Francis reduces sanctions against convicted pedophile priests? How do we define mercy when it applies to predators in high offices but not abused children?

Once we learn about those decisions to protect predators, without commenting or protesting, our indifference becomes part of our daily life. It becomes mainstream or normal to be able to abuse five young boys and then pledge yourself to a lifetime of prayer, as the pope demanded of the convicted pedophile Rev. Mauro Inzoli who was eventually defrocked.

Culture doesn't simply happen. Over the course of a day, billions of individual decisions determine what tomorrow's culture will look like. Which future are we rooting for if we accept that the Southern Baptist Church hides entire databases of pastors accused of sexual abuse—not to help victims but to protect the church from liability?

In October 2021, an independent commission's investigations reported that they had uncovered between 2,900 and 3,200 pedophile priests and other church members. We've heard the stories about multi-millionaires like Jeffrey Epstein and Harvey Weinstein, who used their positions of power to exploit vulnerable women and girls.

Sexual abuse is undoubtedly widespread in large parts of the Western world. What these cases all have in common is the consumption of people as purchasable commodities with utter disregard for their humanity.

Sexual abuse is both physical and psychological, throughout the period of abuse, as well as the aftermath, which can span the entirety of the victim's life.

Understanding consent is paramount to our project of *Freeing Sexuality*. One cannot ethically enjoy themselves sexually at the expense of someone who is not free, and who is not able to provide fully informed consent. This includes the underage, the inebriated, the otherwise incapacitated, as well as anyone who we could use our power over to coerce into sexual interactions.

One of our interviewees, Faith Jones, sexually abused from age six, is the granddaughter of the founder of a religious cult that both abused children and used adults as prostitutes to entrap men and bring them into the cult. While some claim that sex work is oppression, Paulita Pappel became a porn worker as a political act while still in college and now produces and directs alternative porn films depicting real people engaged in real sex.

Together, we try to envision an alternative to the status quo, to paint an image of what our future might look like if we gave it our all. We're not doomed to accept the world we and our ancestors have built and live with the consequences, however dire they may be. When I was four and a half years old, I was introduced to sex by my thirteen-year-old babysitter. The relationship, including sexual penetration and fellatio, continued until I was seven, when my father separated from active duty in the military and our family moved from Eglin Air Force Base, Florida, back to New York City. The physical experience of the sexual relationship was pleasurable, but the knowledge that we were doing something, which needed to be kept secret severely damaged me with an ingrained belief that I was doing something bad and wrong . . . again and again and again . . . bad and wrong, bad and wrong.

Since I was a sixteen-year-old college freshman enrolled in psychotherapy, I have been trying to make peace with these feelings. But no matter how many thousands of lives I have enhanced, with my professional work even saving lives, the dissonance lurks. *I have done something so aberrant, so bad and wrong. How can I still be a good person?*

As difficult as it is for us to come to grips with the unpleasantness, sometimes bordering on horror, of sexual abuse, we must do so, for the numbers of us who have been sexually abused are dramatically high. The Centers for Disease Control (CDC) reports that one in five females (19.3 percent) and one in seventy one males (1.4 percent) have been raped during their lives. The CDC also found that one in four women (24.3 percent) and one in seven men (13.8 percent) experienced sexual violence, other than rape, such as being touched sexually without their consent, at some time in their lives. We must note that sexual abuse is a highly underreported crime as many survivors do not feel comfortable, or safe, disclosing their experiences.

It is my hope that these stories and life experiences, from people in the most diverse areas of life, will contribute to us creating a culture where we can respect each other's differences instead of exploiting them: a future where consent is not a technicality to deal with, or get around, but an integral part of every human interaction, including sexuality.

When we take away someone's choice to consent through a selfish act, we may harm their ability to give enthusiastic consent and be open to the creative, beautiful sex that they want in the future. In order to protect each other, we first have to understand.

15

Paulita Pappel

Alternative Porn as a Mirror for Society and a Political Act

Paulita Pappel is a filmmaker and feminist pornographer who splits her time between Madrid and Berlin. Paulita works as a producer, director, and intimacy coordinator and is an advocate for a sex-positive, consent-based culture.

After studying comparative literature in Berlin, Paulita followed her passion for both cinema and sexuality. She started working as an adult performer and soon explored many different roles, with over ten years of experience balancing between working in the mainstream and adult films industry. She has worked as a producer, director, casting director, scriptwriter, and performer. She's produced feature-length films that were shown and awarded internationally in festivals, and she's also produced, directed, and appeared in many short films.

She is the cofounder of Lustery, a platform dedicated to the sex lives of real-life couples from around the world. She is one half of HardWerk, an independent studio creating cinematic hardcore, where she directs and produces. Since 2013, she has served as a curator for the Pornfilmfestival Berlin. She also works as an intimacy coordinator for mainstream productions.

Dr. Richard Miller (RLM): My guest today is Paulita Pappel, a prominent German filmmaker and creator of the Berlin Erotic Film Festival who has directed and been involved in the production of over twenty erotic films—and, as a political act, has acted in thirteen of those films.

Paulita, when you went to college, you didn't study film, you studied something else.

Paulita Pappel (PP): It's funny, because when I moved to Berlin, I thought about studying film. But I was seventeen when I moved to Berlin, and they had a minimum age. I think you had to be at least eighteen, if not older, to start those studies. So I went for literature and German philology instead. But during my studies, I started to work in independent film productions in Berlin. That's how I got into it.

RLM: Did you start making films in college, or after you graduated?

PP: While I was studying, I became part of this queer DIY community in Berlin within the filmmaking scene. So it was a lot of folks creating films. Then I started acting and, soon, also working behind the camera, producing, casting, and catering. These were all collaborative films. So it was during my studies that I decided to found my own production company.

PORNOGRAPHY AS POLITICAL ACTIVISM

RLM: You went into acting—in pornographic movies, specifically—as a political act. Is that correct?

PP: Yes, I had two motives for why I went into porn. The first one was very personal: I wanted to explore my sexuality, and I was fascinated by the idea of performing in a porn film. But the second one was a political conviction. I believe that there was room within pornography to show different bodies and sexualities and to re-create or reclaim sexualities that are not usually shown in mainstream media.

RLM: How do you see the difference between the films that you acted in or made and what you might call mainstream pornography?

PP: When I talk about mainstream media, I don't necessarily mean mainstream pornography; I mean everything—even romantic comedies and Hollywood movies. Things have changed a lot in the last ten years. But if you look at what kinds of sexual identities, gender identities, sexual practices, and relationships are portrayed in Hollywood films, romantic comedies—even in music—we get a very limited offering. Sexuality still is repressed, but it was even worse when I was younger. So for me, creating porn movies was not an act. My narrative is not that I watched mainstream porn, didn't like it, and wanted to do another kind of porn. It was rather that I lived in this *world* and I didn't like it. I wanted to figure out whether we can do something else to create different narratives around sexuality in general.

SEXUAL STIGMA MADE IN HOLLYWOOD

RLM: Would you say that Hollywood mainstream portrayals of romance and sex are facilitating or encouraging the sexual taboos and stigmas that we have in our culture?

PP: I very much think so. If you think back to the fifties when you would show a bedroom with two separate beds for wife and husband, that was decades ago, but it's a good mirror to show the sexual standards in our society. How much do you show? How much is portrayed in those movies? I do think that the way sexuality is portrayed in those mainstream films reflects how society sees sexuality—and that it is still a taboo. We haven't been showing much nakedness or authentic portrayals of sexuality in movies. The common script is, "Guy looks into girl's eyes, falling in love . . . no words. Suddenly, they're together and *whoop,* they're fucking, without any foreplay."

Even if we do see it, it immediately goes to penetration and then fades to black. The next morning, we're in bed, covering our breasts with our sheets. This is a typical scene we've seen a million times. So when people say porn gives you the wrong idea about sexuality or gives us the wrong scripts, I'd counter that at least it gives *different* scripts. The only sexual script we've gotten from mainstream film is,

"Look into each other's eyes—no communication, no safer sex, no foreplay—straight into this brief sexual moment. Both people are getting together. . . cut to the next morning." That ellipsis—not showing what sex looks like—is as detrimental as anything can be. Not talking about sexuality and creating that taboo is harmful to all of us.

RLM: The only thing you left out of that portrayal is that the actors used to roll over and smoke a cigarette after they were done with having sex.

PP: But they don't show that anymore.

RLM: I used to see the actors smoking after sex and think, *We're teaching millions of children that the first thing you do after sex is to smoke a cigarette.* Maybe they didn't realize that they're encouraging smoking.

PP: I would love to know if the tobacco lobby was behind those scenes.

RLM: Anytime they showed a package of cigarettes and you could read the brand, you knew that the company was in on the marketing deal; showing the cigarette brand wasn't an accident.

ALTERNATIVE PORN FILLS A NICHE

RLM: I hear you saying that you're very much part of a political movement to destigmatize sex. We're talking about three different kinds of movies. We have what we call mainstream Hollywood portrayals of human sexuality, the porn industry—showing what they think sexuality is—and then we have your brand of alt porn. So please talk about all three and give us some perspective.

PP: That's an interesting way of dividing those. There's a lot to these three pillars where we get sexual information. Obviously, other factors in society also influence the way we experience and understand sexuality, but if we're talking about the *representation* of our sexuality, and we're focusing on films, then I love the idea of these three different categories. It's important to say that there's a barrier between what we're calling the mainstream porn industry and my movement—or what people call alternative porn, post-porn, cyber-punk porn, or feminist porn. That line is not as clear as the media tries to portray it. A lot of times when a journalist interviews me, they say, "So why is what you do better than mainstream porn?"

I always tell them that I'm not doing it because I think it's better. When we phrase the question that way, we're reinforcing the stigma against porn. You hear people saying that porn looks all the same, and there is this idea of a shady industry where not everyone wants to be there, folks are manipulated, and women are exploited.

It's important to say that this is not true. You cannot talk about the whole porn industry and give this picture of it, because it doesn't do any justice to it. That is not the reality. It's a vast industry, and there are a lot of standards—the way a shoot works; to establish consent before, during, and afterward; signing contracts—communication is ongoing. There's so much that the rest of the world could learn from porn about consent and doing things right. Reproducing this idea of a shady industry where bad things are happening is very problematic.

At the same time, the idea that all porn looks the same isn't true either. Mainstream porn is a huge industry, and you have a lot of different genders and niches within this commercial, profit-oriented form. In mainstream porn, you see much more variety in bodies, identities, and sexualities portrayed than in Hollywood films. It has always been changing over the last decades. But so many people today, especially queer folks, say that the first time they saw themselves represented as desirable—the first time their sexuality was acknowledged and celebrated—was in porn. That's important because they were not seeing their identity and sexuality in films, so it becomes an important part of building identity and coming to terms with it.

RLM: If I understand your last statement correctly, people with different sexual orientations than heterosexual don't get to see themselves very much in Hollywood films, and they see themselves only a bit in mainstream pornography. So the only place people with different orientations can see themselves in films and feel represented is alt porn. Did I understand that correctly?

PP: Yes, but I would be careful; I don't want to categorize things in a black-and-white way. I don't find that line of where mainstream porn stops and alternative porn starts productive. There is more representation of non-heterosexual sexualities and a disregard for normative standards of bodies in mainstream porn than in Hollywood. We don't recognize enough the value that mainstream porn has in terms of representation. Not all representations are great. Of course, there is a big problem with creating racial stereotypes, reducing folks, fetishizing certain sexualities. There's a lot to it, and we can certainly reflect and improve within the industry. But I'm not keen on drawing this clear line between alternative porn and mainstream porn. We gain so much more from being solidary with each other within the sex industry, saying, "Hey, there is a huge stigma against porn, and it doesn't matter if you do alt or mainstream porn." That stigma is pervasive.

VARYING LEVELS OF STIGMA IN EUROPEAN NATIONS AND THE U.S.

RLM: I've interviewed enough people in the sex industry to know that that stigma is pervasive in the United States. I know that porn actresses' children are stigmatized and bullied in school. I know it's very difficult for retired porn actresses to have a normal life when they retire. There's a huge stigma on porn performers. I'd like to talk in a moment about the stigma and overcoming it, but what can you tell us about the stigma in other countries? You're in Europe, and we're talking about the huge stigma here in the United States. The U.S. sets a tone for the rest of the world. Please tell us, is there the same stigma against porn workers in Germany and France? What about the Scandinavian countries? And Russia?

PP: First of all, stigma against sex work and porn is everywhere. But there are no answers to it, and there are differences. Generally speaking, the U.S. has a big Puritan tradition. If you take Germany—especially East Germany—the way they deal with nudity is very different than the way you would in English-speaking territories like the UK, the U.S, and Canada. There is a wider acceptance of non-sexualized nudity. I'm generalizing, and it doesn't apply to everyone, but I've experienced people having a more, for lack of a better term, *light* relationship with their bodies in terms of nudity. If you come to Berlin in summer, you can see some people in the parks basically naked, and it's not a big deal. I think that would be unthinkable in other parts of the world. Now, the thing with Europe is there are so many little countries, and each has its own idiosyncrasies. I originally come from Spain, which is a very Catholic country, like Italy. Catholics also don't like sex or nudity. Spain also has a Catholic fascist legacy. So I would say sexuality is seen in an even more limited way, especially if you're talking about women's spaces and them leveling up their sexuality. There is an even bigger stigma and more social control surrounding what you do and who you have sex with. However, I would say that, in general, there is more acceptance of nudity and openness towards sexuality in Europe. Generally, acceptance and openness are bigger in the north, and it slightly decreases in the South. So even though Scandinavian countries are extremely negative against sex workers, because they have bad laws—especially in Sweden—they still approach sexuality and nudity more openly. As you go all the way to Spain, it gets worse. But every small hub will have its own different way of approaching it. It is true that there are no good laws anywhere. All European laws are still discriminating against pornography and sex work; they have a lot of hurdles to go over to create a sustainable business. Of course, nowadays, we rely on so many software platforms based in the U.S. such as Instagram and Facebook that their terms and conditions affect all of us, and they are very anti–sex work and anti-nudity.

RLM: Paulita, do the films that are created in these different countries reflect the culture and the religion of the particular country, or is there a similarity across countries?

PP: That's such a good question. Unfortunately, I do not have a comprehensive, scientific answer to that. But I'm speaking from my own experience. I am also one of the curators of the Pornfilmfestival Berlin.

RLM: Yes, I know you created that film festival. Congratulations.

PP: Thank you. One of my colleagues created it, but I joined ten years ago. So, again, I don't have the data to give you a scientific answer. But, from my experience, I would say that pornography is a space where people also deal with the issues that they've had growing up and develop their sexuality. It can be a place of reclaiming. So for example, I see that Spanish or Hispanic films tend to deal a lot more with religion because religion has indoctrinated us so much around sexuality. So I see way more films that work with fetishes, religious paraphernalia, or churches there than in Germany. So I do think that, in pornography, we do see a reflection of the influences that have been informing our sexualities; it's a lot of rebelling against it.

PORNOGRAPHY AS A MIRROR OF SOCIETY'S PROBLEMS

RLM: There's been a lot of commentary here in the United States about women being portrayed poorly in pornographic films, which continues the domination by males that has been going on for thousands of years. One of the people I've interviewed, Katherine Rowland, talks about what she calls the pleasure gap. She draws an analogy between disparate levels of sexual pleasure and the income gap between women and men. She's saying there's a pleasure gap, where women have been subjugated sexually to such an extent that they experience less pleasure than men. Katherine reports that the data suggest that men orgasm five times as often as women in the United States while making much more money. The argument is that there's a correlating pattern between the income gap and the pleasure gap. Speak to us about that particular issue.

PP: I love that. It's such an important topic. When we talk about things like the pleasure gap or orgasm gap, people tend to present porn as the uniform source of this problem: "It's because we're getting these scripts that women do not orgasm as much." Whereas I'd say, "Wait, women weren't orgasming as much before porn was everywhere."

I believe that a big part of this is that porn mirrors current sexual standards in society. So I think we should see it rather as a mirror than the source or cause. Still, I would argue that porn can be a place for fantasy. I don't think it always necessarily needs to portray a realistic group. There are different genders, but I don't think it must represent a realistic representation of sexuality. I would argue that this idea of women being portrayed badly in porn is informed by the idea that women generally don't enjoy sex. That is a problem. It's something that we need to look into because when I look into any type of porn, I see a lot of lustful women that are enjoying whatever they're doing. You can argue about whether all women like having cum shots in their face, but I still am seeing sexually powerful women. Now, the critics are saying, "It represents women as always willing." That's a great fantasy if you compare it with the other portrayal of women as people that don't want sex, that only want sex for different reasons other than sex—like getting pregnant, having a partnership, love, or security. I think porn is a space where most women are presented as lustful creatures, and that's great. So addressing your question: yes, there are representations in porn that mirror sexual standards in society, where we're creating male-dominated spaces and where male pleasure is at the center. But I would not say that is more important than in any other medium. Again, we're back at Hollywood films. I would argue that there is more of women's pleasure in porn than in other representations of sexuality.

RLM: You made an astute comment about American porn, where so often, the scene consists of a look in the face, a quick grab, penetration, and it's done. One of the things that one sees very often in American porn—which you pointed out—is that they end it with the man ejaculating all over the woman's face. What's the message there? What's your take on that? Does this lend credence to the belief that some people have, which is that American porn is a bunch of creepy men in Los Angeles warehouses deciding, based on their own sexual interests, what the whole country is going to watch? Another view is that they're using algorithms to find out what people want to see and simply providing the public with more. Please comment on both, the cum-on-the-face phenomenon, and on the types of porn that are most prevalent.

PP: I think what is being provided indeed has to do with what the algorithms tell us, but also with what people think is going to sell. So it's a mixture of both questions. One of the problems is that we might have too many of the same kind of people with similar sexual preferences in power positions deciding what to shoot. At the same time, the industry has changed so much since the internet. Now, a lot of content creators are deciding for themselves how to stage themselves, and they're selling their videos directly to the end consumer. That has completely changed the dynamic. This idea of a bunch of creepy guys in LA deciding what we do is not the reality of the porn industry today. A lot of folks all over the planet are recording themselves with their smartphone. Some people talk about the "democratization" of porn because all of these folks are their own bosses. Nobody is telling them what to shoot. But again, a lot of them will look at what is selling best and try to reproduce that. Now, because doing porn is such a stigmatized position, there is little room for creativity and exploration. In the States, it works differently than in Europe because you don't have state funding for films. But in Europe, we have state funding for culture. If the porn industry were to have, not even half, but a little bit of support, it would allow for producers to not have to go for the easy sell and maximum profit, but to try out different things for different audiences. Porn is not only stigmatized if you do it but also if you watch it. A lot of audiences don't watch porn because they think it's a bad thing. But if they knew how diverse porn can be, they would look into it and find things they like. That would change the demand and allow for more space for different niches. So back to the cum shot, I think there's nothing wrong per se with a cum shot in the face.

PORN IS FICTION

RLM: There may be ten different perspectives on this and I can think of two immediately: On the one hand, having somebody ejaculate on your face might be exciting and a lot of fun. On the other hand, it might be degrading, especially when you see it happening so often, and you wonder what the message is. What are they trying to tell us by showing men coming on women's faces? That's what I want to know. Is this indeed meant to show women being degraded? Or is this meant to show women getting sexually excited because of this wonderful sperm on their faces? Let us look at the message we're sending to the public in these films?

PP: I 100 percent agree with you that we need to be looking at and questioning these messages. But I also think it's important not to analyze them in a simplistic, casual way. Sexuality is obviously more complex than that. A lot of people demonize facials as being degrading to women or portraying women as submissive. I don't fully go with this narrative, because I don't think that there is anything sexually that degrading there per se. Thinking in those terms is not understanding that sexuality and fantasies can be many things, and that there is a safer space where we can live out these fantasies where it can be wholesome. For example, I have gangbang rape fantasies, and that never means that in real life, I would like to experience someone doing anything to me against my consent. But sexuality is like an adult's game. It is the place where you can play. Therefore, demonizing any practice—whether it's facials, cum shots, or gangbangs—and saying, "This is wrong. This is exploitative of women," means presenting limiting ideas of what a woman or a man *is* in terms of sexuality. On the other hand, if we get only these images, that is also limiting. So why don't we try to have more diversity? Why don't we try to create and offer different images without demonizing the other ones? We need to be able to simply say, "No, this is fine. If you're into this, great." Shame is the worst when it comes to sexuality. So instead of portraying this as a war, I would say, "This is fine, as long as everyone involved is into it. But let's have also this and that other thing. Then, people can choose." Does that make sense?

RLM: It makes sense. You made an important point that we haven't talked about yet: Within the context of the gangbang, you mentioned consent. I think you and I agree that within what I call *sober consent,* any sex act is okay, and any sex act can be fun and pleasurable and no sex act should be shamed or looked down upon. But the keywords are *sober* and *consent.* Correct?

PP: Amen.

RLM: And A-women! I'm not sure to what extent sober consent is portrayed in American pornography. Namely, I'm not sure that the sober consent is clear when you look at a gangbang or some of the other ways women are treated such as being choked or slapped. It isn't clear that the women gave consent. In fact, in some of the mainstream porn movies, they make it appear as if the woman is being taken *against* her consent. Portraying women being taken without consent gives fuel to those who want to stigmatize sex. They can say, "Look what they're doing—they're raping this woman, and they're making it look good, as if there are women out there that love to be raped."

PP: That is such a difficult topic. Obviously, we don't want to put out a message that in any way ever would encourage someone to do any harm. I think we agree on that. However, as I was saying, porn is still a place of fantasy. In the same way that we as humans are able to enjoy art and films that portray shocking things or that might stir complex feelings in us, porn should also have the liberty of portraying scenes that portray things like that. Obviously, there is absolutely no arguing that the production needs to be created with consent. Anything else wouldn't be pornography in my eyes—it would be a crime. But what's important is porn *literacy*. We need to teach people that pornography is, in some ways, the same as an action film. If you see a superhero flying out of the window, but you and I know that's a fantasy, we know that we can't just jump out of the window and fly. As grown-up people, we're able to differentiate between seeing a film and reality. I understand that there's some magic happening behind the scenes. They do tricks so that it looks like someone is jumping out the window and flying. In the same way, we should have the capacity of differentiating when watching porn. So I'll go, "Okay, I'm going to watch a fictional film with scenes that are going to stir some things in me. But I understand as a grown-up person that this is fictional and not a real scene. Weirdly, we don't make that basic distinction when it comes to pornography, although you would teach it to your five-year-old by saying, "That's Superman. He can fly in films, but you can't." I think it has to do with a taboo and stigma. The more openly we talk about pornography, the clearer these lines are, and the less we need to fear being sinful. Once we accept that sexuality is complex and that we as grown-up human beings are able to enjoy things that can be extreme, that doesn't mean we'll go out into the world and do anything bad. But the more we shame those kinks and fantasies, the more we're pushing people to not speak openly. The key is open communication, talking about consent, teaching people about consent, and teaching people why porn is fictional and why it needs to be seen as fiction.

WHO PROFITS FROM STIGMATIZING PORN AND SEX?

RLM: You're talking about serious cultural change, and I happen to agree with you. Change needs to come because the hypocrisy with which we treat sexuality in America is contributing to mental illness in almost every person in the country and I mean that quite sincerely. Our cultural views and actions regarding our sexuality are messing with people's heads, because of the mass confusion about what's okay and what's not okay. Our belief systems about sex have created a cultural divide between those who view sexuality, and the pleasure it provides, the same as air, water, ingesting and eliminating, and those who view it as a base, sinful act other than when engaged in by heterosexual married couples for the purpose of procreation.

Along with all the ghastly events in our world, we received a magnificent gift, which is getting immense pleasure from sexual activity. All it takes is touching ourselves or each other in various ways and we feel this intense pleasure. In addition, sexual play can be healing when it's done with sober consent and respect. We do not yet know to what extent the vibrations which go through the body during sex are healing. But instead of allowing ourselves to benefit from sex, we've gone the opposite way. We've stigmatized sex, including demeaning women for their natural sex drives by slut-shaming.

I know much less about sexual hypocrisy being the case in Europe, where you live, but we certainly have sex problems here. Our cultural hypocrisy is widespread and dangerous. I diagnose it as Cultural Hypocrisy Neurosis (CHN). The hope is that people like yourself and the movement you're part of will grow and have more effect.

Let's talk a bit more about politics. I'm going to ask you a tough question: Who benefits financially from stigmatizing sex and keeping sex workers illegal in so many places? Who is making money off this?

PP: It's a tough question. I love how you're putting it, but I'm not sure that I have the answer, to be honest. I'm doing porn; I'm not creating the laws.

RLM: Yes, you're a filmmaker, not a lawmaker, but you *are* a political person, Paulita. I can hear it and feel it, and I appreciate that. I respect you for that a great deal.

PP: Thank you. Again, I come from Spain. So I know how much money the church has made throughout the centuries by controlling people's sexualities. Stigma against sex workers is one side of controlling and repressing people's sexualities. So I would definitely say that religious institutions are one of the parts of society that benefit from this. We can see it clearly in how aggressively some of these organizations all over the world, but also in the U.S., have been attacking the porn industry and the sex-worker community. We see it in laws like FOSTA-SESTA,* with organizations like Exodus Cry, and NCOSE,

---

*Editor's note: Passed in 2018, FOSTA-SESTA was an attempt to shut down websites that facilitated sex trafficking, but sex workers say that it put them in danger by removing their safest and most reliable sources of income.

the so-called National Center on Sexual Exploitation. That sounds good, but it's not. So I would say that a lot of religious organizations have benefited economically and politically from creating stigma and harming sex workers.

DOCUMENTARY AND CINEMATOGRAPHIC PORNOGRAPHY

RLM: Let's switch topics now. I want to spend some of the time that we have left talking about alt porn because we don't know about alt porn. We know about Hollywood, Los Angeles porn. I've already learned a little tidbit from you because I saw a couple of trailers of your work. The one thing I saw immediately—that was quite impressive—is that people in your movies don't look anything like people in the porn movies made here in the United States. This is a whole different genre. So talk to us about alt porn, how you're portraying humanity, and what people really do sexually.

PP: It's important to say that there are different genres in alt porn. Each filmmaker or director has a different focus and set of ideas that they're most interested in. I found two genres that I personally like. One I would like to call documentary porn. I like to use the word *documentary* because it's a word from film. Again, porn is nothing but film, so we can use film terminology to describe it. When I say "documentary porn," it's what a lot of people call "amateur porn." But I think *documentary* describes it much better. Instead of having a script, someone playing a character, or following choreography, these folks decided to portray their own sexuality the way they would have it if the camera wasn't there. They're basically documenting their sex lives. That was the idea behind Lustery, one of the platforms that I run. These are couples all over the world who want to share their sex videos with the community. There are no rules on what should happen or what is not okay to do. The only rule they follow is to do whatever you feel like and enjoy yourself. That applies to a lot of, what I would call "porn proposals," in the alternative scene that are trying to encompass as much diversity of human sexuality as possible. You try to show as many different bodies, identities, sexualities, and sexual practices as possible to give an idea of how diverse and incredibly rich human sexuality is. Alt porn is a wide category, and there are many differences, but generally, there are not so many scripts or choreographies to follow for portraying sex. Instead, the films are centered around the performers and their preferences. So for example, in the other genre that I enjoy, the sexual part isn't scripted either. I would call this genre "cinematographic," because it is more aesthetically pleasing and complex—we work with scenarios, costumes, and makeup. It is hard work, but I don't tell them, "Okay, now do this; now you go to doggie; now put your leg up." Every scenario is created based on the preferences that the actors have communicated to us in advance. So we've asked them what they like to do. From the list of things they like, we create a scenario where we give them a frame, but they do whatever they do and follow their impulses. We're trying to focus on the actual pleasure and sexuality of the performers, rather than following something that we think is going to sell. Those are the important components of a scene. I am not saying that this does not exist in mainstream porn. I think a lot of mainstream porn also focuses on the preferences of performers, but the space for creativity and trying things out is way more narrow. That's because you need to sell and tick off boxes. You're pushed into re-creating something over and over again, rather than seeing where an idea takes you, if that makes sense.

RLM: It does make sense. Is anybody integrating porn into mainstream film? Are there movies with a script, costumes—maybe a detective movie or a cowboy movie—where they're integrating pornography into the film the way you describe it?

PP: That is happening and that is one of my favorite parts of what's happening right now. It already happened before. We had the golden age of porn back in the seventies and eighties, when movies were playing at cinemas. Everyone remembers *Deep Throat*. In a way, the internet killed porn. All of these big productions weren't profitable anymore at a moment when the internet was offering thousands of video clips. Now, there is this evolution of amateur porn with content creators publishing material that is true to them. They're presenting their sexuality, but on a low budget, mostly with a phone on a stand. There's a new time coming for big feature films with sex, and producers are creating them. For me personally, it's a dream. I want to keep making good movies with explicit sexual content in a way that feels organic. That's where sex carries the narrative forward, so it's embedded in the story of the film.

RLM: I want to ask a personal question. Tell us about how you and your family get along in relation to your career.

PP: Of course, that question comes very often. Because it's you, Richard, I'm happy to answer that. I actually have a good relationship with my parents. I didn't immediately tell them what I was doing when I started as a performer. It took me a while because I wanted to be sure whether I was going through with this before opening up this box. But once I knew this was my career, I wanted them to know from me and not from someone else. So I told them. I always say that sex workers have a different way of coming out than queer people. The first moment wasn't easy. My mom was especially worried because of the idea of a shady industry exploiting people that we get from the media. But we had a long conversation. I gave her books, and we had discussions, cried, and hugged each other. We're at the point where my parents fully support me. They understand what I do, and they believe that it's right for me. They know that I'm happy doing this, and they support that. So in those terms, I'm very lucky, I have to say. Now, my extended family is another story. We didn't talk about it.

RLM: I see. Are your parents proud of your involvement with the Pornfilmfestival Berlin?

PP: In general, my parents are proud that they know I'm doing a lot. I'm a workaholic, and I manage several projects. They know that, and they know that my work somehow has an impact, even if it's not for them or they're not necessarily interested in what I do. They wouldn't necessarily *watch* my film or come to the festival, but still, they understand that it has a political layer and that it has value. They see I can support myself and I would say they're proud of me.

ADVICE FOR ASPIRING PORNOGRAPHY PERFORMERS AND DIRECTORS

RLM: So what advice do you have to a young person who wants to either become an actor or an actress in pornography or wants to do what you do—which is produce, direct, and write films?

PP: I would say watch porn first. A lot of people come to the industry wanting to do porn, but they don't know it. That happened to me. I didn't really know what was out there. Nowadays, it's easier to access and see how diverse and interesting different genres are. So first, I would watch a lot of porn and find out what I like. That's especially necessary if you're going to be a performer. You need to decide whether you want to *produce* content yourself. Then, I would say, start trying out stuff for yourself and see what you like. If you want to work with bigger companies, search for the ones where you relate to the content and can imagine yourself being there. Generally, go for what you enjoy most because that's where you're going to have the most fun. Don't go for what you think is going to sell best. Try to do videos of what you enjoy most, because that's going to sell best. If you are having a good time and enjoying yourself, whether in front of the camera or behind, you're going to put more passion into it and have a better time, and that's going to show in your products.

RLM: Now, there's one liability that porn thespians would be exposed to that mainstream actors and actresses don't have, which is the possibility of contracting some form of disease. How does one protect oneself from disease as an actress or an actor in pornography?

PP: It's such an important question, because a lot of folks have this idea that performers are way more exposed to diseases, and that it is dangerous territory. Actually, both in the U.S. and Europe, there are strict standards that require each performer to have a test before they go to shoot. There's a standard. They need to include HIV, chlamydia, gonorrhea, hepatitis, and syphilis, and the test cannot be older than fifteen days before the shooting. This provides a safety net. I don't have the actual data, but I'm pretty sure that porn performers have less STIs than the regular civilian. That's because we're getting tested so regularly and we're controlling our sexual health so much more than other people, who are not as aware of it. So I would say follow industry standards, inform yourself, and use the available resources. If you're going independent, still inform yourself on a day-to-day basis about industry standards.

RLM: You recommend finding out what the other performers' standards are and following all the recommended health protocols. Does the testing include testing for herpes?

PP: Not as far as I know, currently in Europe. I'm no doctor, so you might have better information about this than I do. The testing for herpes is complex. There are different kinds of herpes, and as long as it's not showing as worse, the risk of being contagious is lower.

RLM: Correct. But if there is a pustule or any kind of an outbreak, then the risk is much higher.

PP: Yes. That's why one of the tests is visual, seeing your partner's genitalia. You should be informed, and I'd say people in the industry here are. If you would recognize an outbreak, that would obviously be a game-breaker where a shoot might be canceled.

RLM: In your experience, alt-porn performers are following protocols, and they're tested?

PP: Yes.

RLM: Following testing protocols is critical for all sex workers.

PP: One-hundred percent. Those tests and protocols are absolutely non-negotiable. I've never heard of a set in Europe, where those weren't standards.

RLM: We're coming to the end of our interview, and I'd like to give you an opportunity to pause. If you'd like, tell us anything that we might have missed.

PP: Maybe there is one thing that I think is also important, and that's the way people consume porn. It's slowly getting into society, but a lot of people still have this idea of free porn. "Why would I pay for it?" That has to do with the stigma we've been talking about. So when people ask me, "If I want to consume ethically produced porn, how do I do that?" I'd say there's a simple way; just pay for it. You don't need a bio to trade something. Nowadays, you can see who's behind the platform. Obviously, I don't mean platforms with pirated porn, which also exist—and you can also pay for those. I mean platforms that clearly state who the producers and content creators are. You can easily pay for your porn and support the porn that you enjoy, either by paying the content creators directly, or the platforms and production companies. I would like to send out that message. If you are worried about what the porn industry looks like—or you're not worried but want to keep seeing the porn you enjoy—it's an easy way to support it. It just needs to be said more often so that people understand that, the same way that you would pay for music or Netflix, you should be paying for porn, because it's a cultural product that needs to be created.

RLM: So let's segue from that and give you an opportunity for a commercial. Tell people how they can access some of your films and some of your platforms.

PP: *Lustery.com* is a membership-based platform. You can pay for a monthly membership to access a huge library of real-couples porn.

PP: For HardWerk films, you can go to *hardwerk.com*. Prior to the launch, we had our films on third-party platforms. Now you'll be able to buy single films or also have paid memberships and access the full library. Thank you so much for having me, Richard. It was really nice. And thank you for all the work that you do spreading sex-positivity to this world.

16

Faith Jones

Escaping a Sex Cult

Faith Jones graduated from Georgetown, summa cum laude, after having been raised in and escaping from the Children of God cult, which she describes in her book, *Sex Cult Nun*. Founded by her paternal grandfather, the group was notorious for its radical practices, which required members to become full-time missionaries, forgo income and formal education, and submit to *the Law of Love,* a doctrine which encouraged spouse sharing and, for a time, sexual relations with children. The group also conscripted female disciples as sex "bait" to gain followers and supporters.

Faith says: "I was able to emancipate myself at twenty-three and, through self-taught study, was later accepted into Berkeley Law School. I give an intimate description of life inside a secretive cult, and most importantly, the framework of how to set oneself free of mental and spiritual manipulation in hopes of helping others stand up for themselves."

"Both inspiring and disturbing, *Sex Cult Nun* unravels Jones' complicated upbringing, the trauma she endured as a result and her path to liberation"—*TIME* Magazine

Dr. Richard L. Miller (RLM): Our guest today is Faith Jones. We're going to be talking about her life, her memoir called *Sex Cult Nun,* which openly describes her twenty years in a sex cult, and her present legal career. Faith, why did you title your book *Sex Cult Nun?*

Faith Jones (FJ): When you read the book and you see how we grew up, living communally, we didn't have personal possessions. Our lives were devoted to service; we spent hours a day memorizing scriptures and reading the group's religious teachings. Basically, we lived like a religious order, except there was a lot of sex involved. I remember when this hit me: I was doing a ten-day meditation retreat in Sri Lanka, many years after I had left. I was an attorney with Skadden Arps and worked out of Hong Kong, doing international IPOs and M&A deals.

At the small monastery in the mountains, I saw these two Buddhist nuns in training—maybe thirteen years old. They were homeschooled at the plastic kitchen table, spent hours chanting Buddhist scriptures, and doing chores. They were living this isolated life in the mountains. I thought, *Wow, this seems so familiar. Where have I seen this before?*

Then it hit me, *Oh my God, I grew up like this.*

I said, "Someday I'm going to write a book about my life and I'm going to call it *My Life as a Sex Cult Nun.*"

RLM: The word *nun* comes with the implication of chastity, of course. So the counterpoint of sex in the title of your book is provocative. You're the granddaughter of the founder of a Christian evangelical religious order that became a sex cult. Is that correct?

FJ: Yes. My family—not just my grandfather—started a group that was initially called the Children of God. It had a variety of names during its fifty-year existence. It started out of Huntington Beach, California, in 1968 out of the Jesus People movement, which consisted of hippies from that era dropping out of the system and rejecting "the Man."

My grandfather was a pastor and came from a long line of evangelists. His message was not well received by the churches that he was trying to pastor or attend because he was talking about dropping out of your lives, leaving the system, devoting yourself full-time to being missionaries, giving up all possessions, and living a type of Christian communism—claiming this was how the early Church lived. His message resonated with hippies and young people. They had already left home, dropped out of the system, and were living in communes. That's where it gained traction.

Initially, it was well-received because people said, "He's getting these hippies off drugs and cleaning them up. Now they're becoming Jesus freaks." But then other practices emerged. My grandfather had other revelations, which, I think, justified his predilections, perversions, or desires. He was using God and the Bible to turn them into a doctrine. That's where the group veered off in a way that was different from most evangelicals and Christians. This had to do primarily with sex.

RLM: If I'm not mistaken, what distinguished the sexual practices at the Children of God from other groups referred to as cults is that sexual activity, in the Children of God, was out in the open. It wasn't hidden, is that correct?

FJ: Yes. That's one of the differences. A lot of religious groups try to control two sources: money and sexuality. Sometimes that control is about not having sex, or sometimes it's about forcing it onto the group. Along with the control of money, those are two powerful levers that people use to manipulate and control their populace.

My grandfather had these revelations he called the Law of Love. He claimed that all of the Old Testament law was abolished, and that there was only one law left: if it's done in love, then it's okay with God. But he expanded this to everything. He then had another revelation: that the wife of one is the wife of all. So everyone is married to each other, and everybody should be having sex with each other within the group.

For some time, these practices—sexual liberty slowly turning into sexual exploitation—were extended to children. It was presented to us as, "Kids should grow up with a natural attitude towards sex." My grandfather had grown up in a restrictive religious environment. His mother threatened him with a knife when she caught him masturbating at six years old. He had also been sexually fondled and abused by a nanny as a two-year-old child, and he enjoyed it, so he thought this was okay.

This is the issue when you have charismatic leaders who take their personal experiences and then say, "If I liked it, then this is fine for everybody." They're not using an objective standard to say, "Is this right or wrong? Is this going to be harmful to people? Is this a violation?" Basically, he promoted sexual activity with children and declared it normal and natural.

FROM SCHEDULED SEX TO FLIRTY FISHING

RLM: What age were those children, Faith?

FJ: There is a whole history attached to it—how my father and his siblings were replaced as the "heir to the throne" by my grandfather's second wife and her baby, Davidito.* They wrote a book about Davidito and his child-rearing. Starting from babyhood, his caretakers were hyper-sexualizing him, and playing with him in a sexual way. That's what the leaders taught as the standard for how to raise your children.

RLM: So did you grow up in a community in which virtually everybody was having sex with everybody else?

FJ: Yes. It was done in an interesting way. Basically, people were on a schedule to have sex, like your chores on the wall. Particularly for women, it was considered an obligation and your duty to God to sacrifice your body and have sex with the men as a way of taking care of them.

RLM: You say in your book the women were taught that whenever a man approached them and asked for sex, their default answer had to be yes. Is that correct?

FJ: Yes.

RLM: I would imagine, not having ever lived in such a situation,

---

*Editor's note: Davidito's life ended on January 9th, 2005, as tragically as it began. Ricky Rodriguez, also known as Davidito, killed himself at the age of twenty-nine, along with his former nanny Angela M. Smith, after filming an extended video where he explained that he needed to take retribution for the abuse he experienced.

that there must have been a great deal of sexual activity, particularly amongst people in their late teens or early twenties, because men must have been approaching women whenever they felt like it.

FJ: Yes, there was. But, in its own strange way, it wasn't allowed to be a complete free for all. It was all so regimented. You would be told who to have sex with or not. So you couldn't do whatever you wanted.

RLM: But it sounds like a situation where a young woman, by the time she reached twenty, would have had sex with hundreds of men.

FJ: No, I wouldn't say that. It's not that many. You lived in small communal homes, and you were not allowed to have sex outside of the group, so options for sexual partners were very limited. For about ten years, there was a doctrine called *flirty fishing* when I was a child, where the women were supposed to go out and recruit members using sex. I wasn't part of this. That's when you were supposed to go out and have sex with people outside the group. With the advent of AIDS, my grandfather completely shut it off. So members were not allowed to have any sexual activity—not even kissing somebody—outside of the group.

RLM: I read in your book that during the period of flirty fishing, according to research, women had sex outside the group, in order to convert men, 275,000 times.

FJ: Yes. I don't know if the number was that high for actual sex because they would also flirt or use their sexuality. But it was high, and women were expected to do that. That gets to the heart of what went wrong. I give examples in the book of my own experiences with child abuse or being pressured into having sex with people I didn't want to. The heart of this issue was that they taught us we didn't own ourselves—our own bodies. Therefore, we didn't have the right to refuse because our bodies were a vessel for God.

God, through the leaders, was telling us to have sex with a person. That was our duty. That was the core violation. I took a long time to figure this out. It wasn't like everybody was flirting or having sex all the time. It was a regimented religious organization with a strict schedule. Everybody had chores. People had to do missionary work and proselytize. Sex was a relatively small part of that, but it was also highly promoted within the literature. That was important to my grandfather, the self-styled prophet.

They used Bible verses to take away people's sense of self-ownership, like "You are not your own. You're bought, with a price—therefore, glorify God with your body and in your spirit, which are God's." They said, "You don't own yourself; you shouldn't have any say in this. Just give yourself over and be submissive." When people gave themselves over like this—their sense of self-ownership, freedom, and choice—it allowed them to give over their sense of moral responsibility.

THE ABUSE OF SCRIPTURE

RLM: The argument of this religious organization was powerfully persuasive for people who believe in God, since it's commonly believed that we are all expressions of God, along with the earth, trees, and animals.

FJ: That was a serious misinterpretation of that scripture. In the historical context, Paul was actually saying, "Don't sell yourself into slavery, where another human will have the right to direct your actions because your loyalty belongs to God first." I explain it like this: "You fully own yourself. Your body is your property, and it's your inalienable right. Nobody can take this right away from you." People who believe in God often say, "God gave me this life as a gift." What is a gift? A gift is a transfer of a property right. When we receive this gift, we own our body—the rights, and the responsibilities—and we have to choose how we're going to use it. Am I going to live in accordance with moral laws, with what I believe is right, with what the Bible says? We choose how we're going to live according to our moral standards.

But for another human to tell us we don't have that right and that our body "belongs" to the group, or we that have to follow this leader who inserts themselves between us and God, saying, "This is what God wants you to do" and using the scripture to imply, "You don't have the right to say no"—that is true violation.

RLM: I can see why you refer to this as Christian communism because there's an aspect of communism where one gives up one's identity in the name of the group. I think we're seeing that in China right now.

FJ: I grew up in China and they've done that forever—it's not new. All the communist countries, socialist countries—any type of cult organization—will do this. They'll tell you that you don't own yourself. One of the main arguments they use to make this sound noble is that it's for the greater good. That's what the cult did. "You need to make this sacrifice to help your brothers in need. This is your sacrifice, your duty to God."

They always use this greater-good argument. In communism, the concept is "Everybody belongs to the state." So it doesn't matter if we kill you, murder millions of people, or take away your rights, because you as an individual don't really matter. In the Declaration of Independence, Americans were trying to escape the tyranny of a king who declared, "I own your body." That's why the Declaration states, "I have the right to life, to liberty, and the pursuit of happiness." Because under the monarchy law, the king owned all the land and people; he could put you in the tower or kill you for no reason. There was no due process. The king or landowner had this horrible right to rape your wife on your wedding night.*

There are many systems of government in which one person or even a group states or implies that they own the people. All of these create massive human rights violations. The first violation is the violation of my body—things like rape, murder, and slavery. We've unanimously decided as a modern society that these are wrong. It's not a leap. What we don't see is the clear, logical way in which this framework moves out to encompass other forms of violation.

---

*Editor's note: The practice commonly referred to as *Droit du seigneur.*

This ethical framework I define in the book and my TEDx Talk, "I Own Me," encompasses everything we consider the moral law in countries all over the world. The core is that we each own our bodies. Otherwise, it wouldn't be morally wrong for the strong to take what they want and kill you. You have to have a hook—a toehold—that creates the basis for a violation. Our moral awareness, our consciousness, our spirit—whatever you call it—uses this vehicle of our body to experience this world. This is our property. It's our first right.

Once we understand this, the next right follows: if I own property, I also own everything I create with that property. In the cult, they said we didn't own anything. When we worked hard, raised money, and got donations, we couldn't keep any of it. It all belonged to the group. If you had something that somebody else needed, you were expected to give it to them. We didn't have any sense of earning something, working toward attainment, or even owning intellectual property like songs we wrote.

Violation of our property right in our creations is theft; slander is destruction of our reputation—something of value that we've created. Anything we create that has value is our property. If a tree on your property grows pears, you own them. Once you own something, you get to exchange it for something else. I call this the Deal—it's the level of exchange, of relationships and contracts. There are five principles that must exist in any valid exchange or deal. If one element is missing, the exchange is tantamount to theft, blackmail, or fraud. When people don't clearly identify these five elements, they can be blinded to the extent that they can agree to all kinds of terrible violations. This includes child abuse, sexual abuse, or submitting to the manipulation of a cult leader.

JUSTIFICATION FOR VIOLATING CONSENT

RLM: On that tack, tell us about physical rape and also verbal or coercive rape without a physical attack.

FJ: I give examples in my book because I've experienced all of those things. Within the group, nobody was going to hold you down and force you to have sex. They weren't going to rape you in that way.

I didn't understand what I'd experienced until after I had left the group in my early twenties, when I was going to college and I had a boyfriend who was a lawyer. He explained this to me. I give an example of what happened to me in the group when I was in Kazakhstan and the leader of the home said, "You need to have sex with this young man."

I didn't like him, and I was repulsed by the idea. So I kept trying to avoid it. The leaders were telling me, "We all need to share." They were trying to make it sound all sweet and nice, but when I wouldn't go through with it, they upped the pressure. The entire home would gather for two hours to read these daily devotions, called the Mo Letters, which were my grandfather's religious writings or from the Bible.

At one of these devotions, the leaders announced to the home that I was rebellious and they had gotten prophecies for me. They had me kneel in the center of the living room and everybody had to pray over me. It was a public humiliation, a kind of breaking. They even made me change my name to strip me of my identity. Then they asked, "Now, are you ready to be yielded to God and do what we've asked?"

That's using coercion and fear of punishment to make you agree to sex, even though it was a circuitous route to get there. They weren't saying, "If you don't have sex, we'll punish you." They said, "If you don't have sex with this person, you're being unyielded. We're going to punish you for being unyielded." If you didn't comply after that, the punishments would escalate.

When you're coerced or feel pressured into having sex with someone when you don't want to for fear of punishment, that's still rape—even if you willingly walk in the room. When we're talking about child-sex victims and sex trafficking, oftentimes these young girls are forced to pretend they like it. But they're being forced to do it at the risk of their life. It doesn't even have to be as severe as that for it to be rape. If you're not freely choosing this, knowing that you've got the uncoerced option to do this or not, then that's rape. That was a huge revelation for me.

RLM: With this kind of sexual activity going on, how did the organization prevent young girls from getting pregnant?

FJ: The goal was to have lots of children, not to prevent them. The group started out with mostly young people. They were encouraged to marry and have kids. They didn't believe in birth control, so families grew very fast.

RLM: You state that the Children of God church grew to tens of thousands of people in seventy countries.

FJ: It did, but it also had a lot of babies. My older siblings and I were in the first batch of children born in the group. We had a different experience than the kids that came later because the group's policies were constantly changing. For around ten years, my grandfather was espousing these sex-with-children policies—girls as young as twelve, boys even younger—having sex with adults.

As these kids got older, the authorities started getting involved. People who had left were reporting on it, which led to police raids. Then the leadership sent around a questionnaire for all young teens. They discovered in these detailed questionnaires that nearly all of the female teens who had been subjected to sexual interaction with adults reported trauma due to these policies. They were terrified of adult men who tried to be sexual with them. So they began to see that these policies were not bearing positive fruit in the lives of these kids.

RLM: You mean the leaders of the organization actually began to see the problems created by allowing sexual relations between adults and children?

FJ: Yes. I think it was a combination of external and internal pressure. At one point around the mid-eighties, they banned all adult-child sexual contact.

RLM: "Child" being defined as what age?

FJ: At this point, I believe it was under sixteen, but the ages would keep changing over time. The UK court case was instrumental in creating new regulations. Then it became under eighteen, but with various caveats. Teenagers younger than that could be with each other, but not past a certain age point. They put in place a lot of strict regulations, which I was happy about. When the first ban came in, I was ten years old and not far from hitting that limit of twelve in which kids were expected to engage in sexual activity with adults.

So it didn't exist the whole time. Kids that grew up after that period would not necessarily have experienced it unless there were unrepentant pedophiles who continued to abuse in the group, and those definitely existed. But the practices were still around; sex was still coercive. That came from this core concept of not owning yourself.

RLM: How did women in the organization know who the fathers of their children were if they were having multiple partners?

FJ: They didn't always.

LEGAL AUTHORITY OVER CULTS

RLM: How is it that the cult was allowed to continue these practices given that they're so distant on the normal bell curve from the sexual behavior that's allowed by governments? How is it that governments didn't arrest the leaders of the organization?

FJ: The organization itself was very secretive. We didn't go to school, and members didn't hold jobs. We raised money with donations and moved from place to place. My family was different in that we had a foundation in one location for quite a long time. We built a whole farm in a village, but that was unusual. A lot of families moved regularly.

RLM: How often is *regularly*, Faith?

FJ: Maybe every year.

RLM: Would they move as a group with fifteen or twenty, so they would all be together, or were you talking about the movement of mother, father, and a few children?

FJ: It would depend. Sometimes the whole home would move; other times, it might disperse and families would go to other homes.

RLM: How would a small family support themselves?

FJ: It was difficult. The concept was that we lived communally. So you had a lot of help. Certain people were assigned to watch kids, others to cook meals or do the cleaning. Some people were assigned to go out and raise money. You would do this by selling the group's posters and CDs. Oftentimes members might have people who would regularly support them as missionaries. We called them Friends of the Family who would send donations as you do to a church. Other than the leadership, the rank-and-file members constantly lived on the edge of poverty. They did not have fancy lives by any means. We were barely scraping by.

RLM: Were the church members extremely modest?

FJ: Yes, very modest. You all lived crammed together. A family would have one room, not a house.

RLM: Of the tens of thousands of followers, would you say the vast majority of them were city-dwellers rather than idealistic communards living in the country on a nice farm?

FJ: A lot lived in cities, but they would usually rent a larger property so that multiple families could live together on one property. Most members, in fact, lived in cities. Our family was unique in that sense. My father had this vision of what he wanted to create and he was bullheaded about it. Not a lot of people wanted to stand up to him— at least not until later.

RLM: Faith, what is the difference between a religious organization— such as Christianity or Islam—and a cult?

FJ: Oftentimes when I talk about this, people say, "Then all organizations are cults." But I think there *is* a definition of a cult, with key characteristics. One of them is isolation from society and cutting yourself off from outside input. We weren't allowed to read outside books, we didn't go to school, and we didn't hold jobs. We were seriously cut-off. Another big aspect is control of finances. If you can't support yourself outside of the group, or they take all your money, that's a big red flag. I experienced this when my mother, myself, and my two younger siblings were accidentally cut-off from the group for a year and she couldn't support us. I was begging in parking lots for money to feed my family when I was twelve. It's taking away people's ability to support themselves economically apart from the group. Besides that, any sort of strongly coercive group is going to somehow undermine your sense of self-ownership and free will.

RLM: Speaking as an experienced lawyer, talk to us about religious freedom and government control. What is a religious group allowed to do in terms of their own sovereignty, in the name of freedom of religion? When do they come under the aegis of the government? There are those religious leaders who say, "We have a right to make our own rules because we're a religious organization." In the United States, religious organizations don't generally have to pay taxes. That's astounding when you think about it. Everybody pays taxes, but religious organizations don't. For example, the Catholic Church and the Presbyterian Church of the United States—both very wealthy—don't pay taxes. They're not subject to the law of the land in that regard, but in other areas, such as their sexual practices, they are subject to laws—but only if the government finds out what they're doing. It looks like there are difficult areas to discern, and it has implications for what these cult leaders can and cannot do.

FJ: I created a framework that simplifies all of that. The framework becomes a lens. You know how when you're trying to see things without your glasses and everything is all blurry, then you put those glasses on and, all of a sudden, it's clear? You can see all the boundaries, read the text, and see what's going on. That's what this framework does. You literally hold up a lens that allows you to compare and clarify people's actions. Remember: laws and regulations are different. Regulations that govern non-moral issues—like what side of the road you drive on or how much you pay in taxes—hold a different position in the hierarchy of law than moral issues, such as child sexual abuse.

The other thing we have to remember is that the law is not always moral. We've had—and still have—many immoral laws on our books as a government. Slavery was legal for a long time; women were considered property. There are many times in which the law itself is immoral and is creating a violation of our rights. So I don't assume that the law is correct. The framework applies equally to religious groups, the government, and individuals. If they're violating your rights to your body, creations or deals, it's wrong.

We have a constitutional law that says states cannot abrogate or limit the right to contract. That applies to the principles of the Deal. If I own something, I get to contract for it. But for a contract to be valid, I have to follow five principles. Every time you see abuse, they're violating one of these principles.

Let's look at child sexual abuse. One of the things that a perpetrator would say is, "I asked this twelve-year-old boy if he wanted to have sex and he agreed. So this is his free choice." Is that true? Let's look at the five factors. For a deal or exchange to be valid, you have to have an offer—to clearly know what's being exchanged. You have to have willing acceptance. There has to be an actual exchange of value. You have to have the mental capacity to understand the impact of what you're agreeing to, and to be able to agree without undue pressure.

A child does not have the mental capacity to understand what they are giving up. They don't know how this is going to impact them in the future. They don't understand the undue pressure inherent in an adult-child relationship based on a power disparity. The child is biologically programmed to want to please the adult, to obey, or to gain approbation. So if they feel like that's what their caretaker wants them to do, they're almost biologically compelled to go along with it. This is not free consent. This is why we have regulations about bosses who are not supposed to have sex with their employees. There's a power disparity that creates the risk that that person feels pressured to do something. So it's not a free choice.

RLM: Yes.

FJ: We see undue pressure everywhere; it's huge. So when you're talking about how these religious leaders are running their organization, look for the undue pressure. If that exists, then it's going to create a moral violation and real crimes—crimes like child abuse, rape, murder, theft, fraud, or blackmail. Each crime falls into one of the circles of the framework diagram.

RLM: Based on what you're saying, you could make a strong argument to classify it as rape when the CEO of a company makes moves on a secretary and is successful.

FJ: That depends. I'm a lawyer, so I recognize that things are context-driven based on a particular set of facts. When sex involves a child, it's 100 percent sexual assault—a child cannot contract. We don't ever allow children to enter a contract because we understand that. For an adult, as in your example, you need to ask: What if the secretary is chasing him down? Maybe she wants to get him in bed to get a promotion? That happens, too.

With adults who are in different positions of power, it's not a violation in every single circumstance, but the potential for violation is so huge there that you're better off not engaging in it. If you do, the parties often have to sign an agreement and state that they did this of their own free will and didn't feel pressured in any way. That's why HR departments have all of these regulations. They're trying to create an atmosphere where the other person knows, "I can decline sex and walk away with no repercussions." If you can't create that genuine feeling in the other person, then you're at risk.

So how do you create the atmosphere that lets the other person know, "If I say no, it's not going to jeopardize my job?" That question is why so many companies have rules against inter-office relationships. In the military, there are rules against a superior officer having sexual relations with someone junior to them. It's because of that inherent power disparity, which can create undue pressure to agree to something they might not otherwise agree to if it was a free, open playing field. That's why our processes and procedures have to try to level that playing field.

THE CONSEQUENCES OF TRAUMA

RLM: Talk to us about the consequences of predatory, noncontractual behavior. You report that adults in the Children of God church/organization had sex with children. What do we know then about the lives of the children later on? What do we know about their ability to form relationships or have healthy sex lives?

FJ: I don't know that somebody has done research specifically on these kids. Even within the group, kids had vastly different experiences. It might have depended on what home they were in, which adults lived with them, what their parents did, or whether their parents protected them. I know some kids whose parents were extremely protective, so they didn't experience anything like that. Other kids were abused by their own parents. But it wasn't only the kids who were traumatized.

In my work, I've seen that how people deal with trauma is incredibly individualized. Some people may have something seemingly insignificant happen to them and it completely derails their life. Others may have things happen to them that seem so extreme, you can hardly imagine it, and yet they are happy and functioning and they move on with their life.

This led to exploring the deeper question: How do we set ourselves up for resilience and the ability to deal with trauma? How do we teach our children those skills? People often ask me, "How are you so normal after experiencing all this? You're happy and productive." This led me to analyze my own experiences and coping techniques. Aside from the fact that I pursued my personal healing with a vengeance, I realized I also used certain techniques, even as a child, that helped me. This got me asking, "How can we teach these resilience techniques to children?" Because, as a parent, you're not going to be able to protect them from everything.

From what I've heard in conversations and seen in my own life,

I do know early sexual experience impacts a person. The extent to which it affects them negatively is going to be different for each person. I remember that the boys in the group would boast about their sexual experiences when we were kids. The boys seemed like they were happy about it; they didn't seem upset like the girls. But when you talked to the boys later in life, they said, "I realize now that did have a negative impact on me. That wasn't helpful. I didn't recognize the emotions I was having, the embarrassment, or the feelings. I wasn't fully aware." They were so young at that time, but as adults and parents, they recognized it. So it's never okay, and it's not a choice that you should give a child.

RLM: I was engaged in sexual activity by a babysitter when I was four-and-a-half years old. The physical and psychological experience at the time was not unpleasant at all—in fact, it was very pleasant. However, there was an immediate psychological impact that I had done something wrong, which was an extremely heavy burden to carry until I finally got into psychotherapy when I was a 16-year-old freshman at the University of Illinois.

I have learned that the nature of sexual trauma varies greatly from person to person. I wasn't physically or psychologically injured by the event itself yet the psychological impact of the sense that, even at that young age, I knew I had transgressed created the trauma that I lived with. By the age of four, we know that there are certain things we're not supposed to do, and I had done one of them. Therefore, I carried that weight.

You've been quite transparent about your life experience of growing up in a sex cult. I read the section in your book where you talked about how sexual intercourse was painful for you for a period of time after you left the cult. Of course, this pain came from the trauma that you experienced while in the cult. I commend you for your openness in talking about these intimate experiences, both here and in your book.

FJ: Thank you. I'm sorry you experienced that, and you're right: for a lot of people, the physical experience is pleasurable because it was designed to be. But it's like picking fruit. When you pick it too young, it's never going to ripen the same way. You've damaged its growth process and development. It's not going to fully develop into what it might've become after that point. People only recognize that later.

A lot of times, people who did have sexual interactions with adults at too young an age carry the guilt and think it's their fault. That also happened to me, when I was six and again when I was ten. We somehow feel like we agreed to it. Other people carry around guilt because they enjoyed it, and that's incorrect. There is no guilt. When you're a child, you cannot make those decisions. The adults are there to make those decisions for you. You're not responsible.

When people understand this framework and get clarity on those five points, especially the principles of mental capacity and undue pressure, it takes away that sense of guilt. Because there's no way you could have understood what was happening to you at five, six, or even ten years old. If something like that has happened to you, it's important to talk about it, go to therapy, or see other experts.

I wrote another book, which is on my website, *www.faithjones .com*. It's called *I Own Me*. It's my guide about reclaiming your body and your property, alongside healing exercises that I found to be the most helpful after traumatic experiences like rape, abuse, or child abuse. I wrote that book before I did my TEDx Talk. It's written specifically to women because I'm a woman, so I feel I can better speak from that perspective.

If you look at the statistics, 91 percent of rape and sexual abuse happens to women. But it definitely happens to men—particularly boys. In fact, the more that I've spoken about it, the more female and male friends have told me about their experiences of abuse. So I know that child abuse is a more common experience for boys than we as a society acknowledge. Even though in the book I'm speaking to women and the societal and psychological aspects that make this abuse more prevalent for them, the healing exercises can work for anyone.

HELPING OTHERS ESCAPE FROM CULTS

RLM: If people are reading this and they know someone who's in a cult, or if someone believes they're in a cult, what can you tell them about extricating themselves? You did something amazing—you spent twenty years of your life completely taken over. You didn't own yourself as you do now, and yet somehow you managed to get out. It must've helped to get accepted at Georgetown—a major accomplishment, given how little education you had prior—but what can you say to people about extrication?

FJ: When I left the cult, Georgetown wasn't in my vision. I left just hoping to get into community college. My desire to learn was paramount. I couldn't stand the restriction of my mind anymore. So I had to figure out how to get a job and support myself, to register for a community college, to take SATs, and so on. I had to figure out how to exist in a whole new world long before I got to Georgetown.

RLM: Even knowing there was such a thing as an SAT was quite an accomplishment.

FJ: I guess I've always been good at research. What I didn't have—that I wish I did at the time—is what I've created: how to understand these principles of self-ownership. I also have videos on my YouTube channel, FaithJonesAuthor, walking people step-by-step through these principles and applying them to their situation and their leaders and asking, "Are these principles being violated?"

If you think you're in a cult, the first thing is to get clear on these principles. Once you get that sense of self-ownership in your bones, you won't be able to take it anymore. You won't be able to allow people to railroad you when you believe that you own yourself. That will help give you the impetus to make the changes because it takes a lot of courage, hard work, and determination to pull yourself out of that situation. Oftentimes, you don't have any money.

You need to have a strong internal conviction that will help guide you. You can find help and resources in lots of places, like shelters.

Today, I realize how important the mental aspect is—getting clarity on your rights and principles, who you are as a human being, and what your boundaries are. That's what this framework does. It allows you to define everything within clear, healthy boundaries, even if you've never had them because you didn't grow up with them like myself.

The second piece is learning how to achieve financial stability and independence. Without that, you're still going to be subject to people abusing you or discriminating against you. When you can achieve economic independence, that is a huge step towards your personal healing and regaining control of your life. I teach people how to use different financial structures for business and investing. That's been my focus for the last few years: "How do we take our money and create passive streams of income to protect ourselves?" Look at how many people lost their jobs during the pandemic, which we couldn't have foreseen. Making sure that you're set up for that so that you can still take care of yourself and your family is important, even more so in this healing process.

RLM: I couldn't agree with you more. I think you know the statistics as well as I do that 70 percent of the people in the United States are only a few weeks away from not being able to pay their rent or not being able to put food on the table for their families. Financial desperation makes it more difficult for people to believe that they own themselves. May your concept of "I own me" spread!

FJ: Thank you for interviewing me so that I can share my story and, hopefully, encourage more people to claim themselves and their power.

17

Laura McGuire

Teaching Consent and Its Broad Impact

Laura McGuire (they/them or she/her), Ed.D., is an internationally recognized sexuality educator, consultant, trauma-informed specialist, survivor, researcher, seminarian, and author of the books *Creating Cultures of Consent: A Guide for Parents and Educators* (Rowman & Littlefield, 2021) and *The Sexual Misconduct Prevention Guidebook* (Fielding University Press, 2022). McGuire was named as one of the 2022 Champions of Pride by *The Advocate* magazine and is regularly featured in media outlets for her expertise and approachability.

McGuire is also the founder of the National Center for Equity and Agency. In 2019, McGuire created the world's first certification in trauma-informed care for legal professionals and in 2021 expanded it to include the insurance industry. McGuire currently teaches at both Widener and Dominican University and works as a trainer, mediation advisor, and author.

Please be sure to check out the website: *www.drlauramcguire.com* and follow McGuire on Instagram @drlauramcguire.

Dr. Richard L. Miller (RLM): Our guest today is Laura McGuire. Welcome, Laura.

Laura McGuire (LM): Thank you so much for having me, Richard. I'm so happy to be here.

RLM: I am so happy you are here. Laura, let's begin by having you tell your story. How did you go from being a Catholic, evangelical-raised young woman with a most interesting background to writing a book called *Creating Cultures of Consent?*

LM: Our origin stories are always one of the most interesting things, I think, about all people. I was raised both Baptist Evangelical—with a little bit of Methodist in there—and Catholic. A lot of people will say they were raised Catholic *or* Baptist, but I got a double whammy. It was an interesting upbringing because I got a lot of messages about consent and sexuality. But they were not the kind of messages we're promoting now, or certainly that I would be promoting in my book. But they were still there; they were just not helpful. A lot of them were based on concepts such as victim-blaming and shame-based narratives. Those created the foundation of my wanting to find something different.

At the same time, though, there were good things about that upbringing. One of them was that, for many years, I was preparing to become a nun. At the heart of that vocation was this desire to be in service of humanity 24/7, 365 days a year. I very much feel that what I do now is in that vein. I go around the world to talk to people and change norms, trying to get people to think about tough topics in an approachable and engaging way. So, on one hand, that upbringing pushed me in the opposite direction to look for the alternative to its negative parts and create a career around that. On the other hand, the good parts did help me to formulate that I wanted to make this my full-time life and job. I'm so fortunate to be able to do that.

PROTECTING BOYS FROM SINNING

RLM: At the beginning of your book you tell a story about going to the swimming pool as a teenager. I want you to talk to us about what you had to wear over the bathing suit and why you were told that you needed to do that.

LM: Many people will relate; this was in the 1990s. Even today, there are still a lot of spaces—and we're not talking about faith-based youth spaces—where they will talk about protecting others in the community from sinning. They'll say—particularly to young women, people assigned female at birth—that they need to cover parts of their body. It's often said that God designed young men to have this natural lust that they can't control. So to help them not go to hell, we have to make sure we're not enticing them to think lustful thoughts or to act on them. When I was in that world, they would have a beach day or a pool party, and they would tell only the girls that they could wear bathing suits. But if they were going to and it wasn't what's called a modest bathing suit that would cover from knees to shoulders, they would have to wear a shirt over it. Even if it was a one-piece, there was too much showing, it was too tight. They would need to wear an extra-large T-shirt over it that would cover everything. Then they would say, "You can still swim in that. But you won't cause your brothers to stumble and fall."

RLM: So they acknowledge that the boys in the swimming pool are getting sexually excited, but there's no recognition of female sexuality and lust whatsoever.

LM: No.

RLM: What you're talking about—putting on a shirt over a one-piece bathing suit that goes from the knees to the shoulders—sounds to me like one step short of a *Burqa*.

LM: Let me clarify a bit. If your one-piece bathing suit didn't cover you from the shoulders, they would ask that you wear the T-shirt. Some bathing suits in those communities do cover more and then you don't have to wear something on top. It's equally important to say that, if that's someone's choice, if that makes them feel comfortable, there's nothing wrong with that. If someone *wants* to wear a bathing suit that covers from their wrist to their ankles, that's great. But it's wrong when it's framed in a way that shames people, saying that you're responsible for someone else's thoughts or actions, and that your body is inherently going to cause them to do something negative or violent.

RLM: With due respect, Laura, we're not born wanting to cover up; we're born naked, and then we do cover up. So I don't know how much choice these young women have, in terms of wanting to wear their suit, particularly in a world where if they go to the movies or see television, they're going to see women prancing around in bikinis. Young people, even those shielded from the larger culture, can't help being influenced by the world at large. But let's move on now to the history of consent, because your book is about consent.

DO RAPE-FREE CULTURES EXIST?

LM: There's an important history, and we can look at it from two perspectives. We can look at it globally, and we can say that, around the world, we have cultures that anthropologists have designated as "rape-free." That means that they don't have a culture that has an expectation that sexual violence is part of the human experience or part of a community. They don't have that in their history, which is fascinating. So that's one perspective.

RLM: You're saying there are cultures on the planet where you don't get rape?

LM: Right. Those cultures also don't have high rates of domestic violence. There's not a lot of interpersonal, intimate, romantically linked violence. That just doesn't exist, and this is exciting because some evolutionary biologists have argued that this is just part of human nature. They've said that, if people are going to have these desires, then sometimes they're going to violently act on them. That this is just the way people are. But these indigenous communities have proven that that is wrong.

RLM: I see. According to the National Sexual Violence Resource Center, we have about 1186 rapes every single day, or 49 per hour, or about 1 every single minute. We might say at this very moment a woman is being raped in the USA.

LM: Right. There are a lot of figures like that. This is a huge problem.

RLM: The National Sexual Assault Resource Center reports that one out of four women in the United States has experienced some form of sexual contact violence at some time in their life and one in five women experienced completed or attempted rape during their lifetime.

LM: Yes. For boys, it's one in six. It's not that far apart.

TEACHING CONSENT

RLM: That's an interesting number, too. So how do kids learn about consent?

LM: That's the ultimate question. When parents see what's going on in the world, you start thinking about how to prevent this, like, *How do I address this?* So many parents just don't know where to start. You start by talking about communication. At the same time that we teach our children to say please and thank you, we want to start talking about consent. If someone's saying "no"—or maybe they're not even saying no, but they're uncomfortable—that's a "stop." We don't try to convince or manipulate them. We honor their discomfort, especially if they're saying no. Then we also want to teach them about enthusiastic consent, saying yes and speaking up about what we *do* want, and honoring that in any interpersonal connection. Far before this gets into the realm of dating or sexuality, it's in every part of interpersonal communication.

RLM: Who teaches this consent? Parents? School? How do we convey this information, Laura?

LM: That's why the book is titled "for Parents *and* Educators"—in an ideal scenario, they're working together. Parents are modeling these things at home. In the book, I break down some examples of what that looks like. Then the kids go to school, and they're hearing the same messages. So they're getting more lessons on it. Throughout their life, they're having this as part of conversations about interpersonal skills, emotional intelligence, and communication. Then it comes into health class when they start talking about sex and dating. So ideally, it's in all those spaces. Faith communities—churches, synagogues, temples—should also be having this as part of their youth education.

RLM: If both the parents and the schools are teaching about consent, what is taught in the curriculum? How is that decided? Let me give you an example: a couple that I'm working with have two children in school, and they got invited to a discussion about the sex education curriculum. They told me that many of the parents in the room were very uptight about the mere thought that their children are to be given sex education. When they got into discussing things like consent, it was not a pleasant scene; it was very awkward. How does one deal with that, and who creates the curriculum?

LM: Excellent question. A lot of parents will have fears and valid concerns because they didn't get this education growing up. It's scary for them. One of the things I suggest in the book is to start with the parents—having sessions where they can learn the curriculum, view it, talk to the teachers, and ask questions. The teachers can give them an overview of the consent culture they're trying to create. They would not only bust a lot of the myths that they might have, but for a lot of parents, it will be the first time they hear these messages. That's so important. Once you get the parents onboard, you're more likely to get the school and the school district to say that this is integral at any age to have this understanding. As the kids get older, they learn more and more. But teaching the parents first, making sure they're safe in understanding it, and asking questions—that's the foundational piece. You can't move forward without that.

CONSENT BEYOND SEXUALITY

RLM: Maybe we jumped too far into the future and we need to go back a bit. Give us a basic definition of consent. What does that mean when you say "consent between two or more people"?

LM: Consent is an enthusiastic and informed, ongoing verbal and non-verbal agreement to anything. If I'm taking on a project at work, I need to know what I'm getting into, and I need to enthusiastically agree to it or not, not just say *yes* because I have that pressure on me, or because I'm supposed to say yes without knowing what I'm agreeing to. It means that, when people are dating, before they ever have any physical contact, they're enthusiastically agreeing to text each other or call each other. We see a lot of cases of harassment where that wasn't in place, and that becomes a consent issue. Especially when people are going to have an intimate relationship, making sure that each aspect of that is agreed to and understood, that people know that just because something is a yes at one time, that doesn't mean yes moving forward. It can be rescinded at any time, and continue to be discussed and negotiated.

RLM: In your book, you talk about how a significant percentage of females in this country are taught courting behavior, and they're taught that when the man moves forward, they move away. The standard being taught is: "Don't immediately jump into sexual intimacy by any means." They're taught to play or act hard to get, and to keep things moving slowly. That's how our culture trains women, "Move the whole thing slowly, and don't just jump right into bed with the boys." But the boys also know that the women are trained to do that. So when the woman is moving away or saying "slow down," how is the boy to know that that isn't just what she does as part of the courtship game? Aren't we training the boys to think, *I'm supposed to move forward even* more *now that she's moving away, so she can make believe I'm convincing her to do something that I know she wants to do as much as I do.*

MOVING AWAY AS CULTURALLY LEARNED COURTING BEHAVIOR

LM: In social sciences and psychology, we call this *token resistance* and *token compliance.* Token resistance is what you just mentioned. For people who are socialized as female, there's an expectation of, "I can't say yes," or, "My partner will call me too eager. They'll use negative terms for me like *slut* or *whore*." Those are powerful insults for people assigned female at birth. So I have to make sure I appear like I'm pulling back, even if, deep inside, I want to do this. It's equally important to note that token compliance includes the other side, which is, I have to say yes or I'll be put down and ostracized. People socialized as male most often receive that. If boys are dating a girl and they say, "I'm not ready yet; we've got to slow things down." The girl will ask, "What's wrong with you? Aren't you attracted to me? Who are you attracted to? You're weird." Everybody gets this, and it's toxic. It's awful, unhelpful, and it creates rape culture, which is the opposite of consent culture. So what do you do? When we're training young men who might say, "How do I know if the girls are just playing hard to get?" you say, "If there's any *question* as to whether this person is saying *no* in any way or a question, that's a *no*." You have to say, "Based on what you're saying, on what you're showing me with your body language, I'm not going to move forward, because I need to know you enthusiastically want to do this. I'm not going to shame you for that." But I need to know because if it's any kind of a gray area, if I'm not 100 percent sure you're saying, *Yes, I definitely want this,* it's a no for me. "That changes that narrative, because then the person can say, "No, I'm saying I'm unsure; *I really am saying no.*" So they say, "That's okay. You're safe to say that with me." Or they say, "Thank you for saying that. Because there are things I want to do with you. But I have these cultural messages and real fears." So here's how we can have more authentic communication. It is about honoring any *no,* any question mark as a *stop,* but then making sure that you're switching the paradigm to have communication be more honest.

RLM: So here's a question from my clinical practice: A young man says to me that he's engaged to a young woman he's courting. They're making out, and he pulls up his shirt and then he starts to unbutton her blouse. She says no, and he stops immediately. She says, "Why are you stopping?" He says, "Because you said *no*." She says, "But sometimes *no* means yes." He says, "Is it *no,* or is it *yes?*" She's saying, "*Well no, but yes.*" So he comes to me and says, "I don't know what to do with such a situation. She's telling me that *no* means yes." You've been teaching me that you don't go against a *no,* that you just leave it as a no-deal. This story seems to tie in with what you're talking about. Have you come across the way women are trained to give a *no* in the beginning, sliding right over into the *yes* very quickly? It's very confusing for a young man who wants to be respectful.

LM: Absolutely. We see this, especially generationally. The teens and young adults I work with now don't have this as much because they've started to make consent culture more of a norm. But for generations past, it's certainly a huge problem. But it's also geographical. I was born in Tennessee; I still live in the Deep South. In some pockets, there's still that token resistance—that pervasive sense of, "I have to perform in order to be accepted or seen as a good person." So if I was talking to that client of yours, I would say, "You're doing the right thing. You're stopping when there's any note of doubt. Even if this person says, 'Well, it's complicated,' you have to sit down and say, 'I can't function that way.'" We've seen this in movies; we've heard this in song. But it's not good. We have to change the way we communicate about this. If you're saying "no," but not pulling back at all, I don't want to play around with that. That's not okay. I need you to be very clear in what you want to do. What *do* you feel comfortable with? Tell me—say *yes.* The biggest thing is to affirm to his partner that there's not going to be any shaming that comes along with this. "I'm not going to go back to my friends and say, 'I had a date with her,' and we're all going to laugh about it and call her names." That's the root fear, and that's culturally conditioned. That's very real. So that's how I would counsel him. He has to change that narrative. Particularly boys and men, who have power in our society, are such an important piece of taking the lead and saying, "I believe in consent culture. I'm going to require an enthusiastic *yes.* I'm not going to exist in any gray area."

THE CONTINUUM OF HARM

RLM: In your book, you talk about a concept called *the continuum of harm*. Tell us about that.

LM: The continuum of harm is a concept of how we get to the point where we see things in the news. You mentioned what's going on with the Southern Baptist Convention, and reports of decades of horrible abuse. People see that and they say, "How on earth did a group of faith leaders in a conservative denomination get to the point where they were condoning, covering up, and excusing sexual assault?"

RLM: Seven hundred cases of sexual abuse were uncovered, which took place over a period of twenty years by the leaders of the Citizen Southern Baptist Convention. This group is the largest Protestant and second largest Christian denomination in the United States.

LM: Exactly. So when we get to the point that that's the headline, we have to realize there was a continuum of behaviors that laid a foundation that allowed the situation to progress to that point. The continuum-of-harm principle says that, before we ever get to a point where someone is physically assaulting someone else, we have to stop and address things. You can imagine it like a pathway or a pyramid, like you're building something on top of something and there's this pinnacle point, which is the worst case. But think about that wide foundation that was built first. So those are: comments, jokes, blackmail. We now have things like revenge porn. Someone sends a picture or video to someone, and they blackmail them with it. "I'm going to use this against you. I'm going to manipulate you. I'm going to ask for money from you." But before that, friends may be doing jokes about someone's sexual history or putting them down by saying they're gay. Homophobia is a route on this continuum, too. If we're able to stop it there and say, "Hey, not funny. Wait a minute—no, that's not okay."—when that becomes the culture, then those behaviors don't escalate. We can say, "Hey, you're texting this person and they're not responding. I think they told you to please stop texting, and you keep bothering them." And we don't get to a place where predators can prey on people and the people around them are going to excuse it or protect them. We even see it in the example you gave, when young people go from reflexively saying *no* to feeling empowered to accurately reflect how they feel with *yes, no,* or *maybe*—but ensuring that it's clear any which way. The aim is for the yes to be clear yes, enthusiastic yes. *That's* how you prevent things from becoming what we're seeing in the news.

RLM: So in this continuum of harm, there are all these variables— little comments, little pictures, all having to do with aggression— *suggesting* going ahead with sexual moves even without getting a definite yes from the other person. When we look at these suggestive variables in totality, they're building the foundation towards making sexual abuse acceptable. Within that context, what did it say to the young people in the United States when they heard a tape of presidential candidate Donald Trump saying to a reporter, "I can grab women by the pussy, and they can't do anything about it because I'm a celebrity?"

LM: I'll tell you a quick story. I was working at a university in Texas at the time of that presidential election, a few months after that sound bite had come out. I was working on a project where we had created a consent education curriculum specifically for international students, because a lot of them were still taking their TOEFL, their English competency exam. So we made sure the whole curriculum was translated into multiple languages. We were talking about expectations and cultural differences. The day after that election, because of that tape, I walked into a class for that group, and a lot of young men from around the globe said, "You're telling us that, here in the United States, you believe in consent, and we can't do this without asking and making sure the person is comfortable. But look at who you just elected. There's no way we're going to buy into this now." So that's the impact. It's not even just U.S. citizens. The globe looks at us and says, "You don't care about consent. You support sexual predators." Even if it was only a joke and he never acted on it, that's a predatory statement. It's not funny. So it becomes part of culture, part of expectation, and it even leaks into our legal system. We see this with judges, attorneys, and police officers, who are then less likely to believe that someone is a victim. Or they tell them it wasn't that big of a deal. All of these subconscious messages seep into the back part of our brain and become the way that we view all the situations we're faced with. The detrimental effect is massive and long-lasting.

MOVING FROM RAPE CULTURE
TO CONSENT CULTURE

RLM: You say in your book that, in addition to the child sexual abuse we're learning about now, which has taken place, and continues to take place, in the Catholic Church and the Southern Baptist Church, we grew up in an even larger rape culture. Talk about growing up in a rape culture.

LM: That's a powerful phrase. Sometimes people hear that and they'll say, "What do you say here, Dr. McGuire? It sounds terrible." I didn't coin the term *rape culture*. It's been around for a couple of decades. But it is a powerful phrase because it's an important concept for people to think about. A rape culture is not a culture that outwardly accepts or condones rape or sexual violence. It is a culture that has *subliminally* put in place these scripts—with token compliance, non-compliance, and token resistance—that this is okay, funny, or not that bad. When a culture has that ingrained in it, it will by default allow things like rape, harassment, and stalking to take place. It entails people turning a blind eye and saying, "I don't see this. This isn't that big of a deal"—or outright blaming the victim. That's what rape culture is. Understanding what that is is the first step. We first have to get that place if we want to move to a consent culture. If we want to shift that, we first have to say, "What is the problem we're looking at? What would the opposite of this look like in action?"

RLM: When you teach young people, do you get a different reception about consent culture from females than males?

LM: Yes. The biggest difference for women and people assigned female at birth* seems to be that they believe it if you say these things but males often require convincing. This is a problem. This is prevalent. The people who are facing violence, harm, and trauma all the time say, "That's real. I think about this all the time. Either I've experienced it, or my friends or family members have. I see it all around me." But for a lot of people assigned male at birth, the reaction is oftentimes, "Are you being hyperbolic? Are you blowing this out of proportion? Maybe it's not that bad? Maybe it's not this level of danger. Maybe I don't have to think about it that much." That's the biggest gap, and that's why it can be good to have cohorts of students learning together from different genders, sexual orientations, races, ethnicities, and age groups. Because then they hear from each other: "Maybe you don't get this in your experience, so it doesn't seem like a prevalent problem. But maybe you're limited by your experience. If you heard how I have to navigate the world, you would have a different understanding."

TEACHING CONSENT TO RELIGIOUS STUDENTS

RLM: If I correctly understand the teaching of the evangelical groups that you grew up with, they're teaching no sex before marriage, and that sex is only sanctioned between a heterosexual married couple. So how did they relate to what you're teaching about consent? I'm thinking they could be looking at Dr. Laura McGuire and saying, "Consent? She's nuts. There's no such a thing as consent. We're saying *no,* period, there's no consent. Consent implies a possibility of

---

*Editor's note: Laura uses language deemed inclusive by proponents of Gender Identity Theory, which posits that it is kinder to use anatomical language, than the biological descriptors of male and female, among other linguistic preferences. This theory has continued to gain social prominence, with its tenets adopted by the Biden administration. Thus, a new debate about consent has arisen, since the time of these interviews, as to whether children are capable of providing informed consent for *medicalized* transition of their gender, which can include being prescribed drugs to stop puberty, cross-sex hormones, and extend even to elective *gender affirming* surgeries.

saying *yes*. So why is she teaching us about consent when it's pretty simple? *No* is *no*. Until you're married to a person of the opposite sex, it's all no. Even when you're married to that person of the opposite sex, sex is for procreation, that's it."

LM: I do get this a lot. I'm in seminary now. So I'm actually going for my master's of divinity to talk about these things in faith communities specifically. When I worked at the university in Texas, one of the first things I did when I got that job was I started connecting to the local student Baptist and Catholic organizations. Because I knew that they probably did not feel connected to the messages that the university had been sending, before my arrival, about consent. And, yes, when I talked to students, that's what they said: "This is not about us. We have nothing to do with these consent talks because we don't have sex against our religion." It's so important to address this. Consent isn't just about sex. It's about any two or more people communicating with each other in any way. So, are you talking to somebody? Are you asking to text them? Are you asking if they'd like to spend time with you, if you're pressuring them, if you're manipulating them, if you're not being clear about your intentions? That all falls under lack of consent. Consent has to be part of *all* of those steps. So whether you want to save sex for marriage or not doesn't matter—consent is still part of it. Also, one of the most overlooked aspects of this conversation in faith communities is that marital rape is very real. It didn't become federally illegal until the early 1990s. This is terrifying. As a culture, we've condoned and accepted marital rape for most of our history. So, for faith communities that are saying, "Sex is for marriage," I'd say, "Great. So you're talking about consent with engaged couples? No? Are you talking about couples who've been married for years and maybe haven't got this education before? No? Well, that's an enormous problem." It doesn't matter *when* you're going to have sex—or *if* you're ever going to have sex. Consent is integral to human relationships. That's one of the biggest areas we still have to move into in all different faith spaces.

RLM: To what extent are young people who are taught not to have sex actually following that direction? Do we have data on this? Are they truly not having sex? Or are they feeling like they're sinning, but still sinning? Because sex is such a powerful drive, particularly when you're in your teens and early twenties. I've read that over 90 percent of women engage in premarital sex.

LM: That's an important aspect, too, even if they're saying that abstinence is part of their spiritual practice. Often, it's not playing out that way. They're still human beings who engage in physical activities. So, statistically, it's rare that people don't have sex *at all* before getting married. That does vary across different religions and denominations. But the percentage of people who would profess that belief versus people following through on it is quite large. About 98 percent of couples in the United States have premarital sex. That includes religious *and* nonreligious people. So even if someone says, "I don't want to do this," if they're doing it at all, they're either doing it consensually and emotionally safely, or they're creating harm and assaulting someone, or they're manipulating or abusing them. This has to be part of every young person's learning about communicating—from children learning to compromise and share with playmates, to teens who are getting into the dating world—whether they think they're going to have sex or not—to adults, and even seniors. We're seeing a lot of consent issues with seniors in nursing homes. This was not something they grew up with. They have to get this education, too. It's for everybody.

TURNING 98 PERCENT OF THE POPULATION INTO CRIMINALS

RLM: I hesitate to say something that might sound critical of religious beliefs. But listening to that data you put forth—that 98 percent of couples have premarital sex—tells me we're creating anxiety and depression. We have a concept in sociology and psychology called *socio-cultural lag*. Socio-cultural lag occurs when the laws of the land—in this case the laws of religion—are opposing a significant percentage of what the population is actually doing. When we tried to get people to drive fifty-five miles an hour on superhighways to reduce gasoline use, it didn't work. People kept driving seventy miles an hour. So we effectively turned ordinary citizens into scofflaws, because all those people driving over fifty-five were not obeying the law.

In the world of psychedelic medicine, we've turned tens of millions of U.S. citizens who use marijuana, LSD, and MDMA into criminals. A very high percentage of these people are good citizens who pay their taxes, obey other laws, raise their kids well, work, and do everything to be a good citizen. But, say, they smoke marijuana instead of drinking alcohol. As soon as they smoke pot, they become criminals at maximum and scofflaws at minimum. In many cases, especially people of color, they go to jail. In addition, we've instilled anxiety and depression in these honest people, because a good citizen is aware when they're doing something illegal and it bothers them. They're scared that if they get stopped while driving, for even a broken taillight, they could go to jail because there's marijuana in the car. Now, you're saying the same is true about religious beliefs and creating sinners. If 98 percent of the people who get married have had premarital sex, then 98 percent of the Baptists who've been taught not to have sex are "sinning." They don't feel good about sinning. They're nice people. If they want to be part of the religion, they don't want to be seen as sinners. But now, in the back of their minds, they live with: "Every time I have sex with my boyfriend or girlfriend, I'm a sinner." That is crazy-making.

LM: It is. What's fascinating from the sexology side is that we see this even in physical issues during marriage. So even when they're told, "You're safe, you're not sinning anymore," we see high rates of erectile dysfunction and vaginal dryness. Particularly, people with vaginas have been told for so long that sex is terrifying and they're going to be in Hellfire for eternity. So when they are given permission to have sex, their bodies don't catch up. Their muscles contract out of trauma.

So they have painful intercourse—or they can't have intercourse—and they face various other issues. So they say, "But I'm allowed to do this now." But you're traumatized. If you're told that something is so bad, so shameful, and so evil, your body won't just turn that off. It's tricky, because we want people to follow whatever practice is right for them. If someone says that premarital sex isn't right for them—if they want to cover up, or if they don't want to have any physical contact with their partner before marriage—that's all important and part of consent culture. We affirm that. But we also have to look at the messaging around these issues and the damage it's causing. So it's a tricky balance. But I think we can find it; all people can, no matter their religious or social framework. They can find a place in a consent culture where their needs, rights, and autonomy are fully honored.

ENTITLEMENT, BOUNDARIES, AND *CHILDISM*

RLM: Talk to us about the relationship between consent culture, entitlement boundaries, and personal agency.

LM: Entitlement is a tremendous problem for dismantling rape culture. So much of the violence we see is based on a sense of privilege and entitlement. Somebody thinks they have the right to someone else's body, and that can be because of their gender, their race, or because they're married to them. "I *own* you now. You don't have the *right* to say no to me." We have to address that and talk about where those messages show up. How do they manifest? How do we address them? Boundaries are the opposite of that. We have to teach people how to have boundaries, especially people assigned female at birth, who are more prone to thinking: *I have to be nice. I can't say no. I have to make this person like me. If I say that was okay last week, but I don't want to do that anymore, I'm going to make my partner upset.* So we have to teach people how to have boundaries. We also have to teach them how to respect each other's right that if someone's boundary isn't your favorite or preference, you don't get an opinion. It's their body and their life. You have to respect that they're saying, "This doesn't work for me"—*agency*. When we talk about creating a consent culture, we talk about two key concepts that we find in research: sexual agency and sexual subjectivity. It boils down to having a right to your own experience: "I have a right to figure out what works for me and what doesn't." I have a right to pleasure. I have a right to physical and emotional peace. I have a right to renegotiate and redecide what those boundaries are. When we give that to young people, they give it to each other, and we then create couples, families, communities, and entire societies that believe each person has a right to their own autonomy, safety, and respect. That's how we get to changing a paradigm.

RLM: How are entitlement, boundaries, and personal agency related to the concept you talk about called *childism?*

LM: We talked about sexism and racism, but childism is not talked about as often. It's the idea that people under the age of eighteen do not have the same rights and needs as someone over the age of eighteen. If we think about it, that's prevalent in our culture. We don't let children say "no" in the same way as adults. If a teenager experiences sexual harassment from a peer at school, we say, "Kids are resilient. That's just how kids are." If an adult did that to another adult, they would lose their job. Their community would kick them out. So that's one of the key pieces. We have to emphasize that you don't just get these rights to consent, agency, and autonomy when you turn eighteen. The right to consent applies for your entire life. Whether we're talking about what's going on with the evangelical community or the Catholic Church, even what we're seeing with several pediatricians who've been charged with sexual abuse for treating children abusively—in all of those situations, kids were told they didn't have a right to say "no." The message is: "You're a kid, and I'm an adult in a powerful position. So your voice is null and void." That's why this is important. It doesn't matter who the person is or what age they are. We all have those same rights.

RLM: I can picture parents reading this and saying, "Is she saying that if I tell my child to go to bed at eight o'clock and not watch television, the child has a right to say no?" I could come up with many other examples that make this idea of children's agency with regard to boundaries difficult to understand.

LM: Exactly. A lot of parents make that jump to: "This means I don't have any rules. I can't say no to anything." No, of course not. Like we just talked about, everyone gets to have boundaries. If it's your home, you can say you don't want the TV on after this time. This is your boundary. Say it's for their well-being, and you know they need to get their schoolwork done, or they need to take a bath. But what is not yours to say you have control over is that child's body. So you don't get to say to them what we used to tell children: "The only people who can touch you here are your parents or a doctor." Statistically, the most likely person to abuse a child sexually is a family member. After that, it comes down to authority figures in that child's life— like physicians and teachers. So instead of saying, "If somebody with this title wants to touch you there, you have to agree," we say, "You can always say no. You can always say you're not comfortable. Even if the person says this is for your own good or they're allowed to do this because of their role."

RLM: What you're saying about childism reminds me of a slogan in my family as I was growing up, and it was probably the slogan I hated the most: "Children should be seen and not heard." Now, that's the ultimate example of childism. It's a way of saying that you have got to keep your mouth shut all the time. For a person like myself, who was born talking, it was a hard pill to swallow. How does one create healthy boundaries? Are there guidelines?

LM: Absolutely. One guideline is to always start with yourself. So often, whether I'm training in a corporate setting or talking to parents, they'll say, "I'm supposed to teach my children or team members this first." That's when you have to say, "No, first, you have to work on yourself." First, you have to discover *your* beliefs about boundaries. How do you model them? Do you follow through with them? Do you *have* boundaries? Is this something you just say to other people?" When you have that in place, it's about saying, "I want you to be able to say 'no' to things. I want you to be able to communicate what you're okay with and what you're not okay with." We normalize that we talk about that openly. The world changes, but it starts with yourself. You can't give that to others if you're not doing it on your own.

CONVERSATION TOOLS

RLM: You talk in your book about tools for creating conversations. What I hear in a thread throughout this interview is the imperative of communication. It's about talking to children, about couples talking to one another, about keeping the conversation going to find out what's okay and what's not: "Am I going too far? Do you want me to stop? Is there a boundary here?" Talk to us about what you call conversation tools.

LM: Yes, communication is the crux of all relationships. We know that one of the key problems for relationships and marriages is a lack of communication. Consent comes down to communication. When I do corporate work, corporations say their biggest problem is communication. This is the thing that we have to address. Some examples I've given in the book are things to start talking about, particularly for parents and kids or teachers and students. How do you even ask these things? Ask the student or child in particular: "What do you think about this? What do you see in the media? What messages have you received about consent?" Maybe watch a sitcom together or listen to a song and say, "What do you think the message is between these characters? Are they respecting each other? Do they have boundaries? Do they have good communication? Why or why not?" Use all of those things as launching points to say, "If it's not what we want, what would we advise these characters? If it's good, how do we amplify that? How do we make this situation more acceptable? What might be things that people have fear around when it comes down to having boundaries or effective communication?" Sometimes people hear that and don't have any idea what to say, or they think their children wouldn't know about these things. But you'd be surprised. Children and teens are so observant. They're so smart, especially in today's world. So engaging with them in these discussions is fruitful.

TEACHING CONSENT DOESN'T EQUAL
HAVING THE TALK

RLM: You have an entire section in your book about how to talk to seven-year-olds about consent. Is that about the starting age, Laura? Or does consent information begin even earlier than that?

LM: Honestly, when people ask when to start talking about consent with their kids, I say, "As soon as they can understand the word *no*," which is around eighteen months old. Obviously, you're not talking to them about sexual consent. But that's why it's important to clarify that consent is not about *sex*. It's about people communicating no matter what. So, with a young child, you can use the example of playing with a friend. "Does your friend want to play hide-and-seek, or do they want to play tag? They said they wanted to play tag, but then you begged them and said you wouldn't be their friend if they didn't agree. So they said yes, but did they really say yes, or did they feel pressure? Did they feel scared to say no?" That's a consent lesson right there. The same goes for children interacting with animals. "Does the dog want to be petted? The dog is backing away from you when you approach it. The cat hissed when you tried to pet its fur. It's telling you it has a boundary. It's telling you, "I don't want to be touched right now. So let's respect that. Let's not try to convince others to engage with us." Those are consent conversations at an age-appropriate level. Sex is never mentioned, it doesn't need to be at all. But you're still putting those building blocks of understanding verbal and nonverbal cues in place, of understanding authentic communication. And you're illustrating how we sometimes manipulate people to get what we want, and also how to address that. So when they grow up, and they're in a more intense, intimate situation, that foundation is already there.

RLM: I want to underline in red your point that teaching a young person about consent and boundaries doesn't have to be about sex. It can come way before even any discussion of sex, because boundaries and consent relate to all kinds of interactions in our world. An essential part of communication does relate to sex a great deal, but part of communication relates to all aspects of everyday life. In your book, you then get to what I consider political. Importantly, you talk about colonialization and consent. Please talk about that.

LM: I think another aspect of the conversation about consent that often gets left out is how history plays into all of this. If we're saying, we want the current reality to be that everybody's boundaries are honored and respected, we have to address the fact that, historically, that has not been the case—not just in the broad sense, but especially for marginalized and oppressed groups. There are entire communities of people in the United States that, for hundreds of years, could not consent to *anything*. Their ability to have autonomy and agency was completely denied.

RLM: Such as women who were virtually owned.

LM: Such as women, people of color, people with disabilities—the list goes on. If we don't talk about that reality, we won't change the culture. Those issues are going to be embedded in the way we think, communicate, and look at victims and their stories. So the work becomes to decolonize that, to say, "What part of this is colonization? What part of this is how overtaking people, controlling people, and manipulating them on a global scale has become how we look at each other and the way we think of humanity? How do we address that? How do we address that in our language, our humor, the songs we sing, or the messages we convey in the media?" Only after we do that can we address the present.

HOMOGENEOUS PERSPECTIVES
CREATING ECHO CHAMBERS

RLM: You talk about a concept called *homogeneous perspectives on sex,* and how those homogeneous perspectives determine how they create problems. Let's hear about that.

LM: When we're talking from our own singular perspective, we often miss most other people's lived experiences. We say, "Everybody goes through this; everyone looks at it this way; or everyone experiences sexuality in this manner." That's not true, especially if we're in communities that become an echo chamber, and we're all confirming our beliefs. We leave out all the people around us, and that becomes part of denying people their reality and failing to address the issues they're experiencing.

RLM: There's a homogeneous perspective—a way of seeing all people the way you see one individual person. Is that what you're wanting to teach us?

LM: Yes, and that can often be like the first-person experience. If I say, "I went to this concert, and it was so hard to get a taxi home. So I walked home. I don't know why this person over here was complaining about getting a ride and the prices, because I just walked home. It wasn't a big deal. Yes, it was dark, but it was fine." That's my singular perspective. You're leaving out the lived experience of needing to navigate getting home late at night, and all the people who don't have that privilege. Maybe a male person will say, it's no big deal. This bleeds into the way we see sexuality and communication. We often have this perspective of, "If I'm experiencing this, if I have this level of privilege, then it must be true for every single person." That denies the majority of people their realities, as well as the barriers that they're having to navigate that we might not.

RLM: Is seeing the color pink as feminine an example of a homogeneous perspective—seeing gender stereotypes? We are taught these gender-oriented beliefs and the behaviors that follow from those beliefs. Is that correct?

LM: Absolutely. So we can say, "All women are attracted to protector-providers." Going back to the example of the bathing suit at the beginning, right, "All boys are so visually stimulated. Girls aren't, but boys are." Of course, people of all genders can be visually stimulated or not, or they can want someone who has certain personality attributes—or not. We're individuals. We don't want to be stereotyping each other, even ourselves. Sometimes people will do that to themselves, as in, "As a man, as a woman, as a nonbinary person, as a trans person, as a person born in the eighties." We all think as if we all experienced the same perspective, and that's not true.

RLM: So that homogeneous perspective is related to a binary perspective.

LM: Yes, you're right.

RLM: You're advocating that we break down this binary perspective? So, advocate for us.

LM: Our binary way of thinking that there are two options for any of these identities—and that there's not a vast swath of experiences in between—is harmful. It puts people in tiny boxes where they rarely fit. It even limits how we think about humanity and our human experiences. We need to think outside of that and think expansively around how people navigate the world—how we're intersectional, that we're not just one thing, but on a continuum of identities—and then layer all these identities together. You are the unique experience that is you. But if you say to me, "No, you check this box. So you have to think this way or have this experience," you will not see me authentically, and I will not have the voice that I need to have in any realm.

GENDER STEREOTYPES PREVENT
AUTHENTIC LIFE EXPERIENCES

RLM: What do you mean when you talk about the *paradox of gender?*

LM: Gender stereotyping—or gender bias—is a huge issue within rape culture. Dismantling that is key to consent culture. What we're just talking about, putting people in little boxes, often comes with assumptions about sexual experience, the ability to communicate, or being able to live authentically. If we don't discuss how we're conditioned by these norms and expectations, we don't get to the root of that continuum of harm and how they're interconnected.

RLM: Even little things like the man being the one to take out the garbage and the woman being the one to do the dishes are stereotypes. Those are gender biases. We have a lot of reevaluating to do, Laura. Talk to us about gender in the bedroom.

LM: This is connected to token resistance and token compliance. Many people socialized as females have the belief and have an experience that they can't say what they want or don't want. We call that sexology. That orgasm gap exists. Even when people are in loving, committed relationships—when they think they're talking, that they know each other, that and they understand each other's likes—so often, people with vaginas don't have orgasms at the rate of their partners with penises. The whole way sex is framed and prioritized focuses on the partner with the penis's orgasm and making sure that they're receiving pleasure. All of this feeds into inequality and thinking less of different people based on their genitals or how they are, the place they are in this galaxy of human identity and experience. That shows up in the bedroom *and* in the boardroom. We know people socialized as female have a much harder time moving up in positions, being accepted as authority figures, and being heard when they have an idea. Does that come down to the way we look at somebody who reports a crime or somebody who says, "I'm uncomfortable with the way this person is talking to me"? Yes, absolutely. These are all intertwined. We have to look at how we're communicating with our partners: How am I prioritizing their pleasure? That will feed into how you respect and respond to people so that violence doesn't occur, and that if it does occur, that people are heard and believed.

RLM: It's going to be quite a movement to free people up so that women who have been taught all their lives to be recalcitrant about sex become unbridled and let their freak flag fly once they're in a relationship that's safe. It's easy to say, "Let yourself be." But how do women let themselves *be* after a lifetime of culturalization saying, "Keep down, keep your sex drive controlled, or else we'll slut-shame you"? We're asking them to break their shackles and turn into free persons. We have a lot of work ahead following hour lead, Laura McGuire.

LM: Yes. Fortunately, I'm not alone in this work. There are so many amazing people in this space, and so many who have gone before me. But the more people hear these messages, the more people take up this mantle, work with us, and go back to their schools saying, "Can we please have a one-time speaker come out? Can we hire them to look at our curriculum and develop something? Can we get this to be consistently offered year after year across different grades?" Together, we start changing things because it has to be a collective effort.

DOES THE IDEA OF CONSENT IMPLY SOBRIETY ALREADY?

RLM: When I think about *consent,* I wonder whether the word is inclusive enough to provide the safety we're aiming for. I want your opinion on whether it would be of merit to call it *sober* consent. Does the word *sober* add enough to make it worthwhile? Or is sobriety implicit in the word *consent?* I raise this question because we cannot have consent without sobriety. What happens to people's agency when they drink alcohol? Does no mean no? Certainly, no always means no. But does yes mean yes when a person is under the influence? What's your opinion on that? Is it worthwhile to expand consent to calling it *sober consent?*

LM: I would say it's unnecessary. If you study anything about consent theory and consent culture ideas, you know it's integral to these principles that people are sober and free from substances in their body where they can't decide. That doesn't mean they've had one glass of wine—but if they keep drinking, or they're drinking hard alcohol, and they're at that level where they're buzzed, then they're not able to make an informed decision. They might say yes, but they don't know what they're saying. So we don't have to add the word *sober* onto it, because it's already ingrained in the concept. But I agree that even adults rarely get this—or they've heard the opposite. They grew up watching movies, where a character would get another character drunk to have a chance with them. So everybody needs to hear that. Yes does not mean yes if the person is pressured, if they're not mentally clear, if they're manipulated, or if they're not sure what they're agreeing to. The person hasn't told them what they meant. For all those reasons, we want it to be enthusiastic and ongoing. I've had more than one student and more than one college parent tell me that the way they were going to get around this "consent stuff" is that before they got somebody drunk, they would get them to sign an agreement, consenting to have sex with them. They're missing the entire point. That doesn't count, because consent is ongoing. If they were sober when they initially consented, that was a yes when they were sober. Now they're drunk. They can't go back and agree or not agree, because they're not in a clear mental space. They're not able to make that decision. So there's no way for them to consent. If they said, "In five hours, I'll still agree to this," it doesn't matter. It doesn't work that way. But it's shocking how many young adults and their parents think that's appropriate.

RLM: So consent is an existential act—from moment to moment, you make your decision. It's not a blank check where you sign on and, for the next week, whenever you want something, the answer is "yes." That sounds important. Consent is ongoing, and you can take away consent at any time.

LM: Exactly, even in the moment. There's no point where they can't say no. If you're in the middle of having sex, and the person says, "Hold on, something isn't working for me," that's it. The consent ended. The other person can't say it's too late. It's never too late to say no. That goes into the marital rape conversation we were having.

If somebody says, "I do," that doesn't mean yes to all sexual activity forever, in every situation with that person. Yes, they're agreeing to be married to them at that moment, in that context. But that has nothing to do with agreeing to everything else. And many people are taught that they don't have to establish consent once they're married or in a long-term relationship because it's assumed. That is dangerous and harmful.

RLM: This is the legacy of the years when women were chattel. The past is what we're dealing with. So what does the future look like? Give us a glimpse of how you see the future and how you would like to see the future?

LM: Hopefully, in the future people will read this kind of material. I have a second book for college campuses to do more work around this. It's called *The Sexual Misconduct Prevention Guidebook.* Hopefully, people will read about this, listen to these things, and start thinking about working first on themselves and considering where they have misconceptions about consent. "Where do I doubt victims? Where do I have bias and prejudice?" We all have to address this by starting to talk to peers, students, and children. This is hard for many people. But the more we learn, the more we know, and the better we can do. So my hope would be that this becomes something that every child receives throughout their lifetime, that these conversations are ongoing for them, that they have support and resources for continuing to work through their questions, misgivings, or confusion. That way, we eventually get to a place where this is the cultural expectation, where people aren't confused, where there aren't mixed messages, where the messaging is clear, and it's all about consent. That is my hope for the future, and it's promising. There's definitely work to do, and there are still a lot of counter-messages going around. But we're getting closer to making this the expectation.

AFTERWORD

Awakened Con-sensuality

There have been numerous times in my life when I've been accused, not without good reason, of wanting the last word. This being one of those times, I offer you some of my afterthoughts on *Freeing Sexuality* . . .

First, however, I sincerely invite you to engage with me on what I say below, or any other topic in the book. You can contact me at info@MindBodyHealthPolitics.org.

My intention in creating this book was to make a sociopolitical contribution to freeing sexuality from its historical—and present—place as a weaponized force. I myself see sexual repression as nothing less than a psychophysical virus that has yielded a worldwide pandemic of neuroto-genetic psychosexual disorders.

Looking back on these conversations with sexperts who have all taught me so much and left me with so much food for thought, my larger takeaway is the painfully glaring, reminder that sex, with its supernatural power, is—like money, with its deified power—another activity in which females are demonically subjected.

From a tactical perspective, the fight for female sovereignty requires a full-court press. The direct relationship between the male/female orgasm gap and the financial gap must be deeply considered. Men are still holding the power. Sex is power, but money trumps sex as a form of power because money can buy sex.

In the name of the quest for sovereignty, women will be best served by bringing their sexual power to the very edges of a new frontier with extraordinary bravery and creativity. The battle for female sovereignty is more urgent than ever at this time in history because, as we all will all soon be forced to realize, we face extinction by our own doing—

whether through industrialization, nuclear war, or any of the other horrors we've placed in our own path. As an experimental species on this planet we have, to a certain extent, failed to live together harmoniously on our planet and our history is one of constant warfare and deprivation. As I write this battles are waging around the world. People are dying in wars and from lack of food and water. And our failing species has little time left to redeem itself before robots move into their developmental place in history. This will occur as soon as we are able to download all the information contained in the human brain onto a chip that can be installed into a robotic body. These brainy robots will then discover how to download human consciousness and they will have it all. Robots will have human information and cognitive processing as well as consciousness. From another perspective one might say we humans have succeeded, for by downloading our information, our cognitive processing, and our consciousness we have become immortal. On computer chips we will live forever. We can literally say "we are in the chips." At that point we will go the way of the Neanderthals. But until then, there is much work we can accomplish to redeem ourselves. There is still time to live as a worldwide collaborative species and I put forth that the females need to lead the way.

When females attain equal power, our prospects for living collaboratively in our remaining time as a species will dramatically improve. I say this so boldly because the data show that males are nine times more likely to commit murder than females. This is de facto evidence that our health, education, and general welfare will be better served when females have equal power. We are only just emerging into the light after spending the last several millennia enveloped in sexual darkness. This darkness has been perpetrated by power-hungry religious institutions and the men who have stewarded their relentless campaign to vilify, suppress, and commandeer human sexuality for their own gain. Sadly, the vast majority of our species has throughout history been relegated to stumbling blindly through a haze of distorted sexuality. Our urges mutilated by a guilt that has metastasized into intergenerational trauma, we now exist as veritable strangers to the most fundamental aspect of our nature.

We have, on so many levels, become disordered and thus the majority of us suffer from Hypocrisy-Induced Neurosis and post-traumatic sexual stress disorder.

How is it possible to harbor such vehement hostility toward the activity to which we owe our very existence? Sex is encoded into us for procreation and, as an incentive for us to continue to perpetuate ourselves, it is one the most exquisite of all human sensations. So what shall we make of any God who would begrudge us for simply enjoying sensations that the same God is alleged to have built into us, and that precipitated our entrance into this world?

As much attention as I've given these questions, I still can't begin to fathom a satisfactory answer.

At the end of the day, I can only sigh and admit that I don't know.

But here's what I do know: just as we have done with our home, our planet, so we have done with the garden of delights bestowed upon us that we refer to as our sexuality. In both cases we have taken a gift of unequaled proportions and degraded it. We have waged warfare and killed, contaminated our oceans, raped our forests, and besmirched our sexuality.

It is time for the greatest change in the way we relate to the gifts of our home, our bodies, our senses.

If there is heaven on Earth, it resides in ecstatic pleasure anchored in authentic intimacy, with another person. It can even be achieved through a healthy, shame-free solo release.

How do more of us get to that exalted place? I'm not sure I have the answers, but I have endless questions. This book is, at heart, a series of questions—questions I put out into the ether before being fortunate enough to receive such gracious, thoughtful answers from such a lovely group of people. Of course, I have more questions. I look at those posed in this book as an invitation to clarity to come knocking on our window.

We heal ourselves when we open ourselves up to conversation about sex, when we are vulnerable. We must allow ourselves to talk openly—everywhere, and with mutual dignity, respect, kindness and love—and peel away the layers of secrecy, lies, doublespeak, and shame. Let us speak openly about sex, share our thoughts and feelings, free ourselves from the straightjackets of our puritanical ancestors, and fully embrace our complete selves as sexual beings.

I mean to be taken literally when I say that our collective survival depends on getting in alignment with all aspects of ourselves, including these desires that have been demonized for too long. By weaving-together our physical and empathic capabilities into a globally minded consciousness, we can reach a state of awakened *con-sensuality* that, I would posit, is the true Garden that Mother Nature intended for us.

Whether or not we ever get there remains to be seen, but I believe we touch the Divine when we aspire to this ideal. It's absolutely worth it—and, besides, you will have a good time trying.

It is my wish that your time with *Freeing Sexuality* is of value in expanding your thinking and feeling about your own sexuality, and about human sexuality in general.

RICHARD LOUIS MILLER

FORT BRAGG AND WILBUR SPRINGS, CALIFORNIA

Acknowledgments

Freeing Sexuality is the product of a collaboration that included our *Mind Body Health & Politics* staff, producer Charlie Deist, associate producer Allison Kelly, sound engineer David Springer, editor Florian Fuhren, financial officer Ezzie Davis; the Inner Traditions staff, Jon Graham, Ashley Kolesnik, Emilia Cataldo, Manzanita Carpenter Sanz, and Courtney Jenkins; and our interviewees, all of whom gave generously of their time.

I also wish to acknowledge my wife, Cherry Blossom, also known as Jolee, who provided me with ten years of the most exquisite, intimate, bounteous sex life anyone could possibly have.

Index